British radio drama

British radio drama

Edited by

John Drakakis

Lecturer in English Studies
University of Stirling

Cambridge University Press

Cambridge
London   New York   New Rochelle
Melbourne   Sydney

Published by the Press Syndicate of the University of Cambridge
The Pitt Building, Trumpington Street, Cambridge CB2 1RP
32 East 57th Street, New York, NY 10022, USA
296 Beaconsfield Parade, Middle Park, Melbourne 3206, Australia

© Cambridge University Press 1981

First published 1981

Phototypeset in V.I.P. Palatino by
Western Printing Services Ltd, Bristol
Printed in Great Britain
at The Pitman Press, Bath

British Library cataloguing in publication data
British radio drama.
1. Radio plays – History and criticism
2. English drama – 20th century – History
and criticism
I. Drakakis, John
822′.02   PN1991.65   80-40678

ISBN 0 521 22183 8 hard covers
ISBN 0 521 29383 9 paperback

Contents

Acknowledgements

Grateful thanks are due in the first instance to Diane Speakman who nursed this volume of essays through its early stages, and to her successor at the Cambridge University Press, Sarah Stanton. The much-appreciated work and advice of Jane Van Tassel also deserve mention. Jacqueline Kavanagh and her staff at the BBC Written Archives Centre in Caversham were a source both of help and encouragement, particularly in connection with permission to reproduce unpublished BBC copyright material. Thanks are also due to the staffs of the BBC Sound Archives, the BBC Script Library, and the BBC Reference Library, and especially to Michel Petheram for his valuable help and advice in compiling the bibliography of published playscripts. The staff of the Library at the University of Stirling were extremely helpful, as always. Finally, acknowledgement must be made of the collective typing skills of Katherine McKenzie, Olwen Peel, and Mamie Prentice, of the Department of English Studies at the University of Stirling.

Notes on the contributors

JOHN DRAKAKIS is a Lecturer in English Studies at the University of Stirling, where he teaches Shakespearean and Elizabethan and Jacobean drama. He has published individual studies of *Othello* and *Much Ado About Nothing* in the York Notes series, and has written articles and reviews on Shakespearean and Jacobean drama as well as on aspects of radio drama.

FRANCES GRAY is a Lecturer in English Literature and Drama at the University of Sheffield. She has published articles on Giles Cooper and Joe Orton, and has contributed a chapter to the forthcoming Peter Lewis (ed.), *Radio Drama*.

CHRISTOPHER HOLME is a former Assistant Head of Features and of Sound Drama at the BBC. In 1962, along with Muriel Spark and Tristram Cary, he won the Italia Prize for an adaptation of Muriel Spark's novel *The Ballad of Peckham Rye*; he has contributed to various journals, and has written, produced, and translated plays for radio.

PETER LEWIS is a Lecturer in English Literature at the University of Durham. He has published widely in the area of Restoration and eighteenth-century literature and has edited an anthology of modern Anglo-Welsh poetry and also the *Papers of the Radio Literature Conference 1977*. He contributes regularly to *Poetry Wales* and *Stand*, and is the editor of a forthcoming volume of essays entitled *Radio Drama*.

DONALD A. LOW is a Senior Lecturer in English Studies at the University of Stirling. He has edited two volumes of essays on Robert Burns, and has contributed numerous articles and reviews on aspects of eighteenth-century literature and Scottish literature. His most recent book is *That Sunny Dome: A Portrait of*

Regency England, and he has written articles on aspects of radio adaptation.

ROGER SAVAGE is a Senior Lecturer at the University of Edinburgh. He is heavily involved in directing plays and operas, has broadcast occasionally on the subject of opera, and has published essays on Shakespeare, Purcell, and Swift.

DAVID WADE was a radio critic for *The Listener*, and since 1967 has been radio critic for *The Times*. He is the author of about a dozen plays for radio and has also contributed other programme material as well as talks and criticism.

KATHARINE WORTH is Professor of Drama and Theatre Studies at Royal Holloway College, University of London. She is a leading authority on Samuel Beckett, and has published widely in the area of modern drama. Also, she has produced her own versions of Beckett's radio plays.

1   Introduction

JOHN DRAKAKIS

> We are not so ready to believe the radio play to be different from the stage play, yet the blind medium of radio in its unique power upon the ear of stimulating the imagination makes for a kind of drama which can embrace subjects film and theatre may never approach. Its subtle and mercurial manipulation of sounds and words, allied to its quality of immediacy and intimacy with the listener, give it possibilities of development that await only the right dramatist. We think now of Mr Louis MacNeice, of Dylan Thomas's *Under Milk Wood* and of Mr Samuel Beckett's *All That Fall* as tentative but real steps towards the discovery of radio drama's proper form.
> (J. L. Styan)[1]

THE SPORADIC AND INCOMPLETE history of the radio play is effectively a history of becoming, dominated from the outset by the search for material, a sound theoretical basis, and suitable forms of artistic expression. From its inception in the early 1920s, radio drama was in direct competition with established theatre drama, and it has always, implicitly or explicitly, sought to measure its achievements against those of the theatre, and of literature generally.

More recently, and especially since its partial eclipse by television, commentators, both from within and outside the BBC, have become increasingly aware of the historical importance of radio, not simply as a medium of mass communication, but also as a primary agency through which our own cultural and artistic values are disseminated. This is likely to prove of particular significance to the history of drama in the twentieth century, since, in addition to providing a new and potentially exciting outlet for playwrights, the intrinsically 'dramatic' nature of radio itself contributed to the more general process whereby the terms 'drama' and 'theatre' began to take on separate meanings.[2] Until the advent of a medium which could approach its audience directly, and in their own homes, drama in the formal sense of the term was the preserve of the theatre, where, indeed, the concept of a 'mass audience' has some literal validation.

1

Paradoxically, however, what was for radio a natural reliance upon 'sound' and the spoken voice was also the condition towards which, *mutatis mutandis*, the presentation of Shakespeare in the theatre had been moving for some time. Begun in the 1880s by the director William Poel, a number of theatrical experiments were undertaken to remove naturalistic stage-settings in an attempt to recreate the conditions of original Shakespearean performances.[3] These experiments involved, as directors and actors, individuals such as Tyrone Guthrie and John Gielgud, who themselves became associated with radio drama in its early stages.[4] But even more important, the terms in which the debate about Shakespearean performance was conducted during the 1920s bear a striking resemblance to those in which the early broadcasters themselves defended the new medium. Issues such as the question of the intimacy of the relationship between actor and audience, the swiftness of the transition from one scene to another made possible by the removal of naturalistic backgrounds, the primacy of poetry and the rhythms of performance generated by the variety of the spoken dialogue,[5] all appeared as part of the early justification for radio drama itself. Indeed, it is tempting to speculate that the first drama broadcast, of three scenes from three separate Shakespeare plays, on 16 February 1923, and produced by Professor Acton Bond of the British Empire Shakespeare Society, was allied to the contemporary debate about the priorities of Shakespearean performance. It is also worth remembering that experiments with literary form, as evidenced in James Joyce's *Ulysses* and T. S. Eliot's *The Waste Land*, both published in 1922, reinforce the view that the development of radio drama requires to be seen in the larger context of experimentation in all the arts during this period.

The choice of Shakespeare for the first serious drama broadcast helps to bring into clearer focus a central paradox which radio, and its successor television, have had to learn to live with. Commenting on the first two years of drama broadcasting, the Director of Programmes, John Reith, expressed his irritation with the excessive 'theatre effect' which much of it contained, and with the apparent failure to discover 'the actual radio effect': 'It seems to me that in many of our productions there is too much striving for theatre effect and too little attempt at actually discovering the actual radio effect when the play is received in distant homes.'[6]

This early and often-repeated assertion of its own uniqueness – a firmly held conviction from the outset that radio had its own 'proper form' distinct from the theatre or from film – existed along with what was to become a more general moral commitment to mediate the entire tradition of literary and artistic achievement. Indeed, within ten years of its inception, the German dramatist Bertolt Brecht commented on the extent to which radio generally in its early stages was a substitute for other forms of communication: 'The radio was then in its first phase of being a substitute for theatre, opera, concerts, lectures, cafe music, local newspapers and so forth.'[7] The early radio adaptations of Shakespeare, carried out by Cathleen Nesbitt under the direction of C. A. Lewis, rather confirm this view. For example, in addition to the quarrel scene from *Julius Caesar*, adaptations included the trial scene from *The Merchant of Venice* (23 May 1923), a recitation by the actress Ellen Terry of the Hubert and Arthur scene from *King John* (31 May 1923), excerpts from *Henry VIII* (7 June 1923) and *Romeo and Juliet* (5 July 1923), and readings from *Macbeth* by John Gielgud and Ben Webster (18 October 1923). The first full-length Shakespeare play to be broadcast was *Twelfth Night* (28 May 1923), produced from Savoy Hill, and including in its cast Nigel Playfair, Gerald Lawrence, and Cathleen Nesbitt. Adaptation in nearly all these cases, it was admitted, took the form simply of 'cutting'.[8] The first novel to be adapted was Charles Kingsley's *Westward Ho!* (April 1925), followed in February 1927 by Joseph Conrad's *Lord Jim*.[9]

This process of adapting plays, novels, and short stories has, over the years, grown to such an extent that radio must be considered a primary means by which many people gain access to the literature and drama of the past.[10] Thus, historical self-awareness and the natural desire to assert an individual identity in the face of alternatives were never clearly disentangled from the larger, clearly irresistible task of generating in radio audiences an awareness of a cultural heritage and the aesthetic judgements that supported it. From the very outset radio drama insisted upon being judged on its own terms, but ironically its appeals, both implicit and explicit, were largely to the courts of established literature and drama; indeed, a good deal of the subsequent theorising about the poetic possibilities of the radio play, and the kind of listener concentration it demanded, did much to reinforce the comparison.

No comprehensive critical history of radio drama exists. What accounts there are usually take the form of personal anecdotal histories by individuals directly involved in the evolution of the medium itself. The result is that, often, technical inventiveness is given pride of place over the business of establishing a clear set of aesthetic criteria by which any radio play might be judged. Nonetheless, such personalised histories offer intriguing insights into the complicated workings of the BBC, described in one such account as *The Biggest Aspidistra in the World*.[11] In each account, however, certain landmarks are clear. Setting aside the broadcast of *The Truth About Father Christmas* on 24 December 1922, it is generally acknowledged that the first play to be produced especially for radio was Richard Hughes's *A Comedy of Danger* (15 January 1924).[12] In July 1924 a separate department for the broadcasting of plays was set up under R. E. Jeffrey, and this was followed in July 1925 by the appointment of Howard Rose. Together Jeffrey and Rose were responsible for much of the early development of radio drama at the BBC.

During the first few years of broadcasting, presentation seems to have been something of a compromise. For example, theatrical conventions continued to be adopted, and actors themselves had some difficulty in coping with the demands made upon them by live broadcasting before a microphone. Indeed, in the early days actors broadcast in costume. Rose's own comment that 'our theatrical upbringing died hard with all of us' and Val Gielgud's account of some of the conventions which continued to be utilised in broadcasting plays up to 1926 indicate the sorts of obstacles that radio drama confronted in its early years:

> As late as 1926 long plays were regularly prefaced with four or five minutes of conventional stage 'overture', and music was always played between the acts. It took a considerable time for it to become clear that the use and value of music to Radio Drama was basic, and not incidental; almost as long as it took to persuade actors that, because the radio audience was a very large one, larger than the audience in any theatre, it was unnecessary for them to project their voices and their personalities as if they were playing in some super-equivalent of Olympia.[13]

In 1928 radio drama took a major technical step forward with the introduction of the 'dramatic control panel'. Hitherto the use of single studios for complete broadcasts had presented problems: handling large casts was difficult, as was the business of controlling sound effects. In these conditions it is hardly surprising that orthodox act-divisions did not disappear immediately, since production itself could not but be stylised. But the development of a device which permitted the simultaneous use of a number of studios, enabling the sound to be controlled from a central panel, and allowing it to be 'faded in' and 'faded out' as required, opened up new possibilities which affected not only the presentation but also the structure of broadcast plays. Lance Sieveking's *The First Kaleidoscope*, sub-titled *A Rhythm Representing the Life of Man from Cradle to Grave*, and broadcast live on 4 September 1928, was the first to use the new dramatic control panel that made it possible for radio to reproduce 'in effect, all the basic grammar that gave the cinema such fluidity'.[14] Nor was the comparison between radio and aspects of film lost on its first users; Tyrone Guthrie, who had used what he called the 'Mixing Panel' (a reference that was to anger Sieveking) in *Squirrel's Cage* (1929) and *The Flowers Are Not for You To Pick* (1930), described its effect as one resembling 'that of superimposed photography in films'.[15]

The introduction of the dramatic control panel enabled radio drama to dissolve both temporal and implied spatial boundaries, thus extending its powers of aural suggestion, and offering parallels in sound only of what dramatists such as Strindberg and Brecht had already begun to explore in the theatre and that film had utilised almost from its inception. The dissolution of conventionally marked scenic divisions, which Poel had adopted in order to sustain the rhythm of Shakespearean performance, also opened the way for montage effects and for the exploration of 'stream of consciousness', both of which have remained structural features of radio drama down to the present time. Moreover, the disturbance of traditional principles of dramatic design, which had relied upon the strictly sequential relationship between plot and character within an action which was temporally constrained, helped to isolate some of the more intricate elements of aesthetic structure. The emphasis upon quality of controlled sound and 'rhythm' – the systematic association of poetically conceived images and effects – slowly emerged as integral parts of the structure required to enable the listener to hold in his mind related sequences of sound for which there could be no objective visual validation.[16] Insofar as particular radio plays sought to recreate by suggestion a *reality* which could be visually apprehended, the activity of visualisation took place in the imagination of the listener.

Notwithstanding the possible advantages accruing from a medium which had dispensed with the faculty of sight, early practitioners remained defensive about radio drama. L. Du Garde Peach, one of the earliest radio dramatists, insisted in this connection that 'Where there is nothing to look at there must be something to think about.'[17] Moreover, this early awareness that radio as a medium of communication sought to extend 'one single sense in "high definition"'[18] made possible the analogy between radio and music. Lance Sieveking, for example, who defended vigorously what are now regarded as the clumsy virtues of the dramatic control panel, conceived of it as a musical instrument to be played by the drama-producer, and his highly personalised account of the broadcasting of his own Morality play *Kaleidoscope* casts the producer in the role of music-maker, and, by implication, the play itself as a kind of orchestral performance:

My fingers knew well enough, even if my head did not. Just as they do on the piano or 'cello. Without consciously reading the directions on my script I faded the tiny football matches out off the horizon, and wiped the narrator off the map with the singer, and then cut the music off sharply. Now it was play, play, *play* the instrument if ever you did anything in your life.[19]

The progress of radio drama in its very early stages was hampered by inadequate technology. Raymond Williams has suggested that in larger social terms the 'public technology' of radio formed part of a larger need to provide kinds of broadcasting 'which served an at once mobile and home-centred way of living: a form of mobile privatisation'.[20] Williams views these developments in technology, and, by implication, in art and psychology, as applications 'of a set of emphases and responses within the determining limits and pressures of industrial capitalist society'.[21] Whatever the precise social impetus, some of the inherent aesthetic potential of radio drama was realised with the concept of the multi-studio principle, made possible through the development of the dramatic control panel and first used by Sieveking. This gave to radio the kind of freedom that in 1929 prompted further exploration of 'the symphonic possibilities of the medium'[22] undertaken by dramatists like Tyrone Guthrie, whose own *Squirrel's Cage* deployed the use of sound in ways that he himself associated with 'superimposed photography in the films'.[23] Thus, by 1930 a basic grammar of radio production had been formulated, with the use of terms like 'fade-in' 'fade-out', and 'cross-fade'.[24] Some of the vocabulary was borrowed from film, but literature, theatre drama, and psychology contributed also. While sound effects could be regarded as aural transformations of the film's camera angle and focus, forms such as 'stream of consciousness' found their way from psychology through expressionistic drama, the prose of writers such as James Joyce, and the poetry of T. S. Eliot into radio's rapidly expanding lexicon of terms and structural concepts.

In 1929 Val Gielgud was appointed Productions Director of the BBC's Drama Department, and he continued the proselytising zeal that had characterised the activities of his predecessor, R. E. Jeffrey. Gielgud's brief was a wide one: 'apart from having to observe the amber warning-lights at the crossroads of Sex, Religion, and Politics, I could drive straight ahead with reasonable confidence of security'.[25] Indeed, it was Gielgud, exacting in his standards, though sometimes quirky in his judgements, who presided over the steady development of radio drama for the following twenty years. In the year of his appointment the *BBC Handbook* set out the case for radio as a national theatre, with its 'means of spanning the unprofitable dramatic ground which lies between the commercial and the artistic; between the business theatre of today and the national theatre of tomorrow'.[26] Already by 1930 the BBC was expected to mount twice as many productions each year as were being mounted on the London stage,[27] and by 1945 some four hundred plays a year, excluding serials, were being broadcast.[28]

This notion of a 'national theatre of the air', providing not only original radio plays, but also adaptations of theatre classics, translations of plays by foreign dramatists,[29] and adaptations of works of literature, was, and has remained, an important part of the philosophy of the BBC.[30] In terms of original writing, during the period 1931–41 productions of radio plays increased some sevenfold, and it was at this time that much of the theoretical and experimental foundation was laid down for future development. In 1932 production moved from Savoy Hill to Broadcasting House, and in October 1933 Laurence Gilliam was transferred from *Radio Times* to undertake responsibility for 'Special Programmes'. A few months later, on 1 January 1934, Gielgud was made Drama Director, and thus began the separation of Drama from Features.[31] Gilliam was to remain Head of Features until 1964 when, after some opposition, the department was abolished, although much of the pioneering work involved in making *use* of the medium of radio for the purposes of drama was done under his direction and during the period 1936–63.

This relatively early division into the categories of radio play and feature, represents in certain respects a distinction without a difference, although the role played by Features cannot be ignored. During the very early years of broadcasting no clear distinction had been made between the two,[32] but despite the formal division of labour which took place after 1934, writers such as Louis MacNeice and Dylan Thomas, and writer–producers, such as Edward Sackville-West and D. G. Bridson, could be claimed simultaneously to be original dramatists and writers of features. While Bridson's *The March of The '45* (February 1936) was a dramatic reconstruction of a series of actual events,[33] and thus best exemplified the principle of the feature, Sackville-West's *The Rescue* (November 1943) was in fact an adaptation from Homer's *Odyssey*, while both MacNeice's *Christopher Columbus* (October 1942), and Dylan Thomas's *Under Milk Wood* (January 1954) are clearly works of fiction. At each end of the spectrum the roles of journalist and dramatist could be clearly distinguished. Both Gielgud and Gilliam seem to have been agreed that the key to the difference lay in the question of dramatic form; Gielgud described a feature as: 'any programme item not basically in dramatic form, designed to make use of radio dramatic technique in its presentation to the listener',[34] and Gilliam, in a more epigrammatic vein, asserted that 'Features deal with fact, Drama with fiction.'[35] The primary value of the feature lay in its documentary nature, although the possibility of dramatisation constituted an option which was always open to the writer–producer, and emphasis was placed upon its full use of the technical resources of radio to accomplish its aim. Needless to say, not all features were successful, as the following report upon the script of a programme entitled *The People Versus Johnny Jones* makes clear:

A feature programme conveys fact and opinion and observation. If it chooses to do so dramatically it can only do so convincingly when the fact, opinion and observation is related to a credible background. This script isn't an individual case history – it isn't a generalized picture drawn from knowledge of several individual case histories. It isn't even a purely hypothetical illustration and reconstruction. It's all of these at once. The author sets out to tell the story of Johnny Jones – what he actually does is enumerate the provisions of the Children and Young Persons Act, illustrate its working in a series of doubtful awards, and he does this against a human background which, to say the kindest, is fanciful. The attempts to generalize from so peculiarly an individual case are, as a result, quite dangerously misleading.[36]

The report's objection is to the distortion of fact to which the process of fictionalising is always prone, and what it describes is a documentary drama, poorly executed, which in its extreme form is distinct from a feature. There does, however, seem to have been no formula for determining the balance between fact and fiction in a radio feature, with the result that there still exists a large grey area within which the terms 'feature' and 'play' are interchangeable. The producer Douglas Cleverdon, writing with a full knowledge and reflective awareness of what had been achieved under the aegis of Features, divided the two forms according to the traditions from which they emanated:

A radio play is a dramatic work deriving from the tradition of the theatre, but conceived in terms of radio. A radio feature is, roughly, any constructed programme (that is, other than news bulletins, racing commentaries, and so forth) that derives from the technical apparatus of radio (microphone, control panel, recording gear, loud-speaker). It can combine any sound elements – words, music, sound effects – in any form or mixture of forms – documentary, actuality, dramatized, poetic, musico-dramatic. It has no rules determining what can or cannot be done. And though it may be in dramatic form, it has no need of a dramatic plot.[37]

Cleverdon's view, formulated with the experience of having produced *Under Milk Wood* behind him, simply reinforces the level of uncertainty involved in the problem of definition. He places his emphasis firmly upon style and method of production rather than upon content as such, and like his predecessors he focuses upon the purely formal distinctions.

On the other hand, a writer such as Louis MacNeice sought to emphasise the dramatic possibilities inherent in the feature form. For MacNeice the feature was more than simply a piece of documentary journalism; rather, the selection of material for both the feature and the play should subserve a *dramatic* function: 'The radio feature is a dramatised presentation of actuality but its author should be much more than a *rapporteur* or a cameraman; he must select his actuality material with great discrimination and then keep control of it so that it subserves a single dramatic effect.'[38] 'Actuality' broadcasting, begun by Laurence Gilliam in 1934, and taken up by D. G. Bridson,[39] involved the recording and broadcasting, unscripted, of the voices of ordinary people. MacNeice's own formula for extending and allying this technical innovation to the principle of a unity of action places him firmly within a dramatic tradition. The two seemingly opposed emphases, the one on dramatic form and construction, with its obviously aesthetic appeal, and the other upon the full utilisation of the technical resources of radio in the task of reproducing reality, are precisely what gave the feature a kind of dual identity, while at the same time allowing it access to the dubious claim of being 'pure radio'.[40] The flexibility claimed for the feature was, and is, a primary quality of radio as a whole, but it required the exceptional talents of a Louis MacNeice or a Dylan Thomas to demonstrate precisely how this flexibility might be enlisted in the service of the creative dramatist.

Throughout its early history broadcasters had been conscious of the competing claims of radio and theatre drama. R. E. Jeffrey, Gordon Lea, and later Felix Felton had all sought to emphasise the unique challenge which radio presented to the dramatist, and the writing of plays specifically for the medium became a *desideratum*. Richard Hughes, Lance Sieveking, L. Du Garde Peach, Tyrone Guthrie, and Val Gielgud himself had all laid something of a foundation, and by 1933 the radio play had established itself sufficiently for Gielgud to consider mounting a festival of radio drama.[41] But writing for the medium was, clearly, not enough; in order for it to attain a status comparable to that of the live theatre, it required its own *avant-garde*.[42] Thus, in 1937 Gielgud felt that the time was ripe to introduce an *Experimental Hour*, designed specifically to encourage new writing for radio.[43] The experiment failed, Gielgud was forced to admit, for lack of good material, and with the onset of war experimentation of this sort faded away. Ironically, the major legacy from these years was the 'microphone serial', begun in 1938, firmly established by the end of the war, and regarded in retrospect with some contempt by Gielgud as 'flattery of the ego of the common man'.[44] Serialisation began with the adaptation of literary classics, but with *The English Family Robinson*, *Mrs Dale's Diary*, *The Archers*, and in 1946

Dick Barton Special Agent[45] a degree of popularisation had occurred which seemed more in harmony with the democratic nature of the medium. Indeed, of all the dramatic forms, serialisation and its extension the series have proved the most enduring products of the modern media, with television taking over and elaborating a pattern begun by radio.

Throughout the period of its early development the call from within was consistently for higher standards in radio drama. In many ways, a theory rooted in a strong sense of theatrical tradition was at odds with a practice which had yet to catch up. Paradoxically, while Gielgud sought to achieve these higher standards, early audience research conducted by R. J. Silvey and inaugurated in 1937 uncovered a distinctly unappreciative audience; a sample of views of some 350 listeners to plays and features during that year revealed the following unflattering conclusions:

Its conclusions were that plays were not often easy to follow, that plays specially written for radio had not on the whole been very satisfactory, that background music was often too loud, that effects were often too insistent, that the construction of features was less successful than the choice of subjects, and that too many narrators spoiled the broth.[46]

It seems hardly surprising that Gielgud, who was committed to the idea of theatre and who sought a comparable prestige for radio drama, should have been disillusioned by 1948. In a retrospective view of the years 1929–48 he observed: 'we have failed to discover more than a minimum of first rate work, and equally to establish any real school of pure radio dramatists'.[47] Such a view, however, disregarded the undergrowth of popular drama that emerged during the war years, and that in any dramatic tradition provides a foundation. In addition to the emergence of the microphone serial, other experiments were already under way. In 1939 D. G. Bridson's highly politicised verse Morality play *Aaron's Field* was broadcast; moreover, with the theatres closed, thus giving radio an unexpected monopoly, Bridson went on with Joan Littlewood to experiment further in 'actuality' broadcasting, which Laurence Gilliam had pioneered, and with Frank Nicolls and Wilfred Pickles set out 'to help the country find its voice'.[48] In 1941 Dorothy L. Sayers's controversial play-cycle, *The Man Born To Be King*, began to be broadcast – a dramatic undertaking which brought writer and broadcaster into conflict, but which managed to translate into a distinctly modern idiom both the format and the unusually direct language of the medieval Mystery plays. This was a novel application of the microphone serial, undertaken by a Renaissance scholar, herself fully cognisant of the tradition of English drama. In radio in the 1940s both the Mystery and the Morality structures, along with that of medieval Romance, provided inspiration for the dramatist. In 1942 Louis MacNeice's documentary verse drama *Christopher Columbus* was broadcast, and later on in the same year the *Famous Players in Famous Plays* series was launched. In April 1943 *Saturday Night Theatre* began, obviously as a substitute for live theatrical experience, with an adaptation of the Dorothy L. Sayers short story *The Man with No Face*. Later in the same year Edward Sackville-West's spectacular failure *The Rescue*, 'A Melodrama for Broadcasting based on Homer's *Odyssey*', with music specially commissioned from a reluctant Benjamin Britten, was broadcast in two parts on successive evenings (25–6 November 1943).

By 1945, some twenty-one years after its inception, radio drama, with all its variety, had come of age. During that year and in response to the variety of BBC broadcasting, the Light Programme was established. In January 1946 Louis MacNeice's *The Dark Tower* was broadcast, and later in October of the same year the *World Theatre* series began with a broadcast of Gilbert Murray's translation of Euripides' *Hippolytus*. By this time different categories of listening had begun to emerge, and also in 1946 the Third Programme came into existence, thus inaugurating a division of broadcasting which, *mutatis mutandis*, has remained in principle ever since. It is perhaps revealing, however, that notwithstanding the difficulty which it presents to the listener, MacNeice's *The Dark Tower* was first broadcast in the more popular Home Service, which continued, even after the division took place, to broadcast a wide variety of radio plays to an audience which was statistically a truly national one. It was also during the late 1940s that Henry Reed, a writer committed to the principle of separating popular from specialised listening, began to write regularly for radio. His impressive adaptation of Herman Melville's *Moby Dick* was broadcast in 1947, and in the early 1950s he emerged as both a radio dramatist in his own right and as a translator of considerable talent introducing radio audiences to the work of Continental dramatists such as Pirandello, Montherlant, and Ugo Betti.

These achievements notwithstanding, there was concern from

within the BBC in the years immediately following the war that the attempts to establish a thriving tradition of radio drama had been less than successful. For example, the Drama Department's 'crime-theme output' was criticised both for its moral decadence and its artistic mediocrity,[49] while the BBC was consistently reminded of its obligation 'to be a means of raising public taste'.[50] On the question of morality, E. A. Harding's instruction to all members of the Drama Department typifies the sort of constraint to which broadcasters were, and still are, subject. On the question of profanity in plays, a subject which had certainly been broached in relation to the broadcasting of Dorothy L. Sayers's *The Man Born To Be King*, Harding observed:

There has been a good deal of correspondence recently in the Press and direct to the BBC complaining about the use of bad language in broadcast plays and I must remind producers that they are individually responsible for cutting all bad language that they cannot give positive justification for on dramatic grounds either of situation or characterization.

It is difficult to give a comprehensive definition of bad language, but the scale ranges from 'Christ', 'Hell', 'Bloody' and 'God' at worst to the comparatively innocuous but still unwarrantable 'Damn' and 'Blast'. The same standards should be observed in respect of plays for all programme services including Third, but producers should bear in mind that the lesser oaths in modern comedies and thrillers for Home Service and Light Programme are most likely to evoke complaint from family listeners. Only too often there is no solid dramatic reason for them and they merely represent careless or exaggerated writing by authors. It would be helpful if play adaptors were told to observe this policy when preparing texts for broadcast.

Unless there is some improvement in this matter there is danger of a flat prohibition on all oaths in all plays and this would be damaging to dramatic values, particularly in serious plays.[51]

It should be observed in passing that Harding's instruction reveals a degree of freedom accorded to radio denied by the Lord Chamberlain to theatre performance; it was a freedom which some twenty years later was to allow a broadcast of Harold Pinter's play *Landscape* after it had been refused a licence for theatrical performance.[52] But there was a degree of dissatisfaction with the general level of artistic achievement too. Gielgud's pessimistic retrospective view was reinforced in specific terms in 1949 by the report of Harman Grisewood, the Controller of the Third Programme; Grisewood conceded:

Our experience to date has shewn that we cannot expect a very substantial flow of worthwhile contemporary radio drama at Third Programme level. We will be lucky if during the year we can find say ten pieces that are suitable. For the rest we must decide what to perform from the corpus of dramatic literature which is written for the theatre.[53]

R. D. Smith, in his tribute to Louis MacNeice, has observed that in terms of technique, all the possibilities of the radio play had been 'discovered and exploited by the end of the 'twenties by Richard Hughes, Lance Sieveking, and Tyrone Guthrie'.[54] With the work of Bridson, Dorothy L. Sayers, and MacNeice himself, a foundation was laid for a generation of radio dramatists who came to prominence in the 1950s. Dylan Thomas, Henry Reed, and Giles Cooper devoted a considerable amount of their time to writing for radio, while Samuel Beckett, like Harold Pinter and Susan Hill after him, was an occasional writer for the medium. It was during the period 1950–60 that the role of radio as regards drama was inadvertently widened by a concatenation of circumstances, not least of which was the fact that television was rapidly becoming a serious competitor for audiences, while there was also a renewal of interest in live theatre.

As early as 1923 the BBC had sought permission to broadcast performances of plays, but had met with initial hostility from the acting profession.[55] In short, the new medium threatened the identity of the old. By 1952, when the then Director of Television, George Barnes, suggested to Val Gielgud the possibility of simultaneous sound and vision broadcasting, it was radio which sought to protect its identity in the face of the threat from a competitor. Indeed, in a somewhat authoritative tone, Gielgud's reply to Barnes's suggestion lays out the principles as well as the practical difficulties involved in such a scheme:

In reply to your memorandum of the 17th, much as I dislike to seem merely negatively unhelpful I very much doubt the practicality of a play S.B. in sound and vision proving satisfactory. I believe that at present there are insuperable difficulties on the Equity front, but apart from that we are up against the fundamental handicap of a complete basic difference of tempo in the two mediums. This was proved conclusively when attempts were made to relay plays in sound from the stages of theatres.
point of view of the listener the thing invariably emerged as
ssion of jerky scenes intermingled with long and for the
mprehensible pauses. This handicap would probably be
e of such formalized works as Shakespeare or even better,
sics in which action is comparatively limited, but even over

these I would have my doubts. To tackle the thing in reverse, i.e. to add vision to a play written for broadcasting, would almost certainly come to grief either scenically or because of the difficulty of getting merely radio performers to learn their lines.[56]

Gielgud was in a strong bargaining position, since, for example, in 1955 *Saturday Night Theatre* (Home Service) attracted some 6.75 million listeners, with *World Theatre* and *The Monday Night Play* attracting audiences of 1.25 and 2.75 million listeners respectively.[57]

Curiously enough, the new, if somewhat loose, alliance which emerged in the 1950s was to be between radio and the live theatre, especially since before the development of sophisticated tape-recording techniques, the former also considered itself to be a live medium. After a period in the doldrums, theatre drama underwent something of a revitalisation following the sluggish success of John Osborne's *Look Back in Anger* at the Royal Court Theatre in 1956. But even before this, and much in the spirit of Harman Grisewood's observations about the difficulty of attracting enough consistently good new drama to itself, radio had begun to take seriously its role as mediator of what was current in dramatic writing generally. For example, Gielgud had asked for a report on Samuel Beckett's *Waiting for Godot*, which during 1953 was taking Paris by storm, but his conservative tastes led him to dismiss the play as worthless, so that its first performance in Britain was at the Arts Theatre in London in 1955, rather than on radio. However, Beckett's concern with the minutiae of linguistic expression made him almost a natural radio dramatist, and largely due to the persuasions of BBC producer Donald McWhinnie, *All That Fall* (1957) and *Embers* (1959) were written especially for radio.[58] But against Gielgud's *faux pas* with regard to *Waiting for Godot* must be set the larger aspects of BBC policy during the 1950s in relation to Continental drama generally, a policy reinforced in the 1960s by Martin Esslin and still very much part of current BBC practice. Reports upon plays being performed on the Continent were regularly commissioned, with a view to translation and broadcasting. In this way, for example, Henry Reed's influential translations of the plays of the Italian dramatist Betti first reached British audiences. Thus, in a very r⸱ radio became, and has to some extent remained, a k⸱ tive *avant-garde* theatre augmenting the sm⸱ experimental theatres, and introducing audien⸱

The period 1950–60 began with the Features Department very much in the ascendancy. MacNeice's plays had been a product of Gilliam's department, and in 1954 Features producer Douglas Cleverdon produced Dylan Thomas's *Under Milk Wood*. But by 1960 the Drama Department had overtaken its rival, and in 1963 Features was dissolved.[59] The variety of drama produced throughout these years was considerable, including popular serials such as Charles Chilton's *Journey into Space* – his use of the medium was effective but unobtrusive – the witty satiric comedies of Henry Reed – some of which were a little too ribald to be broadcast uncensored even on the Third Programme[60] – the challenging plays of Giles Cooper, Samuel Beckett, and the young Harold Pinter, in addition to the broadcasting of Continental plays in translation. The policy of distinguishing between serious and popular drama, however, meant that among committed experimentalists such as D. G. Bridson the Home Service became a byword for mediocrity. Of radio in the 1950s Bridson observed: 'Where the young listener was learning to look back only in anger, the BBC Home Service insisted on looking back in complacency. The age group that it catered for exclusively in the fifties was also in its fifties.'[61] Such a view does not do full justice to the facts, although it does bring into focus the perennial paradox exemplified by the BBC's commitment to providing popular drama on the one hand, and new, technically innovative, and intellectually challenging plays on the other. Incidentally, Bridson's comments on broadcasting in the 1970s are even more devastating.[62]

Ironically, it was during the late 1950s, after the revival of interest in live theatre, and especially when the threat from television began to intensify, that radio drama began to gain ground. Gradually it came to be regarded as a respectable alternative outlet for practising dramatists, giving access to far larger audiences than the theatre could attract. Moreover, in 'extending one sense in high definition' – to recall McLuhan's phrase – it lent itself naturally to drama which expressed its conflicts primarily through language; Samuel Beckett, and after him Harold Pinter, have both exploited to the full this characteristic of radio. Indeed, in the case of Pinter, radio can claim a modest part in his rise to prominence, since it first employed him as an actor[63] and subsequently, between 1959 and 1960, broadcast his three radio plays; Donald McWhinnie, then Assistant Head of the Drama Department, produced *A Slight Ache* (July 1959) and *A Night Out* (March 1960), while Barbara Bray produced *The Dwarfs* (December 1960).

To what extent radio bequeathed anything in the way of formal influence to the development of British drama, or to particular dramatists, such as Harold Pinter or Tom Stoppard, is, and will continue to be for some time, a matter of debate. What is certain is that the radio play has become a viable alternative dramatic form which many of our leading dramatists have, at one time or another, attempted. In the case of dramatists such as Pinter or Stoppard or John Arden, radio is a medium to be mastered, and it does offer an artistic freedom different from that of the theatre, but plays such as theirs contribute only inadvertently to a corpus of specifically radio drama. Part of the problem, certainly, lies in the fact that while dramatists continue to write, a retrospective view of their overall achievement will always be unsatisfactory.

David Wade, in his chapter 'British Radio Drama since 1960', succeeds in imposing a degree of order upon a considerable body of all but intractable material, and his distinction between 'radio drama' as an original form and 'drama by means of radio'[64] is a valuable one. He goes on to distinguish between what is offered by way of dramatic writing on the various BBC wavelengths, although he is less than sanguine about technical and artistic developments in the medium as a whole. Indeed, although technical improvements in the quality of broadcasting pioneered in the 1950s have sought to give radio an even greater flexibility, in artistic terms the paradoxes remain. The Third Programme (in 1970 renamed Radio 3) has become, *a fortiori*, the repository of 'high culture', according to new dramatic writing a minority status more in keeping with the live theatre than with a mass medium. In one sense the wheel has come full circle. As radio itself has grown in confidence with regard to the evolution of its own extensive and varied body of dramatic literature – albeit the distinction is not always an easy one to sustain – so it has sought to reiterate the assertions of its pioneers that the discipline of listening to radio drama is a serious, minority activity, even though the minority of listeners may be counted in millions. Moreover, the broadcasting of classical music, which first began in earnest in 1964 in the Third Programme, serves to provide a context for new dramatic writing which reinforces this view. The present Radio 4 (formerly the Home Service) remains in theory the repository of popular drama, while, in the words of the

Annan Report, Radio 3 is naturally associated with 'more esoteric and demanding plays'.[65]

Of course, writers cannot usually be blamed for the scheduling of their plays on radio, and there is, indeed, a generation of dramatists now writing for the medium who are committed to the radio play as a legitimate art form, writers such as Rhys Adrian, R. C. Scriven, Don Haworth, Fay Weldon, and Jonathan Raban. Moreover, there are some signs that the distinctions accepted in theory are proving less rigid in practice, since there is some interchange of plays between Radio 3 and Radio 4. For example, what in 1959 was considered *avant-garde*, and only fit for broadcasting in the Third Programme, is now accepted into the mainstream of popular taste, as a recent repeat of Harold Pinter's *A Slight Ache*, in the popular *Saturday Afternoon Theatre* series (Radio 4, 29 June 1979) shows. Similarly, Tom Stoppard's own recent adaptation for radio of his stage play *Rosencrantz and Guildenstern Are Dead* was broadcast on Radio 3 (24 December 1978), while an adaptation of his television play *Professional Foul* was broadcast in the popular *Monday Play* series on Radio 4 (11 June 1979). The reverse is also true, with space being found on Radio 3 for plays originally broadcast in the popular *Monday Play* series on Radio 4, as recent examples such as John Arden's extraordinarily challenging play *Pearl* and Tom McGrath's *The Hard Man* indicate. Of course, categories are always open to violation, and radio is no exception to this general rule. But what is certain is that the radio play has now, after a history stretching back over half a century, become firmly established as one of a number of dramatic forms whose collective function is to supply what Raymond Williams has called 'constant dramatic representation as a daily habit and need'.[66]

Considering the volume of broadcast drama – the Annan Report recently noted some 1,250 hours of plays of various kinds broadcast during 1975–6[67] – it is surprising that the radio play has attracted so little in the way of formal critical attention. Many of its earliest critics were themselves practitioners who combined proselytising enthusiasm for the new medium with an almost apologetic awareness of its inadequacies. Much theoretical emphasis was ultimately (if not primarily) aimed at justifying radio's most obvious deficiency: it was a medium which relied exclusively upon *hearing*. R. E. Jeffrey, who first formulated many of the ideas taken up by subsequent apologists, boldly converted this deficiency into a strength by a characteristic appeal to the highest court of drama. In an article in *Radio Times* for 6 June 1924, he enthused:

The amazing advantage of listening without sight to words which are arranged to build emotion-compelling situations is that every person places the emotion in a setting fitted to or known by him. Thus, the emotion becomes a power interacting with a personal experience. Here the artificiality is entirely done away with, and if the ability of the speaker is of a high order, the emotion of the situation is universally accepted – it becomes a personal picture adapted to the mentality of the individual and assumes a reality which can be far greater than any effect provided on an ordinary stage. This is but a development of Shakespeare's idea that curtains of unostentatious appearance should be used for backgrounds.

Jeffrey's inaccurate knowledge of the Shakespearean stage notwithstanding, what he emphasised from the very outset was radio's stimulus to the listener's *individual imagination*. By temporarily relinquishing his sense of sight, the listener could gain access to an experience equal to the best in the culture's literary heritage. The possibilities for lyrical expression existed by virtue of the capacity of words which could be 'arranged to build emotion-compelling situations', and which the listener could complete from his own experience; also the words themselves would stand for physical objects, thus enabling the listener to reconstruct in his own imagination a series of concrete images of (and hence responses to) the real world.[68]

In 1926, Gordon Lea, in a handbook that Jeffrey obviously admired, since he urged all his producers to read it, took up some of these problems and restated them in recognisably Platonic terms. On the question of the relationship between radio and the real world Lea asserted that the radio play was superior to its theatrical counterpart because it was one step nearer reality than the shadowy world of physical forms: 'All art is an expression of imagination – so that at the best a stage scene is a second-hand affair – whereas the radio-scene is beyond art – it is reality itself, not an isolated expression of imagination, but imagination itself.'[69] Tyrone Guthrie, dissatisfied with stage naturalism, was substantially of the same opinion. He declared that the pictures radio sought to create were 'solely of the mind', and that they were therefore 'less substantial but more real than the cardboard grottoes, the calico rosebuds, the dusty grandeur of the stage'.[70]

Rather than simply reproduce with the aid of verbal imagery a kind of quasi-photographic verisimilitude, Guthrie was drawn towards an exploration of 'the purely symphonic possibilities of the medium'.[71] The 'mental pictures' he elicited were an essential feature of dramatic construction, serving exclusively to 'provide the boundaries of the action of the play';[72] moreover, they were a product of the 'atmosphere' created by the 'voice colours' of the actors[73] and were therefore an integral part of the structure of the play's poetic imagery. This emphasis upon dramatic construction led Guthrie to attempt in his own plays for radio formal patterning, repetitions of phrase and incident, ritualised choric reinforcements of the central action, and a careful juxtaposition of detail, all of which were designed to generate a kind of spatio-temporal awareness of the action in the listener's imagination.[74]

From the very beginning, the practical implications of radio's dependence upon one sense only for its effects were fully grasped by dramatists themselves. In a broadcast on 15 January 1974 to celebrate the fiftieth anniversary of the first performance of his play *A Comedy of Danger*, Richard Hughes recalled his own thinking on the matter:

I argued to myself like this. There had never been before anything which people had had to take in by their ears only – anything dramatic, I mean – so it occurred to me that obviously the best thing was to choose a theme which would happen entirely in the dark, and an accident in a coalmine suggested itself. And that's how it came that I wrote this play beginning with the lines: 'The lights have gone out'. And it was hoping that everybody would listen in the dark and get the feeling of the darkness that way.[75]

This naturalising of the play's thematic concerns, bringing them into focus with the listener's own blindness, represents an enterprising solution to the problem, although it left unanswered the larger question of what might happen if the physical setting demanded by a particular dramatic action did not harmonise with the listener's predicament. But even so, the play is more than simply a piece of naturalistic drama. Hughes uses the 'blind' setting as a backdrop for a series of typical dramatic conflicts; youth opposes age, life is threatened temporarily, and the larger metaphysical issues of faith, hope, and despair are neatly worked in. Hughes's characters are stereotypes, thinly disguised secular Morality figures, whose symbolic value is determined by the very economy of the medium itself. The play's delicate ironies work effectively, inviting the listener to share an imaginative excursion into the deeper recesses of the human soul.

Hughes's solution to the problem posed by the blindness of radio has been extended in many different ways by those who followed him. A prominent feature of radio dramatic structure became the interior monologue, conveying to the listener pictures which are, by definition, solely of the mind. The action of Hughes's play was continuous, but a medium which could focus in this way upon mental processes could imitate the flexibility of the human mind itself, with the result that soliloquy, flashback, the cross-cutting of scenes, all became part of the 'grammar' of the radio play. After the invention of the dramatic control panel, the microphone became as versatile as the film camera was later to become, and dramatists such as Lance Sieveking and Tyrone Guthrie rose to the challenge which it presented. In plays such as Guthrie's *The Flowers Are Not for You To Pick* (1930) and Sieveking's *The Wings of the Morning* (1934) this flexibility was fully demonstrated. For later radio dramatists, in addition to swift verbal transitions, the theme of blindness became a kind of reference point; for example, in Louis MacNeice's *The Dark Tower*, the blind seer Blind Peter can testify to the reality of the dragon that Roland is destined to face in such a way that the symbolic nature of the quest is always kept before us. In Dylan Thomas's *Under Milk Wood*, the blind narrator, Captain Cat, is used as one of a number of filters of the sound-impressions which we receive. In Harold Pinter's *A Slight Ache*, Edward's encroaching physical blindness is symbolic in that it represents a moral blindness to his wife Flora's qualities, and leads ultimately to his being rejected in favour of some unseen but ever-present force. More recently, Jonathan Raban's *Will You Accept the Call?* (24 March 1977) returns to a naturalising of the theme by placing the listener in the position of receiving a telephone call from a deranged phone-in fanatic. In all these plays, it should be noted, the listener is, in a sense, created by the dramatist.

By setting *A Comedy of Danger* in a situation where the characters were deprived of the sense of sight, Hughes effectively sought to make the medium itself transparent. In other words, the listener was persuaded to accept unquestioningly the play's rhetorical structure, and this allowed him to share the experience of the characters in the play. Indeed, such was the concern to preserve illusions of this kind that for a brief period Val Gielgud

refused to allow the *Radio Times* to print the names of actors; the
listener had to be persuaded that what he heard was *actually*
taking place and that by collusion in the enterprise he was party
to the action. This general philosophy prevailed for some considerable time, and many objections to the use of the narrator in
radio plays arose directly out of the fear that it would result in the
shattering of the illusion. However, even a dramatist as aware of
the challenge as Tyrone Guthrie could not avoid inadvertently
shattering the illusion from time to time; *Squirrel's Cage* contains
an amusing example of what can happen when dialogue and the
physical setting which it communicates actually collide. The
action of the play demands a visualised physical setting, the
details of which are contained in the dialogue, but in a scene
where Mary and John argue over his son Henry's decision to
break out of family tradition and go to South Africa, the idiom
itself conveys an inaccurate piece of information, which the
dialogue then corrects:

JOHN. That's it – that's like you women – argue, argue, argue. But
reason? No, never.
MARY. Are *you* reasonable? You don't know the meaning of the word.
You're just a stupid, well-meaning, stick-in-the-mud mediocrity. You
always were, and you always will be.
JOHN. I'll thank you, Mary, not to be abusive to me under my own roof –
that is, in the garden.[76]

It would be difficult to justify such a momentary adjustment of
the dialogue, since its effect is to draw our attention to the artifice
itself, thereby breaking the illusion which, at this point in the
play, the dramatist is at pains to sustain.

Notwithstanding a lapse of this sort, the theoretical emphasis
which Guthrie, and after him newspaper critics such as Sydney
Moseley,[77] placed upon rejecting the notion of creating a quasi-
photographic verisimilitude in radio was one which later found
support from the dramatist Henry Reed. In a letter to George
Barnes concerning an adaptation of Thomas Hardy's *The Dynasts*,
he wrote:

It is a MYTH that Radio has any capacity for inducing in the mind of the
listener anything in the nature of PARTICULARIZED VISUALIZATION. You
might, once in an evening persuade him to see *one* of those great stage
directions; but not, I think, more than one. For when radio has to suggest
a *scene* to the listener, it does best to give only a brief powerful hint from
which, with the help of specially written *dialogue designed to an end*, the

listener can without effort and perhaps only half-consciously, construct a scene from the innumerable landscapes or roomscapes (!) bundled away in his own memory.[78]

Reed's remarks take us back to the notion of the listener's creative role in incorporating himself into the action of the play, although he reaffirms that to attempt to overcompensate for the blind nature of the medium would be futile.

While dramatists formulated practical solutions to the problems which radio presented, psychologists showed some interest in precisely what was communicated to the listener and how it was received into his mental framework. The idea that radio appealed to the *individual* raised questions about what kind of experience he might use to supplement the material offered to him by way of dramatic representation. The paradox of radio as a public–private medium was grasped from the very outset, but the question of what the listener could reasonably be expected to receive impinged also upon some of the more detailed issues of form and presentation. In 1931 the psychologist T. H. Pear emphasised that hearing was a cognitive process – 'Let us remember that we hear not with our ears but with our minds'[79] – and that, therefore, a radio play must, *a fortiori*, be an individual as opposed to a group activity, whose effect depended upon the 'mental apparatus' of each listener.[80] Pear recorded his own response while listening to particular radio plays, and he distinguished between those images which he considered to be part of his own personality and experience and those which the rhetorical structure of each production imposed upon him:

Dream-images are often, perhaps usually, symbols of complexes which have been aroused inside the listener's mind, and therefore, from his standpoint, are important. In radio-drama, on the other hand, the experiences evoking the images are sprung upon the listener. His personal complexes may not be ready to leap out, receive them and immediately illustrate them by vivid images.[81]

He concluded that some of the images he received, as a result, were 'diagrammatic, two-dimensional and half-unreal, like a piece of stage scenery observed at close quarters'[82] – the very effect that dramatists such as Tyrone Guthrie sought to avoid. For Pear, radio drama was best suited to representing those experiences which did not lend themselves easily to visualisation. Hence, fantasy and the supernatural presented the radio play with special opportunities,[83] with the strong implication that what the medium could do best was to represent the psychological processes of the human mind, as evidenced in stream-of-consciousness technique, along with those elements of metaphysical 'reality' which could only be imperfectly realised in visual terms.

While Pear concerned himself with the psychology of the listener, and by implication with the larger questions of form, G. W. Allport and H. Cantrill emphasised the ways in which the listener processed particular details which he received aurally. Their concern was primarily with the question of judging personality from the human voice alone, and radio provided a convenient example of this process. They observed: 'probably most people who listen to radio speakers feel assured that some of their judgements are dependable. Often the impression is nothing more than a feeling of favour or aversion, but sometimes it represents a surprisingly definitive judgement concerning the speakers' physical, intellectual, and moral qualities.'[84] In radio drama generally, this is the primary method upon which dramatic characterisation depends for its effectiveness. While at one extreme it might be said that the stereotyping of voice quality results automatically in a stereotyping of character, it is clear from the findings of Allport and Cantrill that a more sophisticated form of characterisation was possible, even though the pressure is always upon the dramatist to give his characters an immediacy of impact upon the listener's imagination. A convenient example of this shorthand method of depicting character may be found in an early Tom Stoppard radio play, *If You're Glad I'll Be Frank* (8 February 1966); in John Tydeman's production of this comedy, the characters Myrtle, Mortimer, Courtney-Smith, Sir John, and Lord Coot are all given immediately recognisable speech-mannerisms which lead us quickly and precisely to make judgements concerning their 'physical, intellectual, and moral qualities'.[85] For Allport and Cantrill, the images elicited from the mind of the listener were both psychological and social, since in addition to reflecting the structures of human thought, they also drew on the listener's own perception of a social milieu. Indeed, in certain respects, the act of listening to radio was becoming analogous to the act of reading.

Practitioners, theoreticians, and psychologists alike all encountered in their various ways the knotty problem of what kind of reality radio drama communicated to its listeners. Gordon Lea's unashamedly Platonic stance received partial support from Tyrone Guthrie and Henry Reed, but it was the theorist of radio Rudolph Arnheim who sought to establish analytically the larger aesthetic context within which the radio play operated. Writing in 1936, Arnheim was fully aware of what constituted the grammar of radio, and he saw 'one of the greatest artistic tasks of the wireless' as being 'the welding of music sound and speech into a single material'.[86] For him, the advent of radio heralded a return to a primitive universe in which the listener should feel himself to be 'back in the primaeval age where the word was still sound and the sound still word'.[87] Arnheim speculated that the purer the sound was, and the more musical its structure, the nearer it approached reality, thus allowing radio to claim a natural kinship with

the poetic word and the musical note; sounds born of earth and those born of spirit found each other; and so music entered the material world, the world enveloped itself in music, and reality, newly created by thought in all its intensity, presented itself much more directly objectively and concretely than on printed paper; what hitherto had only been thought or described now appeared materialized as corporeal actuality.[88]

Here theology and nineteenth-century aesthetics were brought to bear upon the question of the form of the radio play. Indeed, as in music and poetry, the radio play required careful orchestration, with the voices of the actors having to blend together as though it were a musical composition.[89] Arnheim's theoretical framework lies behind the musical content of a large number of radio plays. Dramatists such as Edward Sackville-West (among many others) sought in his play *The Rescue* to give music itself (provided especially for the production by Benjamin Britten) a status coequal with poetic dialogue. Indeed, evidence of its continued currency may be found in the BBC's planning policy for the Third Programme and its successor Radio 3, which habitually juxtaposes drama and classical music.

In certain respects, however, this current juxtaposition is a tendentious one. Arnheim was well aware of the fact that pitch and duration were the primary characteristics of what he called 'the acoustic image'[90] and to these D. G. Bridson added a third, 'rhythm'.[91] Moreover, his general theory of sound, although rooted ultimately in Victorian aesthetics, sought to establish the essentially *dramatic* quality of radio generally and of the radio play in particular. Unlike Sieveking before him, Arnheim did not regret the evanescence of the medium; rather, he viewed it as an indispensable condition of its existence, rejecting as meaningless 'the concept of a timeless representation of sound'.[92]

Arnheim's account is a perceptive one, but the problem involved in linking theories of music or pure sound too closely with what happens in radio is that it tends to play down the more diverse functions of language that are hinted at by Allport and Cantrill. Where music or even unmelodic sound effects are used in a radio play, their function is usually, as all theoreticians agree, expressive, whether they communicate information in some symbolic form or are used to evoke a particular mood. Too great an emphasis upon one particular strand in a complex fabric of sound leads invariably to difficulty, as is shown by some of the abortive attempts made by D. G. Bridson to put his own theories into practice. In his Foreword to *The Christmas Child* Bridson advanced the notion that rhyme and rhythm are what cause the attentive reader to think of poetry 'in terms of sound'.[93] Moreover, the demands made upon the listener by spoken poetry were direct in that they called for 'simplicity, an understanding of speech rhythms and the quality of immediacy'.[94] Such a view was aimed at justifying, and making practical adjustments to, the oral medium of radio, without sacrificing intellectual complexity. However, the results were less than satisfying in practice, as this brief extract from *The Christmas Child* shows:

MARY. [...] It's me that's having the child not you ...!
JOE. I know it lass, – but you'll pull through ...!
It gets you down a bit, sometimes, –
But everyone has it sooner or later ...
Things'll turn out right in the end ...
I'll have a bit more mashed potato.[95]

Not even the presence of Wilfred Pickles in the cast, nor the longest pauses allowable can disguise the pathetic effects of rhyme and rhythm here, both of which contribute to a poetry which confuses simplicity with simple-mindedness. Bridson might have done better to follow the example of Louis MacNeice, who observed that although radio drama's appeal is 'to the emotions rather than to the reason', it nevertheless requires 'a sensitive more than an educated audience'.[96]

Many of the issues rehearsed by Rudolph Arnheim in 1936 were resurrected again, though in a slightly different guise, in 1959 in Donald McWhinnie's book *The Art of Radio*. McWhinnie had been Assistant Head of Drama at the BBC since 1953, he had played a large part in helping to expand the policy of introducing listeners to the work of Continental dramatists, and he had accumulated considerable experience in producing the radio plays of Beckett and Pinter, among many others. Unlike Arnheim, who was concerned to map out what was possible in radio, McWhinnie was concerned to defend what was rapidly becoming a minority mass medium as far as drama was concerned, in the face of the threat from television. But like his predecessor, he too turned his attention to the question of the reality which radio depicts, emphasising along the way the variety of styles of presentation made possible by an exclusive reliance upon sound.

McWhinnie rejected the notion that radio was a naturalistic medium, and he argued that a distinction should be maintained between *realism*, as one of a number of modes of presentation, and reality, which presumably was what a radio play communicated to its audience: 'Sound radio cannot aim at realism but only at the most persuasive illusion of reality.'[97] This echoes the idealism of earlier commentators who had argued that the radio play presented a mimetic reflection of a non-physical reality, and that the microphone itself was the instrument of sincerity and truth. But it also makes possible a formalistic critical approach to questions such as dramatic construction, and detailed matters of style. McWhinnie was mainly interested in poetic imagery and language, the essentially literary elements of the radio play, and thus, for him, reality in the context of radio was determined by his own aesthetic preconceptions and the attendant concern to establish the art of radio as an equal of the literary arts generally.

The question concerning what sort of reality the radio play seeks to reflect is a complex one. In one sense, which cannot altogether be overlooked, it reproduces, by means of a translation, the conditions of stage performance, with a dialogue replete with references to a physical world compensating for the absence of a visual dimension. A convenient example of this might be the opening lines of Pinter's *A Slight Ache*, where a physical scene is painted by means of a dialogue which is also charged with carrying the burden of communicating a sense of the relationship between the two characters, Edward and Flora:

FLORA. Have you noticed the honeysuckle this morning?
EDWARD. The what?
FLORA. The honeysuckle.
EDWARD. Honeysuckle? Where?
FLORA. By the back gate, Edward.
EDWARD. Is that honeysuckle? I thought it was . . . convolvulus or something.
FLORA. But you know it's honeysuckle.
EDWARD. I tell you I thought it was convolvulus.
    [Pause]
FLORA. It's in wonderful flower.
EDWARD. I must look.
FLORA. The whole garden's in flower this morning. The clematis, the convolvulus. Everything. I was out at seven. I stood by the pool.[98]

This kind of relationship between radio drama and theatre may be regarded as 'intertextual',[99] in the sense that each medium complements and is to a degree dependent upon the other. Such a view eschews the concept of pure radio initiated by Lance Sieveking and later taken up by McWhinnie, but it also accounts for the demands made upon dialogue in a radio play. Thus, in one sense, radio drama appeals, as we saw earlier, to the canon of established drama, although its emphasis upon *language* – and McWhinnie rightly emphasised that 'In radio the spoken word is in close focus'[100] – allows it access to another court of appeal, that of literature. And yet it cannot be literature in the accepted sense of the term; rather it must be, McWhinnie indicated, a kind of literature in performance: 'The modern convention is to think of literature as print and to assume that any work which lends itself to speaking or performance is inevitably of inferior quality.'[101] He did not, however, suggest that the radio script might be treated in the same way that formal criticism has learned to treat the conventional dramatic text: as the sum of all possible performances. Indeed, while repeat recordings have latterly become the norm in radio, new productions of original radio plays are by no means common. In radio the relationship between text and performance is a close one, because dialogue is required to be explicit, and it is precisely this fullness of detail, which can be achieved in a variety of ways, that forms the basis of the claim of the text to be literature.[102] Moreover, the ability to preserve recordings has the effect of converting the performance itself into something approaching the permanence of print, whereas in the theatre each performance is unique. To this extent, it could be argued that radio drama is capable of reflecting a literary reality, one which was readily accessible to the very minority of cultured individuals to which McWhinnie appealed as his audience. McWhinnie's general thesis, then, sought to *create* an audience for serious radio drama, and the conditions of its existence harmonised conveniently with a long-standing claim made by the BBC that it was responsible for preserving cultural standards.

A major stumbling-block to this neat apologia was the characteristic which, despite the technological facility for preserving performances, radio shared with its evidently more attractive successor, television; its ephemerality. To be fair, McWhinnie acknowledged this: 'In sound radio there is certainly no turning back; the performance is ephemeral, it dissolves as soon as it is heard.'[103] But then, again, this could be adduced as a characteristic of *all* dramatic performances, and as such need not be given any separate theoretical justification. Moreover, so long as it could be argued that the radio play, like any other work of literature or traditional drama, sought to reflect a fixed reality, then the potential force of this inconvenient fact could be neutralised. Arnheim had sought to solve the problem by an appeal to theology and aesthetics; McWhinnie, attracted to Beckett and Pinter, could explain the metaphysics of radio in more eclectic terms, referring back to the analogy with music, but also taking account of more recent existentialist interpretations of reality: 'The radio act comes out of silence, vibrates in the void and in the mind, and returns to silence like music.'[104] It is interesting to note in passing that McWhinnie did not attempt to distinguish between the different *kinds* of silence which occurred in radio plays. Thus, ephemerality became a means to an end, having no justification of its own, while the concept of radio as a medium of entertainment and therefore by definition subject to the pressures of continuous change, was something that McWhinnie was committed to rejecting on principle.

Part of the difficulty in holding on to the concept of a fixed reality which radio reflects is that it tends to obscure the actual 'stuff of radio'. A radio play, by its very nature, cannot present an analogue of experience in the same way that, for example, a photographic image can.[105] Hence, its imagery must be rhetorical rather than simply iconic.[106] This means that just as the structure of a radio play is man-made, so it refers to other structures of experience outside itself which are also the products of the human mind. To suggest, as Lea, Arnheim, and McWhinnie seem to be doing, that radio drama bypasses the very structures of experience from which it emerges is, in effect, to deprive it of those very characteristics which are its distinctive features. Indeed, its language, which it shares with the listener, is really a kind of mediating system of 'sound-signs' which both parties agree will conventionally represent particular kinds of experience. A crude example might be the sound of the ubiquitous BBC seagull, first introduced in the early days of radio and used conventionally to suggest a particular location and atmosphere. The seagull's cry thus became transformed into one of a large pattern of rhetorical devices. Similarly the rattle of a tea-cup *signifies* 'kitchen', which the listener then complements from his own experience of what a kitchen is; the sound of a door closing signifies 'room'; 'live' and 'dead' sound signify space and intimacy respectively; and so on.

A general view of this sort enlarges considerably McWhinnie's category of realism, while at the same time questioning the assumption which lies behind his use of the phrase 'illusion of reality'. Moreover, in acknowledging specifically both the 'metaphoric' and 'metonymic' propensities of radio,[107] it opens the way for a more detailed formal critical analysis of its particular elements and of the larger social pressures to which they are, by their very nature, subjected. In this way it becomes possible to explain why such plays as Richard Hughes's *A Comedy of Danger* or Tyrone Guthrie's *Squirrel's Cage* strike us now as being dated in their values and attitudes, even though we may applaud their technical accomplishment. It is perhaps worth recalling that Arnheim considered ephemerality as an indispensable feature of radio; by contrast, McWhinnie sought to convert listening into a highly concentrated quasi-critical activity which, in the final analysis, threatened to become self-justifying.

With few exceptions, the majority of the theoretical justifications of radio came from those directly engaged in broadcasting, so that to a very large extent criticism became the preserve of the practitioner. Moreover, whereas early enthusiasm was generated by an awareness of the potential which the medium offered to the dramatist, by the late 1950s when Donald McWhinnie's book appeared, radio was fighting a rear-guard action in the face of the threat from television. Formal criticism was the preserve of publications such as *Radio Times* and *The Listener*, although occasional review columns appeared in the national newspapers. It is hardly surprising, therefore, that those dramatists who published their plays – and the fact that they did publish them suggests a degree of interest in the public at large – invariably felt obliged to justify their endeavours.

Of those dramatists who did, it was, perhaps, Louis MacNeice above all who managed to achieve a sustained critique of radio drama without having to resort to the special pleading that characterises so many accounts. In his Introduction to *Christopher Columbus*, first published in 1944, and in his General Introduction to *The Dark Tower*, published in 1947, he managed to combine lucid critical analysis with practical suggestions for the writer of radio plays. In the Introduction to *Christopher Columbus* he outlined in detail the considerations which determine the structure of a radio play, although he was at pains to suggest that his remarks should not be regarded as 'an *ex cathedra* lecture',[108] and that the rules were there to guide rather than to constrict the creative artist.

MacNeice distinguished from the very outset between the poetic language that a radio play could legitimately sustain and that required of a poem on the printed page. Radio drama could not, in his view, 'aspire to the freedom of lyric poetry written for the page',[109] but on the other hand, it could imbue words with 'those literary virtues which literature itself has lost since it has been divorced from the voice'.[110] Thus, he distinguished between good writing of a strictly literary sort and good *radio* writing, which involved the writer's paying attention to more than just 'words alone'; he insisted that the writer for radio had to consider 'words in the mouths of actors'[111] and that his trade must therefore be 'in words-as-they-are-spoken – and words-as-they-are-heard', with all the pressures that such a process entails.[112] MacNeice's own disillusionment with the ingenuity forced upon the writer of lyric poetry by a progressive vulgarisation of language led him naturally to elevate those qualities of expression still to be found in the human voice and exemplified in dramatic performance generally. Moreover, his attitude towards his mass audience was realistic without being patronising, and he was convinced that simply because of the dynamics of the medium poetry stood a better chance of wide public acceptance in a radio play than did poetry on the printed page. Indeed, one of the unstated premisses of his argument was that radio drama was in fact an intrinsically poetic drama. In this way MacNeice was able to appeal to the 'bardic' function that a radio play supplied: 'instead of prejudging it as a piece of highbrow trickery he [the listener] will, like the audience of the primitive bards, listen to the words, or rather to the sounds, as they come and will like them or not according to their emotional impact'.[113]

In certain respects this recalls Arnheim's theory of sound, and points forward to theses advanced by Marshall McLuhan and Walter J. Ong,[114] although as far as MacNeice was concerned, the reality to which the poetry ultimately referred was the emotional life of the listener. He did not go so far as to suggest exactly how that emotional life was formulated. Also, he appears to have been aware of the inordinately high status accorded to lyric poetry in post-Romantic critical theory,[115] and was concerned to substantiate the contention that the language of a radio play was an adequate, if not comparable, vehicle for the expression of emotion. His emphasis upon sensitivity rather than sophistication was aimed at reconciling the artistic objectives of a radio play such as Christopher Columbus with the fact that it existed above all to entertain its audience.[116]

The Introduction to Christopher Columbus is informed throughout by an intuitive grasp of the oral demands which radio makes upon the writer. It is not simply a question of arranging words in poetic configurations, since the dialogue of a radio play 'must consist of a great deal more than rhythmical patterns of words'.[117] Rather it must form part of a larger structure in which each element combines to produce an overall effect on the listener: 'it presupposes a wider and deeper pattern beginning with a careful and intuitive selection of material culminating in a large architectonic'.[118] Although this does not depart in its essentials from an Aristotelian conception of dramatic structure, what MacNeice offers here is a concise rhetoric of radio drama. The temporal pressures – a perennial issue of debate among broadcasters – imposed certain limits upon the dramatist, as did the fact that the listener could not refer back except through the agency of his own memory. Thus, the dramatist had to avoid over-complicated plots and devices, which might tax the listener's memory, although, of course, a sufficiently strong scaffolding required to be erected in order that the 'large architectonic' might be perceived. For MacNeice, this meant that character and situation had to be clearly established from the outset, and that 'the line of development' was to be kept 'strong and simple'.[119] He believed that narrative or story was important, that the focus should be upon one 'central event or theme',[120] and that the overall framework should be oral rather than literary.

On the question of the oral texture of a radio play, MacNeice was forced to modify his view by the time he came to publish *The Dark Tower*. Earlier, he had suggested that by comparison with other forms of literary language, in the radio play 'the objective elements will preponderate over the subjective, statement over allusion, synthesis over analysis'.[121] But he soon realised that in radio the listener automatically associates what is spoken with a character, so that authorial mediation of the sort that is possible in, say, the novel, could have no real relevance to the problem. Thus, in radio, he argued, there could be no distinction between objective and subjective elements, since each category becomes subsumed into the larger rhetoric involved in the construction of character. In addition to helping to account both for the intimacy and the directness of radio's appeal to the listener, such a view neatly disposed of the many objections to the narrator in radio drama. Having insisted that there can be no objective mediation of the story in radio, then it follows that the narrator becomes a character performing a function similar to that of, say, the Greek Chorus:

When no character can be presented except through spoken words, whether in dialogue or soliloquy, that very *spokenness* makes this distinction between subjective and objective futile. A character in a radio play, as in a stage play, may say things that actually he never would or could say – the author making him utter what is only known to his unconscious – but once he has said them, there they are![122]

In the same way, he later revised his view of the earlier distinction between statement and allusion, accepting that in any spoken dialogue allusiveness could not possibly be eliminated. He went on to suggest that each word in 'all *dramatic* writing' carries 'more than its dictionary weight',[123] so that even when a character seems to be 'talking at random and naturalistically', he is likely to be 'talking succinctly and symbolically, revealing himself – or whatever else is meant to be revealed – by a process of implicit logic'.[124] In this respect, therefore, there was no essential difference between the mechanism of a radio monologue or dialogue and any piece of fictional writing, since what distinguished all verbal *art* from analytic writing was its *implicit* meaning.

MacNeice's concerns were with what was artistically possible in radio drama, although his critical insights were based largely on his own achievements. Thus, in spite of the fact that since 1947 there have been considerable technological advances in radio generally, many of his arguments provide a useful foundation for criticism of a more formal nature. As he himself observed, 'Criticism comes after the event', but even though the event has continued to take place – and in recent years with perhaps greater frequency and diversity than ever – criticism seems to have been unduly chary about tackling the problems which a medium such as radio poses. The result has been that, in addition to its having been left largely to the broadcasters, the enthusiasts have been prone to extravagantly gnomic pronouncements, while the vigorous disapprovers have wished that radio drama would simply go away. Criticism, rightly perhaps, draws back from melodramatically tendentious comments such as 'Radio happens in the mind. It is the art of the unspoken';[125] but it would be equally foolish to disregard one of the major sources of dramatic writing that we possess. This is not in any way an exhortation to think well of radio drama generally. Rather it represents an inducement to think seriously and critically about it.

The evolution of a fully fledged criticism of radio drama has, in some respects, been hampered by a nagging sense of the artistic inferiority of the medium itself. Even an enthusiastic practitioner such as Louis MacNeice could suggest in his Introduction to *Christopher Columbus* that a good radio script, designed to communicate its effects 'through sound and sound alone' may not be as concentrated in its structure as 'a piece of good writing' primarily intended for a reader.[126] Similarly, Sean O'Faolain regarded writing for radio as 'a second, and secondary, though entirely genuine art'.[127] Such views in fact take us to the heart of the critical debate about *all* dramatic writing, since both theatre and radio drama are, by definition, subject to temporal pressures which are minimised in the act of reading.

This volume of essays, although diverse in approach, seeks to focus the critical debate about radio drama more sharply than has hitherto been customary. Specific radio plays (and adaptations) have often been the subject of fairly rigorous practical criticism from within the BBC, as evidenced in occasionally commissioned reports from individuals such as Henry Reed, John Fernald, and M. R. Ridley in the 1950s, while successive Heads of Drama have made frequent retrospective appraisals of their output. However, in the main, the emphasis has usually been on technical advances, associated with particular programmes, and is perhaps only to be expected when the monopoly of criticism is held by the practitioners themselves. Of course, any formal history of radio drama would be required to take a full account of specific technological advances and their implications for the structure of the radio play; innovations such as the dramatic control panel, improvements in recording techniques, and the advent of stereophonic sound would all figure in such a history. This volume does not seek to provide a history of radio drama; rather, each essay focuses upon the work of particular dramatists whose contributions to radio have proved both distinctive and enduring. Although in the case of radio drama a clear historical sense of its development has yet to emerge, it is now possible to evaluate the impact made by the radio writing of Louis MacNeice, Dylan Thomas, and Giles Cooper. It is with a clear sense that such evaluations are overdue that this volume of essays was originally conceived. All of the writers dealt with in the following pages have made important contributions to literature generally, whether it be to the novel, as in the case of Dorothy L. Sayers and Susan Hill, the theatre, as in the case of Henry Reed, Beckett, and Giles Cooper, or poetry, as in the case of Louis MacNeice and Dylan Thomas. In turning their attentions to radio they have all evinced a consistent and revealing awareness of the medium and its artistic possibilities, and can thus be said to have contributed to the establishment of a formal criticism of radio drama.

There are, of course, certain dangers implicit in selection, not the least of which is that an artificial unity may be imposed upon diverse, if not at times intractable, material. In the cases of Louis MacNeice, Dylan Thomas, Dorothy L. Sayers, Giles Cooper, and even Samuel Beckett and Henry Reed, sufficient oeuvres exist to provide the basis for a reliable critical judgement. The generation of dramatists which includes Tom Stoppard, Rhys Adrian, R. C. Scriven, Fay Weldon, Don Haworth, and Jonathan Raban lends itself more naturally to the kind of interim evaluation that the final chapter of this volume seeks to provide. However, the risks

implied in selection are worth taking simply because it is important to acknowledge in critical terms a body of dramatic writing
formidable in its quantity and occasionally surprising in its quality. It can, of course, be argued that every listener is a qualified
critic and carries with him his own personal history of radio
drama. As David Wade rightly implies in the concluding chapter
of this volume, there is no guarantee that the personal history of
each listener is the same, because of the continuing difficulty of
access to plays which have been broadcast. While we are, as a
culture, habitually inclined to a premature conferring of the
epithet 'classic' upon work which evinces literary or dramatic
merit, there has been a certain reluctance to do so with regard to
radio writing. David Wade offers a variety of reasons why such a
movement should not be rushed, although his singling out of a
small body of writers who use the technical and, indeed,
metaphysical dimensions of the medium to the full is an open
invitation to a further structuring of the debate. It is, however,
only through the vital dialogue of critical discussion that reliable
judgement is ultimately possible, and the following collection of
essays represents an attempt to fill what has hitherto been, in
Britain at any rate, a loud silence.

2   The radio drama of Louis MacNeice

CHRISTOPHER HOLME

Poets should be encouraged to write dramatic verse as they should
be encouraged to write narrative verse or occasional verse. It is
particularly likely that they may find a good medium in radio plays.
                    (MacNeice, *Modern Poetry* (Oxford, 1938), p. 196)

LOUIS MACNEICE'S ENTRY INTO RADIO was war work. At
thirty-three, he was an established poet, among the leaders of a
shining generation.[1] Of course he had had to do something else
for a living,[2] and his double first at Oxford had procured him
posts at Birmingham University, and later at Bedford College,
London, as a Lecturer in Classics. He had also been lecturing in
America and had come back from a second visit there because he
decided his place was in England at war.

> Our freedom as free lances
> Advances towards its end;
> The earth compels, upon it
> Sonnets and birds descend;
> And soon, my friend,
> We shall have no time for dances.[3]

MacNeice's first thought was the Royal Navy, where his friend
Graham Shepard was serving, but his eyesight was not good
enough. BBC Features, which he was to join instead, was still
nominally part of the Corporation's Drama Department but now,
under its gifted leader, Laurence Gilliam, was being transformed
by the war. In *Autumn Sequel* twelve years later MacNeice was to
give a light-hearted account of his first interview with Gilliam
and another pioneer, E. A. Harding, and its upshot.

> Remembering . . . that the rent
> Had to be paid . . .
> And that there was a war on, I agreed
> To join this new crusade; the Golden Calf
> Mooed once and Pegasus whinnied.[4]

In its simplest terms a feature was an information programme which used dramatisation. An information programme without dramatisation was the responsibility of another department. Talks, or even possibly News.

The extensive use of dramatisation in news features partly reflected the technical conditions of the time. The BBC had introduced its own disc-recording system in 1935 and an 'actuality' feature *Opping Oliday* (Cockney hop-pickers talking and singing) had been pioneered by Laurence Gilliam, with a recording van down in Kent, as early as 1936. By D-Day (6 June 1944) and before, BBC war correspondents had their own personal 'midget' recorder. Discs were flown home for incorporation in the centralised *War Report*. But apart from these special developments reported speech generally had to be simulated by script writers and actors. Asa Briggs notes actual prejudice against the use of recorded material or programmes in the BBC long after they were technically possible and preferable.[5] Tape recording, which was to revolutionise the whole conception of radio, was a German innovation, already far advanced there during the war, but not available in Britain.

The idea of gathering a team of poets and creative writers to pioneer a new kind of radio journalism did not perhaps present itself whole, though it was not far to seek at a time of manpower shortage in war. And evidently it was a good one, as in this case. By the time MacNeice actually became a member of the BBC staff on 26 May 1941 he already had a number of features behind him.

> To work. To my own office, my own job,
> Not matching pictures, but inventing sound,
> Pre-calculating microphone and knob
>
> In homage to the human voice. To found
> A castle in the air requires a mint
> Of golden intonations and a mound
>
> Of typescript in the trays.
>
> (*Autumn Sequel*)

It was by no means all typescript. Some of his broadcasting assignments were to be close enough to active service and take him far afield. Direct reporting from the scene of events was very much part of the Features job. He was already contributing to a series *The Stones Cry Out*, topical and human accounts of the bombing of Britain. In one night visit to St Paul's he found himself in the midst of it.

> The skies were rent
> And I took notes.

From this series R. D. Smith[6] has rightly singled out for quotation *A Home in Belfast*, as an example of the blend of simple sentiment and irony which MacNeice could infuse into such a news story.

During his first year, 1941, MacNeice scripted nineteen features and took part in one broadcast discussion. They were the first instalment of a personal war effort that was to total over seventy programmes and include his first two fully fledged radio plays. Most of them were news features, providing some sort of background, contemporary or historical, to events in the news. More remote from the news but topical, for instance to give comfort to an ally, or generate warm feelings about one, were the literary and historical features. Two of these in 1941 were occasioned by Hitler's invasion of Russia and were also a fore-taste of things to come from MacNeice's pen. The first, *Dr Chekhov*, was later to be enlarged into an imaginary conversation between Chekhov on his deathbed and his wife and his doctor (*Sunbeams in His Hat*). The second saw MacNeice for the first time associated with an absolutely major production.

Alexander Nevsky, based on the Eisenstein film, was suggested and produced by the film director Dallas Bower, who had come to BBC sound after the war-time closing of the embryo television service. Consisting essentially of linked dramatisations suggested by the Russian film original, it was produced in the grand manner. With Prokofiev's music performed by BBC choruses and orchestra, Robert Donat in the name part, and an opening announcement by the Soviet Ambassador Maisky, this sixty-minute programme was broadcast on 9 December 1941, two nights after Pearl Harbour. It thus happened that Maisky's voice was immediately preceded by those of Roosevelt and Churchill. Bower notes also that it was the first time such a programme had been done in an 'open' studio, 'in distinction' from 'the multi-studio technique then common to features and drama', and that a new film-recording system had been used to ensure a second broadcast.[7] This system was not in fact to supersede disc recording, which underwent a good deal of further development before it was superseded by tape. The open studio, which for a time became general, was in the sixties to be replaced for radio drama, under German influence, by a three- or four-studio block.

Versatility and prolific invention were thus as characteristic of MacNeice in the popular domain as they always had been in his poetry. Auden for one has commented on his conscientiousness in the trade of radio writer and producer which was now his livelihood.[8] R. D. Smith again writes that the radio 'devices of internal monologue, the swift, sharp-cut cinema reel of a life flashing through the mind of a dying person, sound effects verbally placed and primed, music as function not decoration, had been available to the poet for most of his writing life, as a glance at his play *Out of the Picture* shows'.[9]

Smith goes on to argue that the art of radio *documentary* was not so well developed in 1941 and that MacNeice's most original contribution was to that. I am not sure how much significance this distinction between radio drama and radio documentary has. If the basic pattern of a feature or information programme is taken to be narration-with-inserts, a 'string of beads', and that of a play pure dialogue, a 'chain', then obviously there are endless possibilities of modulation from one to the other, and of diversification also with song and music, poetry, inarticulate sound. MacNeice experimented as much as anyone during the war years – and, as we shall see, after them – with these basic forms, but he always seems to have maintained a bias towards dramatic content. The grand, highly applauded features of that era, with their factual substance, their slow pace, and overenhanced voices – I think, for instance, of Cecil McGivern's *Junction X* – were consciously experimental, yet very far from anything MacNeice ever attempted.

Both his meteoric success and the width of his range were demonstrated when 1941 ended with the broadcast by the Home Service of half-hour MacNeice features on two successive evenings. On New Year's Eve itself he was chosen to script a *Salute to the New Year*, a lively succession of small dramatisations representing various Allied groups at their war stations. In *Rogues' Gallery* on the previous evening he offered a 'satirical charade for wartime', an old-style 'smoker' type of light entertainment with verses to popular tunes, songs, and choruses reminiscent of Gilbert and Sullivan. The setting was a night club, a grotesque haunt of black-market dealers and police, and ended in told-to-the-children fashion with a police raid.

The series title *Salute to* . . . was not reserved for MacNeice, but it was one which headed several programmes of his for Home

and Overseas in 1942–3: . . . *the U.S.S.R.*, . . . *the United Nations*,
. . . *the United States Army*, . . . *Greece*, . . . *the Unseen Allies*. There
were other obvious variants like *Homage to Yugoslavia*, a programme of which the main title was *The Undefeated*. From the
latter part of 1941 onward he was becoming more and more his
own producer, though significant differences between his own
productions of his scripts and those of others would be hard to
establish with the evidence we now have. In the cooperative
tradition of the Features Department, with relationships more of
a newspaper kind between originator and end product, they are
unlikely to have been very marked. The case was different with
his first major original radio play.

Following the success of *Alexander Nevsky* MacNeice and Bower
were asked by the Corporation to propose something for the
celebration of the 450th anniversary of the 'discovery' of America,
12 October 1942. The programme which resulted, with original
music by William Walton, BBC Chorus and Orchestra, and a cast
of thirty-two headed by Laurence Olivier and Margaret Rawl-
ings, was essentially of drama rather than feature type. It was
MacNeice's first real radio play. The project from the beginning
had been in the hands of a distinguished producer who had
already worked with MacNeice. His own radio experience did
not yet include a drama production of this type. It was natural
and probably not questioned by anybody that the two should
again function together as producer and writer. There are things,
however, which the writer of a play, for whatever medium, and
nobody else, can contribute to its first production.

These were early days in the evolution of radio drama. The
trappings of the visible stage still hung round it. Not only the
production but also the writing of a radio play were to become
much more like those of a film and its script. Both may be
interrupted for the needs of an audience but neither has much
use for the static encumbrances of the stage. In its writings and in
its production, which can still be heard at the BBC, *Christopher
Columbus*, with a fine performance by Laurence Olivier in the
name part, remains MacNeice's most theatrical radio work. Asa
Briggs records that it 'created a sensation in artistic circles on both
sides of the Atlantic'.[10] The text was published by Faber & Faber
in 1944, with an important Introduction sub-titled 'Some Comments on Radio Drama'. Dallas Bower's own account of the
occasion has also been published.[11]

By 1943 Louis MacNeice was producing nearly everything he wrote, and his output was even increased, with nineteen scripts mostly of thirty minutes or more, nearly all bearing some relation to the war effort. *The Spirit of Russia*, lasting nearly an hour, with incidental music and re-created song settings from the works of Rimski-Korsakov, was produced by Stephen Potter. It has some interesting passages in stichomythia, a device not new to radio but specially handy perhaps to MacNeice from the Greek originals. The New Year's Eve feature, a placing of some importance in BBC planning, was again entrusted to MacNeice, who came up with a dramatised discussion of war aims rather sentimental in retrospect. We may ask how it could have been otherwise in that time and place.

From 1944 onward there was a marked change in MacNeice's output. The change at first simply reflected the progress of the war, which called for the broadcast of more news and operational material – after D-Day Laurence Gilliam was one of the two editors of the new nightly *War Report*, which he had helped to plan – and less and less dramatisation. Indeed, when public discussion of the imminence of D-Day itself became part of Allied tactics, MacNeice scripted a programme of that name in which by dramatised argument and cross-cutting answers were offered to the question what D-Day was all about – within the limits of the case a lively and honest affair. And on 31 December 1944 he again contributed under the title *The Year in Review* the New Year's Eve broadcast to the Home Service.

But what makes the year 1944 significant in any history of radio drama is that in the course of it MacNeice wrote and produced four original radio plays, each in its way indicative of some genre that he was to make his own and yet by no means inferior to his later work. *The Nosebag*, first broadcast on 13 March 1944, was the first of his fairy- or folk-tale dramas, which he, by a final twist of his own, pointed into a direct topical tribute to the Russian soldier then fighting the Nazis. Later the same year it was followed by the archetypal *Cupid and Psyche*, technically the second part of an adaptation of Apuleius' Latin novel *The Golden Ass*, in which this enchanting development of Greek myth is enshrined. *Sunbeams in His Hat* was the Chekhov portrait already mentioned. Finally *He Had a Date* was the first of the plays which MacNeice was later to nickname 'moralities' on the sixteenth-century analogy of those European dramas in which the sacred characters of the earlier Passion or Miracle or Mystery plays were replaced by abstract virtues and vices brought to life. It was, however, only halfway to the genre, as we shall see.

Despite the fact that he was now producing nearly all his scripts himself and was no longer required to supply so many topical war features, MacNeice's list for 1944 still amounts to ten scripts. From now on his output of information and current affairs features, though by no means negligible, may be treated as subordinate to what interests us here, his radio plays. Before we pass to a consideration of these we may ask about his poetry during these frantically busy three years. He was by no means silent. In 1941, the year in which he published his book on Yeats and put together for safe-keeping by his friend Professor E. R. Dodds his autobiography *The Strings Are False*,[12] the volume of new poems *Plant and Phantom* contained, for instance, the unforgettable 'Autobiography'. The next volume, *Springboard*, was published in 1944 and opened with 'Prayer Before Birth'. A more savage contrast with some of those optimistic dramatisations included in his BBC features could hardly be imagined.

And yet I think he need not have felt the contrast himself. A poem, expressing the inmost person, can be honestly put forth by the same man who at a more prosaic craft level can say quite different things. In *The Strings Are False* MacNeice had written about the world outside that 'tended to force creative writers into journalism', not so much for money as 'to beat' the 'commercial bastards on their own ground'. He himself had given way to the impulse, and 'accepted commissions for prose books for which' he 'had no vocation'. In this same passage, however, he insists on man's need for a sanction from outside himself. For MacNeice as for millions of his contemporaries the war provided that. For MacNeice too it provided something more, an opportunity to perfect himself in a craft which had long interested him, the playwright's craft. He had tried his hand at theatre, but in the conditions of the thirties there was not much opening for his, or for any poet's, kind of work. When he came to radio he used his opportunities, at first as an offshoot of war journalism and war propaganda, but very soon in his own right as a poet, and became a leader in establishing a new art form.

As his own producer he had a control over the end product which few theatre playwrights ever get. Indeed, tape recording and other technical advances were to bring the whole production process up to the level of film. MacNeice himself, I think, was never wholly convinced by these developments. A writer could not help remembering the diminished status conceded to his craft in Hollywood, as satirised by Wodehouse and Waugh in the thirties. The director's film and even the director's theatre of the fifties and sixties could already be foreseen. The writer, though more heavily bribed than ever before, was to be thrust to the bottom of the heap in a manner never yet approached by radio. Radio in fact was still, and thanks to the BBC was to remain, a place where the script enjoyed its original primacy. But there were things MacNeice, even as his own producer, found to regret in the performing arts, and in radio especially. In his published introduction to *Christopher Columbus* he wrote that 'radio plays and "features" (dramatic documentaries), when laid on the printed page, tend to lose even more than do plays written for the theatre'. We may note in passing that it is not enough to have written a play to get it published. A publisher will want to know that it has already been performed with success. The publication of *Christopher Columbus* was already an event out of the common run.

From 1945 onward the rate of output was not maintained at the same feverish pace. The list of productions was uneven: in 1945 five features but only one radio play, in 1946 six radio plays and two features, in 1947 three radio plays and one feature. The absence of radio plays in 1945 may be explained by the fact that *The Dark Tower*, a work by any standards major, was broadcast on 21 January 1946. It is worth mentioning also that in these years some at least of the poetry that he had been writing got broadcast. In 1946 there was a short programme of his work on the Home Service and another on the Eastern Service, while the Third Programme in 1947 broadcast substantial selections from *Autumn Journal* with an extract from the Preface. This he himself produced. Both these were improvements on his 1944 exercise, a short talk-down for philistines called *Why Be a Poet?*

What had happened of course was that MacNeice's own life and work, like those of millions of others, had changed somewhat raggedly from war to peace.

> '. . . If you so desire,'
> My employers said, 'this office will now return
> To a peacetime footing where we might require
> Your further service.' I could not discern

Much choice . . .
I stayed. On my peacetime feet. There was little alternative.
(Autumn Sequel)

The biggest event of the peace for radio drama was not given an unequivocal welcome by those already established as radio writers. The start of the Third Programme in 1946 meant that more programme time was becoming available for serious creative work than had ever before been dreamed of. Yet for the established staff writer–producers, such as D. G. Bridson, Francis Dillon, and Louis MacNeice himself of course, whose major works had been pretty sure of a peak-time placing on the Home Service, the new Third Programme alternative seemed merely to mean an audience rating divided by ten or even one hundred, a public of tens or hundreds of thousands rather than millions. These figures almost certainly exaggerate the scale of the change. The BBC's Listener Research people of course improved their methods with advancing sophistication in market research, and thus ratings obtained before the Home/Light/Third revolution are not always strictly comparable with those subsequently obtained. The Third Programme policy of planned repeats was a great mitigation for the loss of audience and in the course of time came to have pecuniary advantages for the writer, once respectable repeat fees had been established.

MacNeice's own idea of the radio play as an art form and means of expression for himself was never to change. *The Dark Tower* was his most demanding original work, and it had been broadcast for the first time on the Home Service. When it was published in the following year with four other scripts, he did add to the General Introduction, itself an important account of his thoughts about radio at that time, a note explaining that he had written it before the Third came into being. The Third Programme, he said, 'for the first time, I believe, in radio history – assumes that its audience is going to *work* at its listening. So there is less question than ever of playing "for safety and to the gallery".'[13] At other times he is defensive about the low esteem in which broadcasting and the BBC are held by his fellow writers and the intellectual world. In the Introduction to *Christopher Columbus* his chief concern had been to persuade some of them to have a go; he wanted to pass on the excitement and satisfaction he had had out of writing for this new medium. In the Introduction to *The Dark Tower* three years later he is already looking ahead and hoping that radio will not be entirely swamped by the advance of television. Fifteen years after that, in the Preface to a volume of two plays published after his death,[14] he fears the radio play may already be obsolescent, but insists that television cannot replace it. Both fear and insistence are echoed by W. H. Auden in his Foreword to *Persons from Porlock*.

During the years 1946 to 1963 MacNeice's radio plays were placed mostly on the Third Programme, at the rate of a little over two a year. He continued to do normal feature work as well. In 1948, for instance, he was sent to India with Wynford Vaughan Thomas to gather material for a big feature series on that country, mostly for the Home Service. In 1950 and during half of 1951 he was given leave of absence to take up a British Council attachment in Greece. From 1961 onward he went on half time. At this stage I have attempted an analysis of his creative works for radio, a first gathering of all those programmes which have some claim to be called plays.

The result is tabulated on pp. 48–9. From more than 160 scripts bearing Louis MacNeice's name in the BBC Drama (Sound) Play Library, I have a selection of 31 provisionally classified as radio plays. It must be understood that the distinction between a radio play and a feature is fluid. MacNeice's own definition of 'feature' is given in the Introductory Note to *Sunbeams in His Hat*[15] as 'the BBC name for a dramatised broadcast which is primarily either informative or propagandist (propaganda here being taken to include the emotive celebration of anniversaries and gestures of homage – or of hatred – to anyone or anything dead or alive)'. It must be clear that some features could be classed as radio plays, just as some of Shakespeare's Histories could be classed as Tragedies.

The six categories I have chosen after a good deal of experiment seemed to me the best fit for the MacNeice case. They would not necessarily be the best for another radio writer. Perhaps some justification is needed for including so many scripts which draw their conversations from historical or literary or documentary sources – features in fact! But theatre from the very beginning has used such sources, and in radio the difference between a play and a dramatisation or feature is not at all rigid. MacNeice's own definition is not entirely helpful. It would make *Christopher Columbus*, an unmistakable play and a good one, into a feature. Besides, of what artistic medium could it be said in the MacNeice era that 'we are the abstract and brief chronicles of the time'? Clearly not the theatre, though the newer playwrights have been trying to inject something more like radio features into it since the fifties.

Returning to our table, we note that the scripts of only twelve of the thirty-one have been published. This has the serious consequence that any account I may give of them cannot easily be checked with the original by the reader. With this warning, we note that MacNeice had already made his mark in five of the six categories during the war years, while his first 'Fantasy', *The Dark Tower*, was broadcast almost as if in victory celebration. We shall see that this was probably not quite accidental. All the categories were originated in a BBC which did not yet contain a Third Programme, and in none of them is it possible to detect a significant change with the arrival of that service except among the 'Adaptations & translations', where the four-part *Faust* and *Trimalchio's Feast* might have had some trouble in ever getting a placing, let alone a commission, on any 'Home' Service, while his memorable translation of the *Agamemnon* despite its suitability for radio had in fact never been broadcast since its Group Theatre performance at the Westminster in 1936. However this may be, the first line of our table does give an even spread, suggesting that the categories offer an immediate perspective of the playwright's work.

The earliest of all those listed, *Alexander Nevsky*, was broadly based on a film script and score, but it represents MacNeice's entry into what was to be among his most fruitful territories, and with its skilful construction could still be good listening. The category into which it could equally be put – 'Histories & portraits' – opens resoundingly with *Christopher Columbus*, an altogether memorable work to which time in some respects has been unkind. First, it was a *pièce d'occasion*, commemorating an anniversary to which the United States entry into the war had given special prominence. Secondly, it used large musical resources, and it was to become increasingly difficult for radio to afford such resources in a play. Thirdly, MacNeice took Shakespearean liberties with history in a way which nowadays would be quite acceptable in a surrealist or expressionist or absurdist play but became unfashionable in radio or stage portraits.

There is a fourth point which could have been put right by MacNeice himself in a new production. In later works, particu-

Louis MacNeice: a tabular selection of radio plays

Fantasies	Popular dramas	Histories & portraits	Folk-tales	Adaptations & translations	Satires
The Dark Tower[a] 21.1.46	He Had a Date[b] 28.6.44	Christopher Columbus[c] 12.10.42	The Nosebag[a] 13.3.44	Alexander Nevsky 9.12.41	The March Hare Resigns[a] 29.3.45
The Queen of Air and Darkness 28.3.49	The Careerist 22.10.46	The Death of Marlow 21.6.43	The Heartless Giant 13.12.46	The Golden Ass 3.11.44	Salute to All Fools 1.4.46
The Mad Islands[d] 4.4.62	One Eye Wild[e] 9.11.52	Sunbeams in His Hat[a] 16.7.44	East of the Sun and West of the Moon[f] 25.7.59	Cupid and Psyche[g] 7.11.44	All Fools at Home 1.4.55
	Prisoner's Progress[h] 27.4.54	Enter Caesar[f] 20.9.46		The Agamemnon of Aeschylus[i] 29.10.46	
	Nuts in May 27.5.57	The Death of Gunnar 11.3.47		Trimalchio's Feast 22.12.48	
	The Administrator[d] 10.3.61	The Burning of Njal 12.3.47		Goethe's Faust, 1–4[j] 30.10–17.11.49	

Fantasies	Popular dramas	Histories & portraits	Folk-tales	Adaptations & translations	Satires
	Let's Go Yellow 19.12.61	Grettir the Strong 27.7.47			
	Persons from Porlock[f] 30.8.63	They Met on Good Friday[f] 8.12.59			

[a] Published in The Dark Tower and Other Radio Scripts (1947).
[b] Revised version broadcast on 14.2.49.
[c] Published in 1944.
[d] Published in The Mad Islands and The Administrator (1964).
[e] Revised version broadcast on 14.11.61.
[f] Published in Persons from Porlock and Other Plays for Radio (1969).
[g] Part 2 of adaptation of The Golden Ass.
[h] Won the Premio Italiano 1954.
[i] Published by Faber & Faber in 1936.
[j] Published by Faber & Faber in 1951.

larly the folk-tales and histories, MacNeice made entertaining and sensitive use of accents and dialects. In *Columbus*, the lines given to seamen and common folk sometimes slip into a sort of simulated stage rustic which in the broadcast did not come off the page. The 'what-be-they's' and 'do-'ee'think's' sound rather unconvincing. This is a pity, for the versification of the script, loose in the dialogue, tight in the songs, is masterly and was very well performed, well matched too by Walton's music in the original production. It is a fine piece of storytelling, and the tension of a well-known conclusion is effectively maintained.

And yet, of course, the Columbus image has changed in the last hundred years. The European conquest of the inhabited world in the fifteenth to nineteenth centuries is nowadays less heroically judged. MacNeice was aware that the celebration of an anniversary of emotional significance in time of war put his probing, judging self in rather a corner. The dilemma is dealt with in his Appendix to the published text. He talks of the 'temptation to debunk the Columbus legend' and describes him as 'a man who like Hitler relied on his intuitions and was rather an offensive character'. What follows is important. Columbus, he says, having become 'a legend first in his own mind, and to all romantics since', and 'radio drama, like all other forms of drama, being primarily directed to the emotions, my first object was to retain the *emotional* truth preserved in the legend'. He claims finally that his tampering with history has been confined to 'some minor transpositions' and 'some minor exaggerations'.[16]

In the same Appendix he makes some technical comments of interest on writing for music (which in those days he thought made it an untypical radio play), on his use of verse forms, with devices resembling the choruses in a Greek tragedy, and his avoidance, owing to the length, of abrupt transitions and surprise twists common in radio plays. We have seen that *Christopher Columbus* is nearer to a stage play than any of MacNeice's other works for radio. It rose to a special occasion with grandeur and excitement and distinguished popular broadcasting in a unique way. In its use of verse forms it clearly owes something to Eliot, whose *Family Reunion* is referred to in the published Appendix, but more I think to MacNeice's own learned and inventive skill in versification. Its lack, as the poet acknowledges, is intellectual, and the question is, Does that matter? There can be no absolute answer, only a pragmatic one. In MacNeice's own work it had no followers. There are delightful verses and songs scattered here and there among the MacNeice feature scripts, but the dialogue of his features and plays was overwhelmingly prose. That particular combination of historical subject matter, the grand manner in verse with music, and a tense emotional narrative development was not to recur, but the historical romance in verse or stylised dialogue in the manner of a folk-tale which took its place did also merge with the Morality in *The Dark Tower*.

We hardly need to remind ourselves once more that the different categories have no rigid significance. They have been chosen as a help in sorting the material. If a programme seems to belong to more than one category it does not necessarily mean that in the author's evolution two or more categories were deliberately combined. It may be simply that the categories in this case are unhelpful. The column of 'Histories & portraits' comprises the most feature-like of MacNeice's radio plays, in the BBC use of that term. Yet it begins in my list with one undoubted 'play', *Christopher Columbus*, and ends with another, *They Met on Good Friday*, in which invention has almost ousted written sources. This has affinities with another group, the 'Folk-tales,' which Auden however would have lumped together with the 'Fantasies', calling them all 'dramatised fairy-tales', from which the 'Fantasies' differed only in being MacNeice's own invention.[17] Yet this last group is itself strongly infiltrated by the 'Popular dramas' and for R. D. Smith forms a common group with them called 'Morality–Quest' plays. However we sort them, the fairy-tales, described by Auden as 'peculiarly suited to the medium', were an influential element in MacNeice's work. The very first of them combined with the war effort on 13 March 1944 in *The Nosebag*. MacNeice made this Russian tale of the eternal soldier into a sparkling short entertainment with a final tribute inserted, more overtly than in the original, to the Russian soldier.

In his Introductory Note to one of the scripts he published in 1947 MacNeice wrote, 'In a programme called *He Had a Date* I attempted the chronicle of a fictitious man of our time and characterised him throughout by understatement, and while I did not succeed with him, I see nothing wrong in the method.'[18] He had been referring to a point made three years earlier in the Introduction to *Christopher Columbus* that 'the radio play can only reach its heights when the subject is slightly larger, or at least simpler, than life and the treatment is to some extent "stylised" '.[19] He now felt that to be an unnecessary restriction. In what sense did he not succeed with the hero of *He Had a Date*? A few years later he revised the play for a new production which was broadcast on 14 February 1949. But a comparison of the two scripts does not furnish a clue. His friend from Birmingham days and younger BBC colleague R. D. Smith, who was to produce the programme once again after the poet's death, calls it an elegy for MacNeice's friend Lt Graham Shepard, RNVR, killed on convoy duty in the North Atlantic. He does not share MacNeice's own sense of failure, nor does he refer to it. Instead he gives a lively and elegant account of the 'Morality–Quest' plays in general.[20]

He Had a Date does seem to have been a key work, and was in BBC terms a great success. It was broadcast several times in three different productions. It was introduced to the listener as 'a private newsreel of episodes from one man's life (some might dismiss him as a fool, a failure, or even a cad)'. Though a fictitious character he was 'typical of his period'. In retrospect it would be both wise and fair to accept and emphasise the author's word 'fictitious', and not to attach too much significance to the personal occasion. MacNeice's acknowledged elegy for Graham Shepard is a well-known poem. Two things are important. First, the theme of the honourable misfit, the hero who for good reasons rejects the roles in which society would cast him and finds fulfilment in death, is fundamental to MacNeice's dramatic work, recurs almost explicitly in *The Dark Tower*, and keeps cropping up in his poetry. Secondly, both in its form and in the quality of the dialogue *He Had a Date* is absolutely continuous with the main body of MacNeice's war features. His standard treatment of any subject he was called on to handle was by rapid cross-cutting of short dramatisations, with perhaps a fragment of narration or verse or a song to keep the story or argument running.

It cannot be said that MacNeice invented this characteristic radio feature style, but in his three years of war work he had contributed a good deal to its evolution. It contrasted at that time with the traditional drama style he had used in *Christopher Columbus*, in which there was a more stately progression from scene to scene. It contrasted also with the big slow-moving documentary feature of *Junction X* type. MacNeice, like Edward Sackville-West, the gifted author of *The Rescue*, and other BBC Drama writers, thought of narration in a radio play as a weakness, a confession of failure by the playwright to tell his story in the

manner of his craft, with dialogue. The use of narration to carry
the story from one dialogue sequence to another, in the manner
of a novel, which was then as now the source of many film and
radio scripts, might indeed seem a clumsy beginner's trick. But
intentional narration or monologue can be just as much a part,
even the whole, of a radio play, provided it *is* intended and not
imposed. If we think of one of Peacock's novels, several of which
have yielded delightful radio adaptations, they might almost
have been written for radio according to the primitive formula – a
narration-with-inserts.

The extraordinary freedom of form which radio gives the
playwright includes this possibility, like that of monologue or of
course a simulated lecture or address, with many others. There is
such a wide range of successful examples that the point may seem
not worth labouring. It is, however, in the case of Louis Mac-
Neice, an instructive example of how severely in his own mind
and practice he felt obliged to limit the possibilities of radio
writing. The extraordinary inventiveness and ready taste with
which he handled the mechanics of the radio play, the variety
and adeptness of his transitions, for instance, were paid for, it
seems, at the cost of intellectual and material scope.

Returning to *He Had a Date*, it was not only in form that its
succession of episodes recalled the dramatisations of his war
features. The actual content of the dialogue in the successive
scenes scarcely rises above the simulation level. It now seems
psychologically bare and innocent with stock characters in stock
situations. Like others for which it became a prototype, it
reminds one of those English Victorian genre paintings which are
now in favour again. It was tremendously apposite to a wide
range of ordinary lives, and in the heightened circumstances of
that time it had a heroic quality and earned its success.

Soon after the first broadcast of *He Had a Date* MacNeice produced for the Home Service *Sunbeams in His Hat*, the revised
version of his earlier Chekhov portrait which he later published
with *The Dark Tower*. It had originally been produced by Stephen
Potter and broadcast on 6 September 1941, the subject itself being
proposed to MacNeice by the BBC planners. It is thus an early
example of his skill in fashioning an original work out of transmitted material. In the past history of drama, audiences have not
worried whether their playwrights used literary or historical
sources for their plots or invented them. In MacNeice's case, too,

the distinction often seems academic. *Sunbeams in His Hat* has the characteristic technique of a chain of scenes flashing back and forth between the death-bed and the past life, just as in *He Had a Date* a month before it. A still earlier example of a literary feature deserves mention for the liveliness of its Elizabethan speech and sharp movement. *The Death of Marlow* compares well with some more recent attempts at that period of history on television.

In the same volume as *The Dark Tower* were published two linked programmes from my last group, which the author himself called 'satirical fantasies' or 'topical satirical fantasies'. They were broadcast just before or on All Fools' Day 1945 and 1946. MacNeice was much attached to them, as appears from his Introductory Note and from the fact that he wrote and produced a third one in 1955. They are nonsense plays with lyrical elements. One can never tell with jokes – they may fall flat at the time and be appreciated later. But these have attracted few supporters and little praise. Nearly twenty years later MacNeice was to write, 'In some modern writers, such as Beckett, this satirical element, or on occasions an odd kind of slapstick humour, can get inextricably intertwined with the lyrical element.'[21]

In his General Introduction to *The Dark Tower* volume MacNeice wrote, 'My own impression is that pure "realism" is in our time almost played out.'[22] Towards the end of his life he expanded this point: 'In the twentieth century, it seems to me realism in the photographic sense is almost played out and no longer satisfies our needs.'[23] When we consider the long column of 'Popular dramas' this remark at first is absolutely baffling. 'Realism' of a prosaic kind is what they often seem to have in common. But, he went on, 'most works of fiction of course will remain realistic *on the surface*. The single-track mind and the single-plane novel or play are almost bound to falsify the world in which we live.' Clearly, then, all these plays were for MacNeice what he calls 'dual-plane work', by which I think he means simply that the dialogue stood for something other than what the characters said. Towards the end of his life he was to return to the subject in more detail. Before we ourselves do so, we must consider one play which seemed at the time and still seems to rise above such arguments.

By an opening announcement included in the text, *The Dark Tower* is introduced directly to the listener as 'a parable play, – suggested by Robert Browning's poem "Childe Roland to the

Dark Tower Came". The theme . . . ancient but evergreen [is that] of the Quest – the dedicated adventure; the manner of presentation is that of a dream – but a dream that is full of meaning.' Browning's poem ends with a challenge blown on a trumpet: ' "And yet / Dauntless the slughorn to my lips I set / And blew *'Childe Roland to the Dark Tower Came'* ". Note well the words "And yet". Roland did not have to – he did not wish to – and yet in the end he came to: The Dark Tower.' In the General Introduction to the published text it is again described as a 'parable play, belonging to that wide class of writings which includes *Everyman*, *The Faerie Queen*, and *The Pilgrim's Progress'*. The author goes on to mention *Peer Gynt*, Kafka's stories, and also *The Magic Mountain* of Thomas Mann.

The play opens when the hero Roland is thirteen or so. He is a member of a family all of whose direct male ancestors and, after his own father, one by one his older brothers have set out on a lone quest never to return. His sixth and last older brother Gavin is receiving his final preparation for the quest. This consists in learning the challenge call from the Sergeant-Trumpeter. After Gavin's departure and a lapse of time covered by Roland's first lesson, merging into the bell which tolls for Gavin's death, we have Roland being put through the same monkish–military education by the family Tutor and the Sergeant-Trumpeter under the Mother's supervision. But Roland, unlike his predecessors, is a sceptic. He does not know whether to believe in the existence of the Tower or the Dragon which rises from it if not opposed, an evil force or social miasma perverting man's minds and actions – or so he is told. His doubts are reinforced by the coming of love. 'Never fall in love. That is not for you,' the Tutor has told him, but he does, with Sylvie, who wants a home and children and pours scorn on his mother. She is 'mad', not altruistic, in sending so many sons to their destruction. 'Each new death is a stone in a necklace to her.'

All the same, after a visit to 'Blind Peter', an ancient and penitent victim of the moral pestilence spread by the Dragon on an earlier foray, he takes his leave of Sylvie and sets out. The temptations along the way are traditional: games of chance, drink, sex (administered on shipboard by the steward, a 'character' whose favourite remark 'Golden days!' shows him to have been modelled on a legendary Oxford scout), but more persuasively also doubt and common sense, represented by Sylvie's reappearance and offers of a normal married life. A marriage between the two is indeed arranged in a haunted chapel in a forest, but when the banns are called Roland's father, Gavin, and Blind Peter suddenly appear to forbid them. Sylvie, more like an older sister than a wife, is dismissed by the ghostly clergyman to return and marry one of her own kind, to 'spread the shining crop on the spare room floor' – a picture which has been identified by MacNeice's sister Elizabeth (Lady Nicolson) as a scene from his childhood in the rectory at Carrickfergus.[24] Roland goes on to the desert, there to be tormented like an old-time hermit by voices from his past and monsters from nowhere, and pursues his quest unwittingly. At last his father and brothers await him on surrounding hills as he comes out of the desert and the Tower grows out of the ground. He blows the challenge.

The Dark Tower has a kind of stature which cannot be shared with any of MacNeice's other radio plays. It is successful, deeply personal, and the one above all in which the poet speaks in his proper language. It has mystery and intensity. The author himself warns us against facile identifications and interpretations. 'I have my beliefs and they permeate *The Dark Tower*.'[25] We have already noticed one picture which takes us back to his childhood in Northern Ireland. Another direct association with childhood no doubt was Browning himself, a favourite of MacNeice's father.[26] The lines about the tormented horse, one of the horrific visions in Browning's wilderness –

> I never saw a brute I hated so;
> He must be wicked to deserve such pain

– which have shocked the literal-minded, were no doubt read by the rector as sarcasm. He himself 'hated hell-fire religion'[27] both Catholic and Protestant, and it is hard to believe that Browning in these lines intended anything but mockery of the Dantesque picture of hell. Visions in the wilderness, the dark tower itself, the challenge, all reappear more or less transmuted in MacNeice. No doubt they too were part of the childhood clutter with which his inspiration was furnished. Browning's poem was first published in 1855. Its title, 'Childe Roland to the Dark Tower Came', is from Shakespeare's *King Lear*, where Edgar in his feigned madness flings out a quotation from an old ballad. In the *Ballade of Burd Helen* Rowland, an old annotator tells us, was the youngest brother of Helen of Troy. With the help of Merlin he rescued her from elf-land, whither the fairies had taken her. Neither Browning nor MacNeice is concerned with any of this. Neither of their two heroes exactly succeeds in his quest, nor is it at all clear what Browning's hero's quest is. MacNeice is more explicit, his hero carefully briefed in childhood. Browning's tells his own story; he too had some kind of briefing, from a 'hoary cripple' who reappeared in MacNeice as the loquacious Blind Peter. This character gives Browning his sardonic and miraculous opening line: 'My first thought was he lied in every word.'

We are bound to feel some regret as we turn from this to the cumbersome and explicit 'three knocks' of old-time radio – the opening announcement already quoted from *The Dark Tower*. Against that it may be argued that Browning's mystery is poured out at once with a heavy hand while MacNeice's is more like a mist rolling up from the sea. Moreover, there is no reason why MacNeice's opening announcement, designed for a Home Service audience at the end of the last war, should not be discarded today. Browning's poem cannot start with a trumpet call; MacNeice's play could and did, as well as ending with one. 'There now, that's the challenge,' said the Sergeant-Trumpeter, 'and always remember, hold that note at the end.' The music of the 'challenge', and throughout the play, was written by Benjamin Britten, to whom the play is also dedicated. It is indeed a magical opening, and a pity that the announcement was printed with the script. The radio listener's ear, after all, is trained to separate the show from the presentation, to divide up the time lapses coming out of the box, but such bits of continuity may well look foolish in print.

In his published scripts, of which there are so few, MacNeice was meticulous in indicating the panel directions in print. In the Introduction to *Christopher Columbus* he had joined in an argument as old as radio with those 'veterans of broadcasting who go so far as to say that no radio script can be more than a very rough notation for the producer'. This he thought an overstatement – a really good script should survive a bad production. But he tried to make sure. As an example of panel directions in print which would be found in few working scripts, at least nowadays, in *The Dark Tower* there is one succession of short scenes each keyed into the next by 'verbal transitions' – the cue words at the end of a scene are repeated, usually by a different character, at the beginning of the next. These are not only printed 'verbal transition' in the text, but explained by a note at the end. The device is more often a comic one, or at any rate 'light' – it might occur in a thriller. In MacNeice's own production of *The Dark Tower* they are delicate and natural and anything but funny.

Generally he was a master of transition. It is perhaps the critical element in a radio play or feature, getting from scene to scene, from episode to episode, from narration to insert or the reverse, and it goes without saying that any of MacNeice's colleagues would have had this expertise, and like him too would have depended on the judgement and expertise of the man at the panel. In the General Introduction to *The Dark Tower* he refers to the 'group experience' of radio and the advantages of being a writer–producer. That is, after three years and thirty of his own productions, his position has shifted somewhat. Radio is still a writer's medium, but radio writers who do not go into the studio and see what happens there are missing something.

And the script of *The Dark Tower* is indeed harder to read, depends more on performance for its full appreciation than *Christopher Columbus*. The sound and meaning of some of the more complicated passages are difficult to imagine from the page alone. Some speech sequences look rather childish in print but in sound they work. Thus for MacNeice at this stage – and I think he was never to go beyond it – the radio script is nearer a film script than a stage play, but it is not a mere notation requiring performance to actuate it. It can be read like a play, with as much satisfaction. With some trouble the reader can judge for himself. Recordings of two different MacNeice productions and one R. D. Smith production of *The Dark Tower* are preserved and by arrangement with the BBC can be heard.

The Dark Tower then is a parable. What does MacNeice mean? An allegory? No. We recall that Browning too denied emphatically to one enquirer that his 'Childe Roland' was an allegory. It was the greatest English puzzle poem of its day, a favourite topic at Browning clubs and the like in England and America, which Browning himself used to visit. MacNeice thought of allegory as implying a one-to-one correspondence between representation and thing. He called this 'algebraic'. He was explicit about 'parable' in his Clark Lectures at Cambridge towards the end of his life.[28] As a word 'parable' was the best of a bad lot: 'symbolism', 'allegory', 'fantasy', myth. The word has to cover a wide range of authors, a multitude from whom he chose six – Spenser, Bunyan,

Kafka, Beckett, Pinter, Golding. What do they have in common? They all create special worlds. It is clear that this definition includes far more than it excludes. An army of names is added to the list of the chosen. The discursive, confidential prose takes us agreeably from one quotation to another. But the idea that parable used thus vaguely can define a special kind of writer, rather than a special kind of utterance which needs to be meaningfully distinguished from all the other kinds, to me is not rewarding.

Apart from the MacNeice trip which this short book so attractively provides, I find that he is here, as several times in the past, disclaiming for himself, excusing himself from writing, a play or novel of character, of personality. Despite its Browning model – for Browning, as MacNeice admits,[29] had a gift for character, was a novelist in verse – *The Dark Tower* is not psychological. The people in it are not personalities but puppets or messages. This must be the meaning of MacNeice's reiterated rejection of 'realism', in one place identified with 'naturalism'.[30] The trouble with people as walking messages or ideas is that they have to act and speak, behave as people. Bunyan, whom MacNeice had absorbed as a child, and who constantly recurs in his critical writings, is the most obvious model for his 'parable' plays. That Bunyan had humour and a gift for what one can only call character had not escaped him, but MacNeice's own humour, puzzling to the uninitiated, was not of this kind and his feeling for character seems always to have remained uncomplicated and childlike. In *Varieties of Parable* we actually find an analysis of Browning's 'Childe Roland' as 'one of the few really successful pieces of parable writing in Victorian *verse*'. Browning's hero is not only plunged into his quest by surprise, he pursues it unwittingly; every step he takes involves him further in it against his will, and his destination, when he has reached it without knowing, suddenly traps him by springing up all around him.[31] The Dark Tower is a 'destination where even defeat is an achievement'. All these features are mirrored in MacNeice's play, which begins not suddenly in the middle like Browning's but in its hero's childhood. This is a gruelling and overloaded preparation for a life of dedication and service in which the hero has come to disbelieve. Yet he sets out. Even his terrible mother who has sent son after son to his death is losing her conviction. Instead of Roland she will bear and sacrifice a 'stone son', that is, she herself will die (as MacNeice explains in a footnote).

I read these family sequences as almost wholly abstract. We know that MacNeice lost his own mother just before he was six, and the heartbreaking aftermath has been described by his sister Elizabeth[32] and commemorated by him in the poem 'Autobiography'. By the time he had a stepmother, whom he soon loved, he was off to school in England. Perhaps the mother of *The Dark Tower* somewhat recalls the Ulster dourness (and real affection) of that Miss MacCready who bridged the gap. But really I think she stands for the educational *alma mater*, the public school that played such an overwhelming part in the lives of children of MacNeice's class. Her choice of death rather than another flesh-and-blood 'son' or generation, would then be explicable in terms of the social changes, the disappearance of the public schools, so much in the air towards the end of the war. The quest then is the career of service, public service, civil, spiritual, military, for which such children are prepared. But such a quest has become ambiguous and may be false. What else? The sententious Sylvie offers a quiet, unambitious, and essentially good life – marriage and so much else. The world is mad, says Roland. Not all of it, she replies;

> Those who have power
> Are mad enough but there *are* people, Roland,
> Who keep themselves to themselves or rather to each other
> Living a sane and gentle life in a forest nook or a hill
>   pocket,
> Perpetuating their kind and their kindness, keeping
> Their hands clean and their eyes keen, at one with
> Themselves, each other and nature.

The alternative is tempting, more so than the distractions along the way. These too are symbolic. Soak, the drunkard who can conjure up cities with music, is explained by MacNeice in a footnote as 'a Solipsist', 'his alcoholism an effect rather than a cause'. No doubt we have here a reference to the lonely melancholy by which he himself was often possessed and may have sought to relieve by drink, the proverbial 'black dog' which was the other side of his gaiety and could ruin a party. The steward with his relentless shipboard game is perhaps the extrovert business life while his associate Neaera is not just sex but the good-time world in general.

What then of the quest? In the war which MacNeice had been helping his country to wage, a quiet life was out of the question.

In his own time he had continued to write as a true poet. At the BBC he had been a conscientious man of his trade, but with three years of war propaganda behind him, it would be surprising if such a probing self-analysis as *The Dark Tower* did not contain some reference to it. We remember that in an attempt to put his childhood behind him he had in 1941 completed an autobiography and given it to a friend for safe-keeping. There he has a passage about the temptations for creative writers to take up journalism. 'Not so much for money as because money remained a symbol of energy. To beat them on their own ground. To show these commercial bastards that one knows the ropes as well as they do.'[33] He himself had given way, accepted commissions for prose books for which he had no vocation.

Many of us were still reacting over-much against Art for Art's Sake, against the concept of the solitary pure-minded genius saving his soul in a tower without doors. Our reaction drove us to compete with the Next Man. But once you come up against the Next Man you begin to lose sight of the sky. The Next Man swells to a giant, you find your face buried in his paunch and on his paunch is a watch ticking louder and louder, urging you to hurry, get on with the job – when the job is finished there will always be another.

By this Kafka-like little picture we are at once reminded of the clock sequence in *The Dark Tower*.[34]

Four years later the war had come to an end. *The Dark Tower* was completed in 1945 and broadcast in January 1946. Its conclusion is that Roland, 'the black sheep, the unbeliever – who never did anything of his own free will' – will blow the challenge to the Dragon in the Dark Tower 'to bequeath free will to others'. We know that MacNeice and some of his left-wing friends at first took a detached view of the war against Hitler. When war broke out he returned to America, where he had a university job and could have continued teaching, but finally decided that his place was in England and came back. His eyesight debarred him from many forms of service and he joined the BBC. In all this area of decisions taken and work done I think we shall find the key to layers of quest, true and false, in *The Dark Tower*.

All three 'Fantasies' may be treated as quests. *The Queen of Air and Darkness* is sombre, and is more or less in verse. It combines an idea of Housman's with one from Tennyson (the Lady of Shalott). The Queen is an evil spirit who once in every generation puts her finger on some man and out of his own good qualities builds him into a bloodstained tyrant. She is blind and has a magic mirror reflecting events on earth, with two handmaidens who report them to her. If ever the mirror is broken she will die. Her latest victim, after having overthrown his predecessor, turned tyrant himself, and been overthrown in his turn, in the Hall of the Catacombs where the political prisoners, victims of his own and previous tyrannies, are kept, learns the cause of his corruption. He seeks out the Queen, whom we may thus suppose to be Power itself, and destroys her by cracking her mirror. We have the false, or perverted, quest. At the very beginning the hero is in a posture familiar in MacNeice, that of a professional man under commercial pressure to lower his standards. MacNeice calls this radio play 'one of the few things I have written where I deliberately attempted allegory'.[35] Without bothering about Housman's intentions he had made the Queen a source of perverted idealism, such as Hitler's. The hero 'accordingly was a self-deceiver'. What the Queen had really given him was the lust for power.

As the play was getting itself written, I realised that the most difficult scene would be the final confrontation and struggle to the death between the Queen and this lover who has never seen her. For in killing her he will, so far as the allegory goes, be killing something in himself, whereas, so far as the drama goes, it takes two persons, not one, to make a struggle.[36]

The Mad Islands was published in 1964, in one volume with *The Administrator*, one of the 'Popular dramas'. It is rather loosely derived from an ancient Irish tale, the Maelduin ('Muldoon') voyage, with seal-men and seal-women mixed in from other parts of the Celtic inheritance. The author says in his Introduction that he did not mean his piece to be 'essentially Irish!' It is, however, in its light-hearted way decidedly Celtic, with two Welsh witches for good measure. Muldoon has been brought up as an orphan. On coming of age he is told by his foster brother that his real mother is alive. He is magically taken to see her in 'the heart of the blackest bogs of Ireland', and she gives him his quest, to kill the Lord of the Eskers, a sea-rover who stabbed Muldoon's father to death in a church. With a strange crew of seventeen, beginning with Cormac and his Jester, whose jokes are anything but funny, and ending with Skerrie, who turns out to be a seal-woman, one of the drowned who live on in the sea, he begins his Odyssey among the islands. He visits such strange characters as the Miller of Hell, who grinds and 'sends away to the West' all the worthless riches of the world. Like Odysseus Muldoon loses all his crew, last of all the loving Skerrie, for he fails to muster the understanding that might have turned her into a real woman and a wife. Before that he learns, in a vision of his dead mother with a hermit on a rock, that his quest was based on a lie. He is the son not of his mother's husband but of his mother's lover who killed her husband. Unfaithful in his turn, he was to be killed by his own son at the revengeful mother's instigation. The vision saves Muldoon from his crime and Skerrie dives into the sea and leaves him to start the boat alone. Where to? His foster home?

We are not told. MacNeice's production was stylish, punctuated with music for Welsh harp.[37] It opens well, but as it goes on the story seems too inconsequential and the MacNeician taste for fantastic humour is indulged rather widely. The most difficult thing, a 'Funster' whose jokes are *meant* to be bad, does not come off, nor do the fantastic jests of other characters in contexts too wild to be mysterious. The fairyland has no thread of rationality to set it off, and the dénouement is rather scrambled. But it is a strange play, not easily dismissed, and may come to be thought of differently.

The clear affinity between the 'Fantasies' and the 'Popular dramas' enables us to use the three former to classify the latter, as it were in ascending order from death and falsehood to life and truth. These qualities are not in the quests, none of which is true, but in their resolution.

First, the perverted quest. The anti-hero can only destroy the evil, identified with the ruthless pursuit of power, by killing himself. In 'Fantasy' we have *The Queen of Air and Darkness*; in 'Popular' prose, *The Careerist*.

Secondly, the uncertain quest. In *The Dark Tower* the doubting hero resists all distractions, acquiesces in a mission he distrusts, and after all finds fulfilment in heroism and death. Here we have the misfits and drifters who for reasons which may be honourable reject the role that society has cast them in (*He Had a Date, Nuts in May, Prisoner's Progress*) or else accept it but succumb to commercialism, then get into trouble (the 'Demon Drink'!), find their way home to death (*Persons from Porlock*).

Thirdly, the false quest. The plays of this group are comedies in the sense that they do not end with the death of the hero, but with some kind of victory, however precarious, for truth and honesty. But MacNeice anticipates what has become almost a convention of popular dramas on television in the seventies in his inconclusive endings. Whether they will be happy or not is left open. The comic 'Fantasy', *The Mad Islands*, shows the hero that his quest was all a lie but leaves him to go on his way questless, without companions or a mate. The three plays in this sub-section are *The Administrator*, *One Eye Wild*, and *Let's Go Yellow*.

The 'Popular dramas' are a special group. Their plots and characters are modern, not adapted from a literary or historical source, their language prose, and for seventeen years, after the first broadcast of *The Dark Tower*, they were MacNeice's preferred form of radio expression. Before discussing them more fully, it will be useful to look at the other groups once more. It is a pity that none of the three Norse saga pieces has been published. They are splendidly exciting and evocative – *The Burning of Njal* perhaps the best of the three. From this 'Histories & portraits' group Auden chose two for publication – he felt that the sagas, being already available in good translation, had lower priority – *Enter Caesar* and *They Met on Good Friday*. The first is a didactic exercise, designed to entertain while it teaches, an imaginative reconstruction of things recorded in history and what might have been said by those concerned. The characters speak modern English, the dialogue often as racy as listeners might hear from their favourite entertainers. MacNeice has even more pointedly underlined the nature of the exercise by bracketing the ancient scenes between schoolmaster speeches in a Scottish schoolroom – a radio substitute for narration. Caesar never appears; the scenes are about him, building up to his arrival. It is all very skilful and lightly drawn but does not rise above the didactic level.

From the same collection, *They Met on Good Friday* has perforce been grouped with the 'Histories', but is far from didactic and has very little in common with *Enter Caesar*. Its source is legend and its supernatural content could well have placed it among the 'Folktales' (just as *Macbeth* and *Hamlet* and *Lear* are grouped with the Tragedies rather than the Histories). It is about the battle of Clontarf on 23 April, Good Friday, AD 1014, nominally between Norsemen and Irish for the control of Ireland, though the races were by then mixed up and it was not always easy to tell which side was which. It has songs and a musical accompaniment (by Tristram Cary) and though mostly in prose the speech is what I think MacNeice would have called stylised, neither quite modern nor pastiche, a supple and expressive language with poetic metaphors, as it might be a translation of Homer or an old romance. A 'sceptical historical romance' is indeed what its author calls an enthralling and evocative piece. One of his very best.

The reuse of our vast heritage of folk- and fairy-tales and other-world characters to give some sort of a twist to contemporary plays on contemporary theses needs no special explanation or even remark. Nor does the revival of such tales in radio, the new medium. For MacNeice the example of *Peer Gynt*, at the very outset of the modern movement, was close and important. More surprising sources, if that is the right word, were the Victorian fantasist George Macdonald, Charles Kingsley's *Water Babies*, and Carroll's Alice books.[38]

The fairy-tale chosen for his volume by Auden was *East of the Sun and West of the Moon*, Norwegian in origin, again with music by Tristram Cary, well told, with rough humour and no obvious moral. When the North Wind has blown down the castle of trolls where the hero was held enchanted, he offers hero and heroine a lift home. Home? Wherever they with their love are is home. As they look around, the sun comes out, the air is balmy, trees put out leaves, and flowers bloom. So there they decide to stay. Less successful in my opinion was the *Faust* exercise on which Mac-Neice spent a good part of 1949. It remains to be proved, I think, that *Faust, Part 2*, though much abridged, is suitable for radio. A great deal of the translation, done by MacNeice from a rough version by E. L. Stahl, is very fine, as may be verified from the published text. Professor Stahl's own account is well worth reading.[39] But so far as MacNeice's own work is concerned I doubt if his long hard grind with Goethe had very much influence.

I return to the 'Popular dramas'. Speaking loosely, MacNeice used to call them all Moralities. In 'olde Englande' of course the best known of the original Moralities was *Everyman*, the play which inspired Bunyan and seems to have haunted MacNeice. For the stage he wrote *One for the Grave*, an Everyman play which was put on after his death, as the first new play to be presented at the rebuilt Abbey Theatre, Dublin, in the autumn of 1966. The action and words, which take place in a television studio, are modern, though often in verse and song. It is a robust and exciting text. The nearest thing in radio to the original model is *The Careerist*, first broadcast on 22 October 1946, a sordid story of a publishing empire built overnight by treachery and fraud and lowered standards, ended by financial disaster and death. Its anti-hero is called Human, there is a male and a female 'chorus' (each played by a single voice) and a collection of Vices and Virtues named in Greek who discuss him at critical moments and seek to influence him. It has great ingenuity of structure, but the whole effect is rather leaden.

The action of *One Eye Wild*, a 'romance in commonplace', lasts only a single day. Things are not well between Roger, a sports writer and commentator, and his wife Margaret. She wants a move to the country, he has a dream woman about whom he fantasises when alone. He gets drunk and is knocked down by a car and all that follows are conversations between him in delirium and the 'Joker', another self, until his wife, who has made good her threat to leave him but then scented disaster, returns to the flat and finds him unconscious on the floor, having in delirium discharged himself from hospital. There is a reconciliation, and Roger recovers.

Prisoner's Progress has a more decided attempt at naturalistic characterisation and psychology than any other MacNeice play. Also it has a heroine as well as a hero. Misfits both, combatants on the same side in a war that never was, they discover their love for one another in an escape attempt. The sole survivors of their party, which has come to involve prisoners from the separate male and female camps, they climb the mountain which is their chief obstacle, only to be intercepted and killed by the enemy guards with their dogs on the frontier. Among the male prisoners are a comic clergyman and a black cook who sings to his own guitar. Among the women an archaeologist (funny foreign accent) deplores the whole escape as vandalism of the Neolithic chamber tomb she has found there. There is also a MacNeice cardboard comic, the enemy commandant. The war, though 'loosely based on data from World War Two, is not a real one'. The prisoners, the Greys, are 'our side', and they are 'prisoners in more senses than one'.

What comes through is an exciting story well told. The escape itself is real and has all the suspense of a conventional adventure story. This rather unusual combination of elements was no doubt the reason why this play was chosen by a BBC committee as that year's entry for the Italia Prize, where it won the second award, the Premio Italiano.

Army life, of which MacNeice had no direct experience, figures also in *Nuts in May*. Here we have a hero born to an inherited quest in the sense that he comes of a line of Indian Army officers and goes automatically to Sandhurst. But he has also inherited a propensity to make a mess of things. A drunken brawl in India gets him sent home, he has a spell in advertising, and so on. The title of course refers to the singing game for picking up sides – in which our hero is always the last to be picked. Finally seizing a lucky chance, he gets on to an Antarctic expedition and there dies heroically on a forlorn journey to save two snowed-up comrades.

The Administrator is one of the two published plays of this group, having appeared with *The Mad Islands* in 1964. For anyone who can look up the original script in the BBC it has two alternative endings, and there may even be a third somewhere in manuscript. The hero, Jerry, is an atomic scientist in a well-known dilemma. The 'career structure' of his profession requires him, as he moves up in it, to do more and more administration and less and less science. It also requires him to become an agent of the misdirection of atomic energy for harmful uses. His indecision has become acute with the offer of a new managerial post which his wife, hard and ambitious, is pressing him to accept. His arguments with her alternate with dreams, hers as well as his. In the dreams is a traumatic episode from his and her past, a motor accident in which he was driving but his friend Robert was killed. Robert, it seems, was the go-getter his wife Martha really loved. Other dreams – a 'Voortrekker', with African beater and big game in South Africa, a German doctor using 'comic' broken English, a trial scene (Kafka or Wodehouse?) – somehow or other convince Jerry, who at last tells Martha he will refuse the post. At least, that is the published version. In the broadcast he told her he would fall in with her wishes and accept it. Originally, MacNeice tells us, he had wanted to leave Jerry undecided but was told that 'the listening public hated this'.[40]

In *Let's Go Yellow* the hero (Rugby and Oxford) wants to make good in journalism, where he is much derided for his education and ideals. He is put on to a rather nasty gossip-column assignment, which as it turns out involves the son of a leading advertiser in his newspaper. Despite warnings he persists and exposes a drug ring. The editor fires him as a sop to the advertiser and takes credit for the exposure at the same time. He arrives at the BBC to offer his story!

Finally, in *Persons from Porlock* the allegorical, or metaphorical, element is provided not by dreams but by a hobby – potholing. The hero, Hank, fails to make a living as a serious artist and turns commercial. The resulting misery of soul drives him to drink and his girl friend Sarah leaves him. He seeks compensation with another girl, who takes over his studio and nearly ruins him with her extravagance despite the large sums he is now earning. The earnings too begin to be endangered as drink takes over more and more. A fresh crisis is provoked by the refusal of his potholing friend Mervyn, who had earlier introduced him to the sport, to take him on an expedition. The inroads of drink have made him no longer trustworthy. He throws out the substitute girl friend and starts painting again. After a show at which he sells nothing his true girl friend and 'muse' Sarah rejoins him. But now the bailiffs are in and the drink still has its hold. Sarah is badly hurt in a car accident caused by his being too drunk to put the car away himself. He takes a cure for alcoholism and Mervyn once more agrees to take him potholing. In exploring a new 'trap' – the 'Stygian trap' – Mervyn is cut off and Hank goes after him. Neither comes back. Death, the last 'person from Porlock', has caused a final interruption. Sarah is left to hold a last, posthumous, and now probably successful show of his new serious work.

This play has all the technical finish of the Victorian genre painting to which I have already compared *He Had a Date* and which this too in its own medium so much resembles. The elements are expertly ordered, the transitions neatly and unobtrusively varied. It was MacNeice's last. As part of the production he went to Yorkshire to supervise recordings in a famous potholers' cave. Walking on the moors he got wet through in a shower, but in his wet clothes spent the evening in Leeds before returning to London. After finishing the production with illness already on him he still did not go to bed. When he was finally seen by doctors a day or two later he was found to have pneumonia and pleurisy. *Persons from Porlock* was first broadcast on 30 August 1963 and Louis MacNeice died on 3 September 1963.

W. H. Auden calls this last play 'a magnificent example of. . .a psychological drama'. Radio, he thought, was perhaps the ideal medium for 'the portrayal of the inner life, what human beings privately feel and think before and after they perform a public act. For its principal characters, therefore, it demands men and women who are by nature self-conscious and articulate'.[41] I must say I find the word 'psychology' misleading to describe such a very articulate, explicit, and *simple* style of playwriting as Mac-Neice's 'Moralities'. They are very deliberately interactions not of character as a subject of analysis in the Jamesian, novelist's, manner, but of moral principle. MacNeice himself more than once compared the schoolroom parade of vices and virtues in his Moralities to a poster or cartoon. The word at once suggests a certain crudity and flatness, a lack of psychology. It takes us into quite a different world of influences from that of any novelist, the world of expressionism, total theatre, and mass indoctrination blown over from the Continent, which in MacNeice's case formed a surprising alliance with his childhood reading in a Victorian library. Or perhaps not really surprising, for the morality of a Victorian genre painting is as much a broad outline as its visual impact is detailed and meticulous.

Obviously some simplicity or explicitness is imposed on radio by its nature. The blind medium is more vulnerable than theatre or film to those wanderings of the attention which can have a more disastrous effect on the enjoyment than losing one's place in a book. MacNeice himself had a remarkable gift for telling a radio tale. His fairy plays, for instance, are delightfully clear and enthralling. But a crude simplicity of characterisation and motivation is in a fairy-tale the natural and usual thing, and in his critical writings he leaves us in no doubt that this was not a chance model.

The defence he would use was exactly like the one he gave of Eisenstein's *Alexander Nevsky* film, the script of which he adapted as his first major radio play. He notices that it 'disappointed some English intellectuals because of its lack of subtlety in characterisation, its complete innocence of psychological conflict, its primitive pattern of "Black versus White" ' and 'was for those very reasons easily transposed in a radio form'. This clear outline of the very pattern which was for nearly twenty years to determine MacNeice's own output of plays on contemporary subjects for the BBC cannot be overlooked.

When he came to the BBC in 1941 he had behind him some vigorous attempts to establish himself as a theatre playwright. The Group Theatre, an experimental company with which

Auden was associated and which had produced Auden's political masque *The Dance of Death*, followed by Eliot's *Sweeney Agonistes* and Auden and Isherwood's *Dog Beneath the Skin*, in 1936 presented a translation by MacNeice of the *Agamemnon of Aeschylus*. With a balletic production by Rupert Doone, masks and décor by Robert Medley, and music by Benjamin Britten, it had the kind of mixed reception which might be expected at that time, but the notices of his translation must have been encouraging to the poet. He had already produced students in Birmingham in an earlier farce, *Station Bell*, and his next play, *Out of the Picture*, was given two performances by the Group Theatre company at the Westminster Theatre on 2 and 9 December 1937. The 'cardboard comic types' disparagingly referred to by *Scrutiny* as mimicry of Auden were in fact among the aims of the Group – in Doone's words 'not portraits but cartoons'.

The critics of those days seem very insular in retrospect. During his last year at Oxford, 1929–30, one of MacNeice's favourite records, which he was constantly playing in his rooms, was a selection of songs from the *Dreigroschenoper*, which he had brought back from a visit to Berlin. It is certain that the ideas of 'total theatre', as we may loosely call the spectrum of innovation from Wedekind to Expressionism to Brecht which was so drastically modifying the heritage of Ibsen and Shaw, became as familiar to him as to his friends, though his lack of German cut him off from many actual sources. He certainly knew the American developments. The fact that the German theatre of those days was so much inspired by English classics, from *Everyman* to *The Beggar's Opera*, did not necessarily mean that when the movement reacted back on English writers it was the German transmutation that was followed. To a great extent the German novelties remained unread and unstaged while English writers simply accepted the redirection to English models. The one writer in German whom MacNeice deeply absorbed and often mentions is Franz Kafka, one of his elect among parabolists.

But the Epic Theatre, too soon a refugee from Nazism, must be the unquestioned standard of reference for the whole theatre movement with which MacNeice had long associated himself. He found there the theoretical justification of the teacher's stance which came so natural to his writing. His plays are didactic, sometimes even politically so, like the Teaching Plays (Marxist Moralities) with which Brecht experimented before the full flowering of the Epic Theatre. But MacNeice was no Marxist. What he always goes back to is a personal morality rooted, with all its differences, in a Puritan childhood. That is why the naturalism so strongly rejected by Brecht for its 'naive criminal instincts'[42] keeps creeping back into MacNeice. Questions of personal morality are not so easily stripped of a psychological context as those of politics or theology.

Louis MacNeice is a poet whose stature has been steadily rising since his death. His vocation was to be a poet. He gave radio what he could. A great deal. His last radio play was among his most personal. It did not have the crystalline perfection of his best poems. Nor could it, for it was itself one of the interruptions it documented in the poet's life. Like lecturing, or writing commercial books. We cannot doubt that from the end of the war until his death the BBC, however warm and indulgent and justly grateful to MacNeice, was his biggest 'person from Porlock' of them all.

3   The radio road to Llareggub[1]

PETER LEWIS

'UNDER MILK WOOD' is easily the most celebrated full-length play for radio, or 'play for voices' as Dylan Thomas designated it, that the BBC has produced in more than fifty years of broadcasting, and it is for many people the outstanding example of the genre, an unsurpassed and virtually unsurpassable achievement. In one of the first reviews of the published text, Gwyn Jones claimed that, whatever its limitations as literature, it 'is surely the best script ever written for broadcasting. One had heard nothing like it before, and we may never hear anything like it again. The richness of one of its minutes would take the water-blue milk out of the average full evening's programme.'[2] Nearly twenty years later another distinguished scholar, Walford Davies, stated categorically that 'it is, quite simply, the best radio play ever written', although his reservations about the work as literature are evident in his comment about 'its essentially low-key ambitions' and his description of it as 'unashamedly a trivialising work in that it reduces a view of life to immediately entertaining details'.[3] Not everyone would agree with these evaluations of Under Milk Wood as a supreme work for radio, since a number of other important writers have written brilliantly for the medium, but its extraordinary popular success during the quarter century since its first appearance has established it as one of the very few generally accepted radio classics, perhaps 'an innocuous classic' as Davies claims,[4] but still a classic.

Considering that the fate of most radio plays produced by the BBC is to be broadcast once, to receive no or, at best, very little critical attention, and to remain unpublished, the history of Under Milk Wood since 1952, when an incomplete version was published as Llareggub, a Piece for Radio Perhaps,[5] is remarkable. Still in an unfinished state, it received three public readings in America in May 1953, one solo performance by Thomas followed by two stage-readings with Thomas as director and major participant. In

October 1953, just before setting off on his last and fatal visit to
America, he gave another solo performance in Wales, and later
that month took part in further stage-readings in New York.
Since these readings were one of the main reasons for his fourth
tour of America, he had tried to complete and revise the play
during the summer, and a few days before his departure he
delivered an apparently finished text to the BBC for broadcasting.
Douglas Cleverdon's original Third Programme production was
first broadcast on 25 January 1954, repeated no fewer than three
times during the next three months, broadcast on the Home
Service in a slightly shortened version in September, transmitted
on the General Overseas Service in two different edited versions
on six occasions in 1954, and released on an Argo disc in the same
year. Furthermore, just over six weeks after the January broadcast, the first translation of the play, Eric Fried's German version,
was put out by the BBC German Service. With *Under Milk Wood*
an Italia Prize winner for 1954, the BBC celebrated the first
anniversary of the original broadcast by repeating it on 25 January
1955, and further repeats followed on the Third Programme in
1956 and (an edited version) on the Home Service in 1957 and
1960 and on Radio 4 in 1972. In 1960 the central section of the play
was chosen for a BBC Stereophonic Experimental Programme,
again produced by Douglas Cleverdon, who was also responsible
for another new radio production in 1963 to commemorate the
tenth anniversary of Thomas's death; this was broadcast in
October and November. Yet another BBC production appeared
in November 1978 to inaugurate Radio 4's *Hi-Fi Theatre* series
and to commemorate the twenty-fifth anniversary of Thomas's
death. This received the unprecedented accolade of being broadcast three times within a week. Indeed, no other radio play has
received anything like the privileged treatment of multiple productions and multiple broadcasts that the BBC has bestowed on
Under Milk Wood.

But if BBC Radio has done Dylan Thomas proud, *Under Milk
Wood* has hardly lacked other outlets. Publication in book form in
England less than six weeks after its first broadcast, and shortly
afterwards in America, was an unusually speedy operation by
modern standards, but one easily explained considering the current epidemic of Dylanmania. However, even before these publications, *The Observer* issued a shortened version of the play in
two instalments in February 1954, while in the same month the

American magazine *Mademoiselle* contained a different abridge-
ment prepared by Thomas himself. If the response to the broadcast was very enthusiastic, the reception of the published text was
overwhelming. Few books can ever have been reviewed so
widely and with such acclaim as *Under Milk Wood*. In Britain,
almost all the leading daily, Sunday, and weekly papers, including those not noted for their literary coverage, gave it space, as
did a number of provincial newspapers, not to mention many
periodicals and magazines, both general-interest and literary
ones. Much the same is true of America, where dozens of newspapers and magazines reviewed it. The chorus of praise was at
least as much a part of the post-mortem idolatry as a response to
the play, and there was scarcely a dissenting murmur. Even John
Wain, who devoted his entire review except for the last sentence
to not reviewing it but to deploring the maudlin excesses of the
Thomas-worshippers, relented at the end to note that 'it is a very
good book'.[6] Nevertheless, a number of the reviews were of a
high quality, being long, thorough, and perceptive as well as
encomiastic, and in his reply to the dissenting Stephen Pike's
'Not good enough',[7] Stuart Holroyd articulated the reasons for
the widespread approval as well as anyone, arguing that *Under
Milk Wood* 'is one of the sanest literary works created in the
present century':

It is this generosity [akin to Chaucer's] which makes *Under Milk Wood* an
enduring piece of literature. Call it generosity or love, what you will, the
quality which enables him to create a gallery of living characters –
rogues, braggarts, drunkards, loungers, scandal-mongers, conservative
old maids and promiscuous young ones – characters not wholly com-
mendable, but all of them redeemed by the humour, tolerance and
beneficence of their creator.
  In an age when most artists either condemn their fellow-men or seek
to change them Dylan Thomas was one poet who could accept them as
they are; accept them with all their faults and failings, their narrow-
mindedness and crudity, accept them and, in spite of everything, love
them with the passionate love of the great humanist. More than any
other contemporary writer he could see and represent the fundamental
greatness, the nobility, the dignity, the divinity of man.[8]

Interest in the play outside the English-speaking world, partly
triggered by the award of the Italia Prize, soon led to translation
into most European languages and into Japanese. Eventually,
even a Welsh translation appeared.

Under Milk Wood rapidly reached a large audience over the air and on the printed page, but it had other channels of communication. Just over a month after the original broadcast, Cleverdon directed the first complete stage-readings in England at the Old Vic. Two years later Cleverdon and Edward Burnham directed the first orthodox stage production, which after opening in Newcastle upon Tyne in August 1956 took the Edinburgh Festival by storm before enjoying a seven-month run in the West End. Cleverdon subsequently directed the Broadway production in New York, which opened in October 1957. The televising of the British production by the BBC in May 1957 gave the play yet another outlet *via* the media, although it had received some TV coverage while at Edinburgh. During the twenty years since the publication of an acting edition in 1958, based on the London production, the play has frequently been staged and stage-read in English and in translation by professional and amateur companies all over the world, and in 1978 it returned to the West End for another successful run in a production by the Welsh National Theatre Company to commemorate the twenty-fifth anniversary of Thomas's death. Not surprisingly, *Under Milk Wood* did not escape the attention of the film industry, and Andrew Sinclair's film version had the honour of opening the 1971 Venice Film Festival.

What the history of *Under Milk Wood* amounts to is one of the greatest literary and dramatic success stories of this century, and for something conceived as a radio play it is unique. In the circumstances there are two surprising facts. Considering that Thomas has been an apparently endless goldmine for scholars and critics, *Under Milk Wood* has attracted comparatively little academic attention, although as radio plays go it has done inordinately well and was the subject of a thesis as early as 1956.[9] Many critical studies of Thomas concentrate exclusively on his poetry or his literary prose, and those that do discuss the play usually devote relatively few pages to it. Even in magazines and journals, little has been published since the spate of reviews in 1954 and 1955, especially in comparison with the verbal Niagaras poured over his poetry. The second point emerges from this one. Apart from the often-repeated truism that *Under Milk Wood* grew out of one of his best-known radio talks, *Early One Morning*, first broadcast in 1945 and revised for a repeat in 1953 as *Quite Early One Morning*, hardly any attempt has been made to relate the play to his other work for radio or to the medium itself; even the chapter 'The Artist in Comedy' in John Ackerman's *Dylan Thomas: His Life and Work* (1964) and Raymond Williams's important essay,[10] which take more account of the medium than most, do not go far in this direction. As a result, critics have often approached *Under Milk Wood* as though it were either a literary text existing only as words on the page or an orthodox drama, and this failure to view it in relation to the sound medium it was written for has led to gross misrepresentations, including one of the first important analyses, David Holbrook's influential demolition job in *Llareggub Revisited* (London, 1962) – in his later book on Thomas, *The Code of Night* (London, 1972), Holbrook's attitude is much more sympathetic. However, Holbrook's attack was salutary in that it questioned certain assumptions about the play and consequently provoked its admirers to reassess it, though it is important to note that critics who answered Holbrook, notably Norman Talbot[11] and Laurence Lerner,[12] did so in literary, not radio, terms.

A common misconception surrounding the play is that it marked a radical change of direction in the career of a lyric poet whose lyric gift was supposedly drying up, and initiated a new phase in Thomas's work that he did not live to fulfil. He was, after all, on his way to California at the time of his death to discuss the possibility of writing an operatic libretto for Stravinsky. Indeed, several reviewers in 1954 lamented the loss to English *drama* as well as poetry of Thomas's early death. The words of one of the first reviewers, the anonymous London correspondent of an Australian newspaper, were frequently echoed in the following months: 'Obviously, had he lived, Dylan Thomas might have become the major poetic dramatist for whom we have been waiting.'[13] This – especially the 'Obviously' – is nonsense since, as *Under Milk Wood* itself reveals very clearly, Thomas did not have the makings of a dramatist in the ordinary sense of the word. As a play, it is singularly undramatic, although this is not an adverse criticism for the simple reason that the play does not purport to conform to orthodox conceptions of the dramatic. Thomas had originally planned a more conventionally dramatic structure for the play with the provisional title *The Town Was Mad*, but discarded both structure and title as the work evolved. It is always necessary to remember that *Under Milk Wood* was produced not by the Drama Department of BBC Radio but by the Features Department; and as Douglas Cleverdon rightly insists, this play is in the very fluid form of a radio feature, whereas *The Town Was Mad*, or *The Village of the Mad* as he calls it, would have been in 'dramatic form', complete with elaborate plot, development, and dénouement.[14]

Furthermore, Thomas's lyric gift was anything but a fast-flowing stream for most of his adult life, and only towards the end of the Second World War did he recapture for a short time something of the extraordinary fertility of those *anni mirabiles* as a teenager in the early thirties. His primary commitment was always to poetry, but he found it increasingly difficult and laborious to produce, as the hundreds of worksheets for his later poems show. After the outbreak of the war, much of his time was devoted to things other than the writing of poetry: film scripts, radio scripts, broadcasting, poetry-readings, and the four American tours. His contribution to the war effort took the form of working for Strand Films as a professional script-writer of documentary and propaganda films, and this led to his preparation of treatments and scripts for feature films, such as *The Doctor and the Devils* and *Twenty Years A-Growing*. However, it was the BBC that proved to be his most consistent patron, providing him with plenty of work and much of his income, even though he was never a staff member. In the period between the end of the war, when his film work was coming to an end, until the end of 1948, he participated in more than a hundred broadcasts, principally as a poetry-reader but also as an actor, programme-compiler, and script-writer. In 1946, his peak year, he averaged just under one programme a week. By the time he began serious work on *Under Milk Wood*, he was an extremely experienced broadcaster who not only knew the medium of radio from the inside but knew it inside out. In addition, he had written several, probably as many as six, scripts of a 'dramatic' nature in that, while not plays but radio features or fictionalised documentaries, they employed characters in action and required actors. Far from being a new departure for Thomas in the direction of drama, *Under Milk Wood* is the culmination of his work as a script-writer for radio and, to a lesser extent, for films. Drawing his basic subject-matter from one of his own radio talks, what he did was to apply to it the methods of the feature, which he had already mastered in *Return Journey*, in order to create a large-scale work for radio. The connections between the play and his film scripts, whether documentary or feature, are much more tenuous, although some American reviewers who wrote about *Under Milk Wood* and *The Doctor and the Devils* together, since they were published within a few months of each other, drew attention to certain stylistic resemblances; but the mixture of narrative and dramatic techniques in the film scripts do prefigure the alternation of exposition and dialogue in the play. In dividing the narration of *Under Milk Wood* between two Voices, with the First predominating, Thomas may, as Andrew Sinclair suggests,[15] have been recalling his use of a dialogue between two speakers, one of whom is dominant, in his documentary film script *New Towns for Old*, instead of the usual single commentator.

Considering Thomas's involvement in radio features, his use of feature techniques rather than conventionally dramatic ones in his play for voices is natural enough, even though he first attempted the latter, perhaps because he 'assumed that for a sixty- or ninety-minute script the BBC would require him to furnish a proper dramatic plot', as Cleverdon observes.[16] The distinction between a radio play and a radio feature is notoriously hazy, and there are exceptions to every definition. According to the Head of the Features Department in its heyday, Laurence Gilliam, the feature, however imaginative and fanciful the treatment, is based on fact, whereas the play is a work of fiction,[17] but his Features Department did produce purely fictional works, including such outstanding radio scripts as MacNeice's *The Dark Tower* and *Under Milk Wood* itself.

The first three scripts that Thomas wrote for broadcasting were short features, although it is impossible to know exactly what form they took, since no trace of them remains and the little correspondence about them in the BBC Written Archives is not particularly illuminating. In an undated letter to Vernon Watkins, probably written in August 1940, Thomas explained, 'I do scripts for the BBC, to be translated into, & broadcast to, Brazil. I've got an exciting one to do next, on Columbus.'[18] The first of these scripts for the Latin American Service, *Duque de Caxias*, was broadcast on 26 August 1940, and the second, *Cristobal Colon*, on 13 October 1940 after a rewrite by someone else. The third, *March of the Czech Legion Across Russia in the Last War*, was turned down, but in a letter to John Davenport dated 8 January 1941 Thomas gives some hints about his approach:

The script uses five announcers. 'War. The shadow of the eagles is cast on the grazing lands, the meadows of Belgium are green no longer and the pastures are barbed with bayonets. War. War.' Five announcers, and a chorus of patriots crying 'Siberia', 'Freedom of Man', 'Strengthen us for the approaching hour' like a bunch of trained bulls.[19]

This obviously indicates feature techniques, and it seems fairly safe to assume that the other two scripts were similar in this respect.

More than five years elapsed before Thomas wrote three more features, in 1946 and 1947, but during this time he broadcast on the Welsh Home Service the first three of his highly individual talks based on personal experience: *Reminiscences of Childhood* (15 February 1943), *Early One Morning* (31 August 1945), and *Memories of Christmas* (16 December 1945). *Early One Morning*, broadcast as 'An imaginative portrait of a small seaside town in Wales', contains episodes, characters and even phrases that were to recur in *Under Milk Wood*, but in all three talks Thomas developed what might be called his radio prose, the ear-catching, exuberant, and witty idiom that culminated in the play, especially in the speeches of the two Voices. It is this idiom that caused Walter Allen to compare Thomas to Nashe ('language is in full spate') in his review of the posthumous collection of radio scripts, *Quite Early One Morning* (1954),[20] and Kenneth Tynan to say of Thomas in his review of the Edinburgh Festival production of the play that 'he conscripts metaphors, rapes the dictionary and builds a verbal bawdy-house where words mate and couple on the wing' and to suggest 'Hopkins with a skinful' and 'Taproom baroque' as possible descriptions.[21] Among the characteristics of Thomas's style are its long, flowing, almost breathless sentences, its helter-skelter rhythms, and its rhetorical and figurative richness. His poet's ear for verbal patterning, involving alliteration, assonance, and rhyme, is obvious in his description of the 'ugly, lovely town' of Swansea at the outset of *Reminiscences of Childhood* as 'crawling, sprawling, slummed, unplanned, jerry-villa'd, and smug-suburbed by the side of a long and splendid-curving shore'.[22]

Indeed, most of the verbal devices employed in the play, such as transferred epithets, invented and compound adjectives, personification, unusual metaphorical identifications, departures from normal word-order, and piled-up lists of incongruous items, are present in these talks. Thomas uses identical devices in his poetry too, but there they are almost invariably employed for serious purposes whereas in his radio prose the aim is usually more humorous, playful, and jocose. Thomas had established himself as a comic prose-writer with *Portrait of the Artist as a Young Dog* in 1940, and much of his subsequent prose, including his unfinished novel *Adventures in the Skin Trade* and the satirical novel written with John Davenport, *The Death of the King's Canary*, as well as *Under Milk Wood*, is entirely or partly comic, unlike his much more intense poetry. High-minded critics belonging to the school of close verbal scrutiny have been quick to condemn such radio prose for being trivialisingly lightweight, superficially clever, and meretriciously attractive; but in approaching all Thomas's creative writing for radio, including these talks, it is vital to remember that his radio prose was written for the ear of a listener, not the eye of a reader, and is therefore not 'literary' prose, however 'literary' its techniques may be. It was primarily designed for immediate aural impact, and any sensitive criticism must bear this in mind, instead of imposing 'literary' criteria on it. To say that it is better heard than read is actually a compliment, not the qualified insult it is often intended to be. It is as wrong-headed to treat radio prose as 'so many words on the page' as it is to treat dramatic writing in this way, but since English criticism is notoriously literary in its evaluation of drama, writing for radio cannot expect to escape the same fate and is rarely respected for what it is.

After failing to write two scripts for the Overseas Service towards the end of 1945 that he had agreed to do, one on Augustus John and one on 'Nationalism and Poetry', Thomas did honour another commission for the Overseas Service in 1946, the last of a feature series of thirteen programmes with the overall title *This Is London*, intended to present different aspects and views of the city. Although Thomas's script, *The Londoner*, first broadcast in the African Service on 15 July 1946, has never been published in England, it is of particular interest to students of *Under Milk Wood*, as only Cleverdon[23] and Ralph Maud[24] have pointed out, because its structure prefigures that of the play. Being much shorter, less than a third as long, *The Londoner* is, of course, less panoramic and introduces far fewer characters, but even so it requires as many as twenty-four speaking parts, just a third as many as the play. Unlike *Under Milk Wood*, *The Londoner* is too short to create a picture of a community; but, as in the play, Thomas shows more interest in social breadth than psychological depth. Both scripts are devoid of normal dramatic form and are shaped by the simple device of taking a representative twenty-four hours in the lives of their subjects, an average working-class family in Shepherd's Bush, Lily and Ted Jackson and their two children, in *The Londoner,* and Llareggub and its inhabitants in *Under Milk Wood.* After short expository introductions, both open at night with dreams, progress in straightforward chronological sequence through the day, and conclude with the return of night, sleep, and dreams. In both cases the amount of radio time allocated to different parts of the day does not correspond to their real-life duration. Well over half of *Under Milk Wood* is devoted to the first half of the day, so that the afternoon and evening sections are highly compressed (Thomas's manuscript shows that he might well have expanded the later parts somewhat if he had lived,[25] but he must have regarded the version he delivered to the BBC as sufficiently complete to stand on its own), and *The Londoner* exhibits almost exactly the same imbalance; although the time-scale is slightly less disproportionate than in *Under Milk Wood,* more than half is given over to the morning so that the rest of the day is relatively telescoped. Both works also consist of a chain of short episodes, the transitions in time and space usually being effected by omniscient narrators who also provide much essential information. The use of a narrator is now thought to be inherently undramatic and untheatrical, but is virtually indispensable in the radio feature and is not unfamiliar in radio drama. Since the purpose of *This Is London* was to convey an accurate picture of contemporary city life to overseas listeners, Thomas's approach is that of documentary, and even though his characters are fictional, he stresses their ordinariness and typicality.

The opening section before the sleeping Jacksons are introduced takes the form of questions and answers, with a Questioner asking about the area and street where they live as well as about the family, and various voices providing replies, mainly objective information. The most interesting feature of this introduction, and one that has a parallel in *Under Milk Wood,* is the contrast between the cold, factual description of Montrose Street provided by officialdom, and the subjective, human view of an inhabitant:

VOICE OF AN EXPERT. It is a grey-bricked street of one hundred houses. Built in 1890. Two bedrooms, a front room and a kitchen. Bathrooms were built into less than half of the houses in 1912. A scullery and a backyard. Rent 28 shillings. Too cold in the winter, too hot in the summer. Ugly, inconvenient, and infinitely depressing.

VOICE OF AN OLD RESIDENT. No, no. You got it all wrong. It's a nice, lively
street. There's all the shops you want at one end, and there's pubs at
both ends. Mightn't be much to look at, but there's always things
going on, there's always something to see, buses and trams and
lorries and prams and kids and dogs and dogfights sometimes
and . . .[26]

In *Under Milk Wood* the official description of Llareggub provided
by the Voice of a Guide-Book corresponds to that of the Expert,
and although there is no specific equivalent to the response of the
Old Resident, the abundant variety and complexity of village life
soon expose the total inadequacy of the Guide-Book account. The
ensuing dream sequence in *The Londoner*, consisting of two
speeches, one each for Lily and Ted, is extremely short compared
with that in *Under Milk Wood* and might be considered gratuitous
as documentary; but it allows Thomas to contrast the fantasy
lives of the Jacksons with the predictable and unexciting routine
of their daily existence, and therefore to introduce a comic
dimension into the feature. In her dream Lily enters the world
of Hollywood romance ('Ooh, what a beautiful dress . . . like
the one Ingrid Bergman was wearing in what-was-the-
name . . . And the music!'), while in his, Ted sees himself as an
indefatigable boxing champion ('There goes the bell for the mil-
lionth round'). Comedy is not the only characteristic of the much
more elaborate night-time section with which *Under Milk Wood*
opens, but it is the prevailing one, and even in the voices of the
dead that arise from Captain Cat's subconscious there is humour
as well as pathos. In both scripts Thomas exploits dreams more
for their comic potential than for any of the other possibilities
they offer.

Indeed, Thomas extracts a surprising amount of humour from
the Jacksons' world, considering the documentary style of the
programme. As the day unfolds with the Jacksons at breakfast,
Ted on his way to and at work, Lily with her gossipy neighbour or
by herself or shopping or with her friend Gwen, the family at
home in the early evening, Ted in the pub, and Lily and Ted
together again at bedtime, Thomas blends a serious exposition of
their preoccupations, problems, and life-style in the immediate
post-war period with frequent flashes of comedy. On the one
hand he emphasises the shadow cast by the war and its aftermath
over the Jacksons in particular and British life in general. Ted's
work involves demolishing air-raid shelters, and during his

lunch break he reminisces to his friend Alfred about his experiences as a prisoner of war, while Lily too recalls the same years in her lunch-time soliloquy. Ted and Alfred discuss that brand-new instrument of war and threat to civilisation, the atomic bomb. There are several references to the current shortages of food, money, beer, and cigarettes. On the other hand Thomas imparts humour to situations he could have treated grimly or sourly, and this presages his whole approach in *Under Milk Wood*, where Mrs Ogmore-Pritchard's obsessive fastidiousness, Mr Pugh's murderous fantasies, and Jack Black's militant puritanism are purged of their realistically repugnant qualities by being treated in a wholeheartedly comic manner. The frustration of shopping in conditions of rationing and virtually unobtainable goods becomes an opportunity for good-natured banter rather than rancorous complaint as Lily negotiates with shopkeepers, such as the Butcher: 'Offal, Mrs Jackson? Now you're asking. As far as *I* can see, animals don't possess no insides these days, worth mentioning.' In this shopping incident, the rapid interchanges among the queue of grumbling women is also comic in tone:

1ST SHOPPER. Last week there was bananas in Humphries . . . saw them with my own eyes. . .
2ND SHOPPER. Keeps 'em for his regular customers, so he says. . .
1ST SHOPPER. All gone when I got there, of course. . .
2ND SHOPPER. If I'm not a regular customer, Mr Humphries, I said, who is then? Mrs Miniver?
1ST SHOPPER. That's right, dear. . .
3RD SHOPPER. Pity the men can't queue a bit. . .
1ST SHOPPER. How long you been queuing, dear?
3RD SHOPPER. I've been here half an hour.
2ND SHOPPER. I been queuing for six and a half years.

Although this episode is less stylised than the two comparable sections in *Under Milk Wood*, the antiphonal chatter of the Neighbours in Mr Waldo's dream and of the village Women at mid-morning, there is a decided resemblance, made more pronounced because in each case four women are involved. Incidentally, such writing is pure radio, since it is perfectly suited to a sound medium but becomes awkward, stilted and unnatural when transferred to a visual medium such as the theatre.

Thomas's penchant for comic incongruities, zany flights of fantasy, grotesque comparisons, and surrealist-tinged humour reaches its apogee in *Under Milk Wood*, but this tendency is evident at times in *The Londoner*, as in Ted's sustained metaphorical description of the next-door neighbour and the bizarre variation of current complaints about the quality of sausages he makes in passing: 'That old barrage balloon. . .I'd like to see Mrs Cooley floating in with a couple of real eggs and some fried liver and. . .sausages that aren't made out of old newspaper and minced shaving brushes. . .Mrs Cooley'll be living here soon. . .Keep her moored in the backyard.' The episode of the children's breakfast is virtually an excuse for further humour in this conversational vein, as sibling rivalry between Carole and Len takes a curious turn after Carole indicates that she wants to wear her hair 'long and straight and half of it right across my face so that I look out mysterious':

LEN. If Carole's going to have her hair all silly like that, can I go bald then. . .
LILY. Eat your breakfast and don't talk so daft.
LEN. Bald like Uncle Vernon. . .
LILY. If Uncle Vernon heard you talk like that . . . and eat properly, Carole, don't put your finger in your porridge, what d'you think spoons are for?
LEN. Eating jelly.

Even the normally sober Narrator provides a touch of humour with his motley list of oddly juxtaposed items, a favourite device of Thomas's and one present in such talks as *Early One Morning* as well as *Under Milk Wood*:

Now, for Ted Jackson, the working day is over; dusty and tired, he waits for his bus, in a queue. Newspaper placards announce a shocking murder: The Cabinet meets again: a film-star has 'flu: a West End play has been running for fifteen years: 'Bishop says shame to mixed bathing in the Sea': the weather is forecasted, firmly, as dry, or wet: nobody scored at Lords. And a workman wants his tea.

The most startling element in what purports to be a quasi-documentary script is the doggerel verse Thomas adopts for Lily's soliloquy about her household chores. The sudden shift from prose into irregular and undifferentiated quatrains has the effect of transforming what might have been predictably dreary complaints into a comic mould:

Empty the teapot – must have a new one –
only this morning the kitchen was *so* neat –
soak the frying-pan – wish it wasn't fish –
oh *why* do people have to eat –

Why do men put fag ends in their saucers –
knives and forks and plates and cups –
think of all the breakfasts in Montrose Street –
and think of all the washing-ups –
I won't scrub the floor this morning –
I wish the plumber'd come about the sink –
I'll just sweep the breadcrumbs up and then –
another cup of tea I think . . .

One of the few unsung passages in *Under Milk Wood* lineated as verse is, interestingly enough, a soliloquy by another Lily, Lily Smalls.

It would be misleading to overemphasise both the comic aspects of *The Londoner* and the resemblance between it and *Under Milk Wood*, since they are so different in some ways; but in writing a radio feature involving characters, dialogue, and dramatic situations, Thomas clearly pushed his script much more in the direction of comedy than might have been expected for a programme of a documentary nature in a series aimed at overseas listeners. If *Early One Morning* is a precursor of *Under Milk Wood* in that it provided the seeds from which the play grew, *The Londoner* is its precursor as far as structure, technique, and mode are concerned.

Thomas's next radio feature, *Margate – Past and Present*, followed very quickly after *The Londoner*, and although commissioned by the BBC it was not intended for broadcasting by the BBC itself on any of its services. It has never been broadcast in Britain and never been published anywhere. The programme was recorded by the London Transcription Service, on 22 September 1946, with a distinguished cast and music specially composed by Elizabeth Lutyens, for transmission in America as part of an exchange deal between the BBC and the New York radio station WOR, which provided the BBC with a thirty-minute feature about Coney Island. The BBC obviously regarded a programme about Margate as a holiday resort near London, emphasising its entertainments and fairground, as a suitable equivalent. Like *The Londoner*, *Margate – Past and Present* is fictionalised and dramatised documentary, designed to convey aspects of contemporary English life to foreign listeners. By building his script around the visit of Rick Johnson, an American ex-serviceman now a mechanic in New York, to Margate to marry the girl, Molly McFee, he met during the war but has not seen for a year, Thomas provides his intended audience with an ordinary consciousness they can identify with. Throughout the feature Thomas uses Rick's relative ignorance of England and its way of life to convey information and local colour to his transatlantic listeners and to engage their interest.

Margate – Past and Present resembles *The Londoner* and *Under Milk Wood* in its episodic structure and in covering the events of one day, as Rick travels to Margate, meets Molly, wanders along the seafront with her, visits her home, then the Dreamland fairground, then a pub, and finally Dreamland again very late at night, now peaceful and deserted – 'suddenly, so *dead, dead quiet* after the hurdygurdies and the barkers and the squealing and the screaming and everything',[27] rather like Llareggub after the hubbub of the day. But *Margate* differs from the other two scripts in that it does not attempt a night-to-night coverage complete with dreams and in that the day is a very special one in the lives of Rick and Molly rather than being a representative commonplace one. Indeed, since it possesses an orthodox plot with plenty of dramatic potential – a man makes a journey to meet both the girl he fell in love with a year previously and her family, whom he does not know, and is uncertain about what his own response is likely to be and about the reception he can expect – *Margate* could easily have been developed as a straightforward play, unlike *The Londoner* and *Under Milk Wood*. This does not happen, since Thomas treats potentially dramatic scenes as opportunities for documentary exposition, but even so *Margate* has much less in common with *Under Milk Wood* than has *The Londoner*. This latter feature may be documentary rather than dramatic in method, but it does concentrate on characters and their concerns, and the play for voices presents a galaxy of individualised villagers, whereas *Margate* sometimes focuses much more narrowly on the town as a beach resort and entertainment centre, thus neglecting the characters themselves. Paradoxically, *Margate* ends up being less dramatic and more documentary-like than the other two scripts.

During the train journey, Rick's monologue of spoken thoughts, which alternates with passages of dialogue in a way that seems quite natural on radio but is usually unnatural in a visual medium, reveals his uneasy state of mind: his anxieties about his reunion with Molly, about meeting her parents, about whether they believed he would return, and even about whether Molly will recognise him. But after the short scene at Margate station, where Molly also reveals her apprehensions about the encounter, this psychological probing gives way to description and evocation of the place, with Rick virtually ceasing to be a character and instead becoming a narrator as they walk around:

I like the way that boat – what's it called? the Golden Spray – I like the way it's kind of riding and rocking on the water like a big boozed bird . . . There's everything in the world I've got to tell you, Moll, when we're together . . . Can't tell you now . . . I like the way the kids are hullaballooing on the sand, and the old guys in the deck-chairs with newspapers over their faces, and the girls all gay and jaunty, and – oh look! – a bunch of old ladies, all fat as barrels, lifting their dresses and paddling – and screaming . . . !

Thomas's fictional framework goes into a state of suspended animation when his characters lose their dramatic dimensions to become voices in a feature, eyes through which we see Margate rather than individuals in their own right. Rick can't tell Molly now because his function here is to narrate. Although there is no official narrator in *Margate*, unlike *The Londoner*, this is because Thomas finds other means of providing information, as in this case and in the subsequent depiction of Dreamland. Interestingly enough, he originally planned to use the blind Captain Cat in a similar way in *Under Milk Wood* as both central character and sole narrator, but eventually shifted the main burden of narration on to the two Voices, leaving Captain Cat only a little of this narrative function in the morning section.

The episode in the McFees' house when Rick meets Molly's parents is an even more remarkable example of how Thomas transforms a potentially dramatic human encounter into a vehicle for documentary. The conversation between Rick and his future parents-in-law quickly turns to Margate, and after the local guide-book has been amusingly rescued from the dog's bed, the scene proceeds with extracts from it, while the characters are virtually abandoned. In a style reminiscent of the Voice of an Expert in *The Londoner* and the Voice of a Guide-Book in *Under Milk Wood*, a Voice of Information supplies facts about Margate, past and present, and other voices, such as a Broadsheet Voice, make further contributions. In the closing stages of *Margate*, the psychological element does return to prominence with Molly's monologue of reminiscence and with renewed emphasis on the lovers' relationship, but in most of the script this is of secondary importance.

If the attempt to render the atmosphere of Margate severely restricts the development of both character and plot, it might also be expected to permit hardly any possibility of comic writing, but Thomas surprisingly overcomes this particular obstacle by seizing any opportunity for humour. The most sustained example is, oddly enough, the opening of the scene at Molly's home when Rick meets her parents. Instead of attempting a dramatically realistic representation, Thomas uses the situation to introduce Molly's parents as comic characters as they reminisce about their lives in show-business:

MCFEE. We used to work the shows with a man that could eat twenty sausages for breakfast, didn't we Flo? . . .
MRS MCFEE [*very deep, very husky*]. And a egg . . .

and chatter at cross purposes:

MOLLY. Dad, you're not attending to your guest – go on, pass him the beer . . .
MCFEE. Help yourself Rick . . . Funny names Americans have, don't they Flo? . . .
MRS MCFEE. . . . gives you wind . . .
RICK. . . . beg your pardon, Mrs McFee?
MRS MCFEE. Gives you wind . . .
MCFEE. Flo means bottled beer gives you wind, don't you Flo? . . .
RICK. D'you ever feel like going back into show-business, Mr McFee?
MRS MCFEE. . . . and palpitations . . .

Even the reunion of Rick and Molly, which could have been heavy with romantic emotion after their long separation, assumes a comic aspect as they joke about their worst premonitions of the meeting, Molly saying, 'I was thinking, "Oh what if he doesn't recognise me at all and I have to go up to him and say 'Good morning, Mr Johnson, d'ya remember me, I'm the girl with the carroty hair you're going to marry, remember?' " ' Margate itself is observed by an eye quick to spot comic incongruities, as in the description of an elderly man building a sandcastle, with 'bowler hat, glasses, bathing-trunks and a tummy like a bass drum'.

Although there is no omniscient narrator in *Margate*, Thomas employs two Voices at the beginning and more briefly at the end as a framing device, initially to establish the opening situation and introduce Rick, and finally to round off the feature. In *Under Milk Wood* he again makes use of two Voices, but this is for the purpose of aural variety, since they play such a large part, and there is no dialogue between them. In *Margate*, on the other hand, the two Voices alternate with questions and answers, and this resembles the opening of *The Londoner*, although there the Questioner receives replies from several voices. But this is a superficial difference compared with the difference in tone. In *The Londoner* the Questioner and his answers are external, social voices, but in *Margate* the two Voices sound like an interior dialogue within the writer himself as the creative process gets under way and he tries to imagine the opening situation of his work without being certain about how it will develop. The rather fairy-tale opening of *Under Milk Wood*, 'To begin at the beginning', also suggests the winding up of the creative process, but the resemblance is slight. In *Margate* the apparently omniscient Second Voice is capable of making mistakes, even though he is short-tempered with the First Voice for not knowing what is happening:

1ST VOICE. Well, where do we begin? Got to begin somewhere . . .
2ND VOICE. Begin in a third class railway carriage.
    [*Background train noise*]
1ST VOICE. Is the train moving?
2ND VOICE. Of course it's moving – are you deaf? The fuming, snorting iron steed with her attendant gallimaufry...
1ST VOICE. ...wrong word...
2ND VOICE. ....of green gay coaches is racing proudly along the glistening rails, her bright, shiny electric engine... sorry, it's a steam train.
1ST VOICE. Where's it going?
2ND VOICE. Margate, stupid.
1ST VOICE. Who's in the compartment we're beginning in?
    [*Murmur of voices in carriage*]
2ND VOICE [*quickly*]. There's a stout, badgered lady with a cluck of children and a thermos-flask wrestling with a sunshade fallen off the rack and a crushed bag of dried-egg sandwiches... There's a small, flat lady with a baffled expression, as though she'd been slammed in a door once and couldn't remember which door, reading the new best-seller...

This very unconventional and even quirky opening is itself comic, partly because of the amusing thumbnail sketches of the people sharing Rick's compartment, who would not be out of place among the gallery of eccentrics in Llareggub, and also because of the deliberately inappropriate pomposity with which the train is described. There is a particularly Thomasish touch of humour a little later when the First Voice asks what the two girls in the compartment are giggling about, to receive an 'exasperated' reply from the Second Voice: 'How do I know? Life, death, Einstein, what the lodger said.' At the end the two Voices return to find a way of concluding the feature just as they had set it in motion:

1ST VOICE. Well, where do we end? Got to end somewhere. Do we end in Dreamland, in the dark?
2ND VOICE. End at the foot of the stairs in the dim-lit hallway of the McFees' boarding-house. End with Molly and Rick saying goodnight.

Considering the documentary purpose of *Margate* and the limitations this inevitably imposed on him, Thomas's way of using the two Voices is startlingly unexpected and seems like a conscious attempt to introduce an element of originality into what might have been predictable and routine. Of course, *Margate*, like *The Londoner*, is essentially a work of Thomas the professional script-writer, which is what the war turned him into, rather than Thomas the poet and creative writer. Both features were commissioned for a particular purpose and for an overseas audience, and Thomas provided scripts which met those requirements. He obviously had much less of a free hand than in the case of his personal talks, but even so one does not have to be an advocate of the *auteur* theory to recognise that he stamped his own individuality on these features. This is particularly evident in the extent to which he created possibilities for humour in programmes that could easily have been completely serious and predominantly factual, and furthermore because he preferred to exploit any dramatic situation for comedy rather than anything else.

During the nine months separating *Margate* and *Return Journey*, Thomas continued to be heavily engaged in broadcasting, and three of the talks he gave at the end of 1946, *How To Begin a Story*, *Holiday Memory*, and *The Crumbs of One Man's Year*, are of some relevance to *Under Milk Wood*. *How To Begin a Story*, broadcast on the Home Service on 8 October as a contribution to the programme *In the Margin*, is not based on personal experience or reminiscence like the other two or the talks mentioned earlier, but exhibits the same kind of verbal flamboyance ('Those flash, brash, cigar-mashing floozy-flayers')[28] as it makes a brief parodic survey of various fictional stereotypes. In retrospect, the part dealing with 'the story of rural life'[29] and burlesquing T. F.

Powys's kind of fiction can be seen to prefigure elements in *Under Milk Wood*, and at this time Thomas himself must have been thinking about how to begin a play for voices. His clarification of the type of story he is making fun of, one 'set in a small, lunatic area of Wessex, full of saintly or reprehensible vicars, wanton maidens, biblical sextons, and old men called Parsnip or Dottle',[30] would bear a strong resemblance to his play if 'Wales' were substituted for 'Wessex'. In Thomas's original conception, *The Town Was Mad*, Llareggub was to be 'a small, lunatic area', and it certainly contains a saintly vicar (Eli Jenkins), wanton maidens (Polly Garter and Mae Rose Cottage), and characters with Biblical associations (Jack Black) and odd names (Lily Smalls, Sinbad Sailors). Thomas's further comment about every character in 'this sophisticatedly contrived bucolic morality' having 'his or her obsession'[31] is also curiously pertinent to *Under Milk Wood*, in which so many of the characters are conceived as 'humour' figures, each with an obsession – Polly Garter and babies, Organ Morgan and music, Mrs Ogmore-Pritchard and fastidiousness, Mr Pugh and wife-murder, Lord Cut-Glass and time. Even more interesting is this passage: 'Cruel farmers persecute old cowherds called Crumpet, who talk, all day long, to cows; cows, tired of vaccine-talk in which they can have no part, gore, in a female manner, the aged relatives of cruel farmers; it is all very cosy in Upper Story.'[32] There is a sense in which 'it is all very cosy' in the self-contained world of Llareggub too, and the bad-tempered farmer Utah Watkins, who 'hates his cattle', tries very hard, though unsuccessfully, to be cruel near the end, while his milk-maid, Bessie Bighead, does indeed talk to her cows, one of whom Utah Watkins urges to gore not his aged relatives but his dog. Despite Thomas's evident mockery of a certain kind of rural writing, his own version of pastoral in *Under Milk Wood* has some affinity with the 'sophisticatedly contrived bucolic' sort.

In *Holiday Memory*, broadcast on the Welsh Home Service on 25 October 1946, and in *The Crumbs of One Man's Year*, broadcast on the Home Service on 27 December, Thomas consolidated the style of radio prose he had developed in his earlier talks and was to use in subsequent Welsh Home Service talks, *The Festival Exhibition, 1951, The International Eisteddfod, A Visit to America*, and *Laugharne*, as his unfailing fertility of verbal inventiveness shows: 'the cow-patched, mooing fields', 'milk-pail handbags', 'the buses gambolled', 'we trod the buried grass like ghosts on dry toast', 'a bicycle by the larder very much down at wheels' (all from *The Crumbs of One Man's Year*),[33] and this extraordinary piece of alliterative, assonantal, punning writing, the equal of anything in *Under Milk Wood* itself: 'I pry back at those wizening twelve months and see only a waltzing snippet of the tipsy-turvy times, flickers of vistas, flashes of queer fishes, patches and chequers of a bard's-eye view.'[34] Both of these talks are remarkable for their wide-ranging sweep, their amused but uncritical and sympathetic survey of human behaviour, and their delight in the sheer variety of life with all its incongruity and *bizarrerie*, as Thomas examines a day (*Holiday Memory*) and a year (*Crumbs*). When he subsequently created a day in the life of Llareggub, he did so in much the same spirit. *Holiday Memory*, which encompasses a typical August Bank Holiday from early morning to late at night, has a further resemblance to *Under Milk Wood* in that it is yet another example of Thomas's use of the ready-made structural device of a single day for a radio programme. Surprisingly for a talk, it also contains a favourite comic device of his, a passage of rapidly intercut speech described by T. H. Jones as 'a kind of stichomythia',[35] which he used effectively in *The Londoner, Margate, Return Journey*, and *Under Milk Wood*.

Although next to nothing has been written about *Return Journey* as a work for radio, it is well known as a source of information about Thomas's pre-war life in Swansea as seen through his eyes, and the passages about the 'bombastic adolescent provincial Bohemian' wearing 'a conscious woodbine',[36] for example, are frequently quoted by biographers and scholars. Nevertheless, it is an outstanding radio feature in a totally different class from the more pedestrian hackwork of its predecessors, and Cleverdon goes as far as to 'doubt whether there has ever been a better thirty-minute radio piece'.[37] The BBC production, first broadcast on the Home Service on 15 June 1947, has deservedly been repeated on a number of occasions on several channels, including the Third Programme and the Overseas Service, and just as it is Thomas's only feature to have been transmitted on the national network, it is the only one to have been published in England. Like *The Londoner, Return Journey* was commissioned for a feature series, itself called *Return Journey* and consisting of twenty-four programmes between 1945 and 1951, in which well-known writers recalled the place most closely associated with their childhood. This was, therefore, the first opportunity Thomas had to write a feature, as opposed to a talk, of a very personal kind, drawing on his own experiences and memories and also dealing with Wales. The series might seem like a prescription for indulgent nostalgia, but from Thomas's point of view the invitation came at a particularly appropriate time because he had been exploring the lost world of his childhood in his poetry, above all in 'Fern Hill'. Since he himself was really the subject of *Return Journey*, more so indeed than in any of his radio talks, his involvement in this miniature *A la Recherche du Temps Perdu* was much more personal than that of the professional script-writer of the previous features. In the production, Thomas took the only really substantial role, that of the Narrator, who is implicitly the Thomas of 1947 making a return journey to Swansea in search of his younger self.

Although certainly not lacking in humour and wit, *Return Journey* is darker, more intense, and more emotional than the talks and features of the previous four years. Yet Thomas carefully balances the serious with the comic so that the script is never in danger of being sentimental or portentous. Significantly, the day in February of the Narrator's quest could hardly be more bleak and wintry, and this establishes the tone of the work just as the warm spring day does the different tone of *Under Milk Wood*. From his opening words ('It was a cold white day') the Narrator repeatedly stresses coldness and whiteness, and the 'white havoc'd' desolation caused by winter only serves to reinforce the desolation of a town whose centre had been completely destroyed by bombing during the war (the former shops are now 'blitzed flat graves marbled with snow and headstoned with fences'). The vivid evocation of the dead of winter is interwoven with an equally vivid evocation of 'vanished buildings' and urban death, of a town with the social and commercial heart torn out of it and reduced to 'flat white wastes'. On two occasions, lists of 'the remembered invisible shops' conclude with the words, 'and nothing', emphasising the contrast between past and present, between memory and observation. But there are other deaths too, including those of the former schoolboys killed in the war whose names are listed as on a memorial during the Narrator's visit to the partly destroyed school; and the recollection of childhood games of Cowboys and Indians with Jack Basset, narrated by the First Voice, is immediately followed by the Narrator's stark reminder of mortality and war: 'Jackie Basset, killed'. *Return*

Journey ends with the word 'Dead' repeated no fewer than six times by the Park-Keeper in reply to the Narrator's question about what has become of Young Thomas. The effect is like the tolling of the funeral bell that accompanies the list of Young Thomas's dead school friends, so that he is virtually added to the memorial. In *Under Milk Wood*, two of Polly Garter's bursts of song referring to 'little Willy Wee', including one immediately before the First Voice's concluding speech, end similarly with 'dead' being repeated three times; and although the play is obviously not an elegiac work in the sense that *Return Journey* is – indeed it is often thought to be a Rowlandsonian romp and a great celebration of life – death makes its presence felt, especially in the voices of the dead.

Return Journey is to some extent a requiem for Thomas's childhood and youth, but it is just as much a requiem for the old Swansea, and the two elements are closely connected, since Swansea in ruins is a physical equivalent of the lost past and makes the sense of irrecoverability even more absolute. Thomas's private world is in fact subsumed into a much wider one involving the whole town. It is partly because of this emphasis on a lost place and a lost world that the feature is not narcissistic and self-pitying, but the amused detachment with which the Narrator and others describe Young Thomas and the abundance of humour are also crucial counterpoises to any sentimental tendency. The Narrator sees him as 'a bit of a shower-off; plus-fours and no breakfast . . . a gabbing, ambitious, mock-tough, pretentious young man; and mole-y too' who 'used to wear an overcoat sometimes with the check lining inside out so that you could play giant draughts on him' and 'slouch like a newshawk even when he was attending a meeting of the Gorseinon Buffalos'. The vignettes of 'Two typewriter Thomas the ace news-dick', referring to Thomas's brief period as a young reporter for the *South Wales Evening Post*, of Thomas and his artistic friends 'arguing the toss' about 'Communism, symbolism, Bradman, Braque, the Watch Committee, free love, free beer, murder, Michelangelo, ping-pong, ambition, Sibelius, and girls', of Thomas the schoolboy who 'garbled his lessons with the worst of them', and of Thomas the would-be Casanova of Swansea Promenade, are all very funny. So are some of the characters in their own right, notably the Barmaid with her breathless, unpunctuated chatter: 'Seen the film at the Elysium Mr Griffiths there's snow isn't it did

you come up on your bicycle our pipes burst Monday.' Even in
evoking the bombed town, Thomas can be far from solemn, as in
the Customer's wry reply to the Narrator's question about a
well-known pub, 'What's the Three Lamps like now?': 'It isn't
like anything. It isn't there. It's nothing mun. You remember Ben
Evans's stores? It's right next door to that. Ben Evans isn't there
either...'

The earlier features are often comic, of course, but *Return
Journey* differs from them in being verbally witty as well, in the
manner of the radio talks. Whereas *The Londoner* and *Margate*
proceed mainly through dialogue and soliloquy with narration
playing only a minor part, about half of *Return Journey* is spoken
by the Narrator, who can be identified with Thomas himself. Not
surprisingly, therefore, he employed the prose idiom he had
developed for his radio talks, although in a fairly subdued and
non-virtuoso way as befitted the material. Even so, his fondness
for 'metaphysical' comparisons, personification, word-play, and
exciting sound patterns manifests itself throughout, as in the
descriptions of the wind 'with a soft sea-noise hanging on its arm,
like a hooter in a muffler' and of the Three Lamps as 'that snug,
smug, select, Edwardian holy of best-bitter holies', and in this
assonantal and alliterative sentence about the icy weather and its
effect: 'Then I tacked down the snowblind hill, a cat-o'-nine-gales
whipping from the sea, and, white and eiderdowned in the
smothering flurry, people padded past me up and down like
prowling featherbeds.' Different, but also characteristic of his
exhilarating radio style, is the rapid accumulation of epithets in
this amusing passage, which also illustrates various other devices
and tropes designed to electrify the ear: 'Fish-frailed, netbagged,
umbrella'd, pixie-capped, fur-shoed, blue-nosed, puce-lipped,
blinkered like drayhorses, scarved, mittened, galoshed, wearing
everything but the cat's blanket, crushes of shopping-women
crunched in the little Lapland of the once grey drab street, blew
and queued and yearned for hot tea.' By combining for the first
time in *Return Journey* his idiosyncratic radio prose and the feature form, Thomas created the possibility of writing something
more extended than a talk in this idiom and therefore prepared
one of the routes to *Under Milk Wood*.

Return Journey prefigures the play in other ways too, especially
in the importance and centrality of the Narrator and the effects
this has, although there are differences. The narrative provided

by the Voices in *Under Milk Wood* is omniscient and in the third person, whereas in *Return Journey* it is in the first person with the Narrator himself appearing as a character, in the sense that he is conducting the search for Young Thomas as though for a missing person – and this leads him into contact with other characters. It is the three Voices introduced briefly in the closing stages to provide information about Young Thomas's childhood who, because of their full knowledge of both past and present, may be called omniscient. Nevertheless, the Narrator is correctly named since he exists less as a character than as a consciousness recording the present and eliciting from the memories of others anything they can remember of Young Thomas. Drawing attention to what is outside himself and to the past rather than to himself, he remains effectively anonymous despite being the voice of Thomas, and is therefore closer in conception to the Voices of *Under Milk Wood* than to either Captain Cat, who aids the narration but is strongly individualised, or Rick in *Margate*, who oscillates uneasily between performing dramatic and narrative functions. The Voices in *Under Milk Wood* also belong to a consciousness, but one embracing the totality of Llareggub, and therefore corresponding to the creator himself. Thomas wrote the part of the First Voice for himself (as he had the role of the Narrator in *Return Journey*), performed it in the American stage-readings, and would have repeated it for the BBC had he lived.

To give the Narrator such a pre-eminent position is a drastic move away from orthodox dramatic methods to a more purely radio form, since it considerably reduces the possibility of dramatic interaction and development. In this respect, *Return Journey* is the precursor of *Under Milk Wood* and strikingly different from *The Londoner*, where the Narrator is not a consciousness but a technical device providing essential bits of information and smoothing the transitions between short dramatic scenes, most of which proceed through realistic dialogue. As a medium, radio is noted for its temporal and spatial flexibility, but the extensive use of a narrator can greatly enhance this freedom from theatrical restraints. In *Return Journey*, for example, the Narrator introduces characters in isolation instead of in social situations, ushers in disembodied voices, and passes rapidly from one character or voice or situation to another without returning to any of them. Like Thomas's earlier features, *Return Journey* is episodic in form, but unlike them there are no central characters apart from the

Narrator, and in this it closely resembles *Under Milk Wood*. *Return Journey* also differs from the earlier ones in its handling of time. Superficially it conforms to Thomas's familiar format of the single day, beginning in the morning and ending with dusk, and as in *The Londoner* and *Under Milk Wood* the pace accelerates after a leisurely opening. But the Narrator's search for Young Thomas moves back in time as well as forward, and as the day advances the memories regress in contrary motion. The first picture of Young Thomas is as a journalist and bohemian just before he left Swansea, and the last is of the small boy in Cwmdonkin Park. Furthermore, the past is itself presented in different ways: sometimes simply being recalled by the interviewee, such as the Passer-By and the Schoolmaster (who speaks in verse like Lily at one point in *The Londoner* and a few characters in *Under Milk Wood*); sometimes as a flashback emerging from a recollection, as in the case of the Girl who springs to life out of the Promenade-Man's memory; and sometimes as a flashback without any intermediary other than the Narrator, as in the case of the dramatised scene with the Reporters. The treatment of time in *Under Milk Wood* is more straightforward, since the play is primarily concerned with the present rather than the past, but voices do appear from the past, especially in the dreams of Captain Cat and Mr Waldo.

If *Under Milk Wood* is approached *via Return Journey* and Thomas's other radio features instead of as an extension of his poetry, the vexed problem of its form and genre may not disappear but does become much more tractable. When reviewed in 1954 and 1955, *Under Milk Wood* was sometimes linked with books of poems, sometimes with stage plays or books about the theatre, sometimes with miscellaneous books, as well as being treated on its own. It was usually discussed in literary or conventionally dramatic terms, not radio ones, so that the emphasis put on its significance as radio by Eric Gillett was most unusual: '*Under Milk Wood* is one of the most important contributions to our literature which radio has made...[It] could only have been written by a poet with a large and varied experience of broadcasting...[It] is easier to listen to than to read.'[38] It was described as epic, although there is nothing epic about it; more categorically as a verse play, which it certainly is not, since most of it is in prose; and even more frequently as poetry or prose-poetry. The absurd attribution of epic qualities or pretensions to *Under Milk Wood*,

partly because Thomas once said that he would like to write a
Welsh *Ulysses* and was influenced by Joyce, has resulted in perverse comparisons with Joyce's masterpiece, notably by David
Holbrook in *Llareggub Revisited* where he actually states that 'this
is Dylan Thomas's *Ulysses*'.[39] Even though *Under Milk Wood* certainly owes something to the Circe section of *Ulysses*, as Holbrook
and, more sympathetically, Raymond Williams argue,[40] the differences in genre, medium, scale, aim, and tone between the two
works are so great that comparison can easily become invidious.

Then again, even if the widespread view that its conception is
essentially poetic is correct – and this arose not only because
Thomas was expected to be poetic but also because a number of
reviewers found it impossible to call it 'dramatic' – *Under Milk
Wood* cannot be called a poem without some qualification, such as
the modifier 'radio' or simply quotation marks. It was because the
work failed to deliver the poetic goods he had been led to expect
that Stephen Pike expressed such disappointment with it in his
argument with Stuart Holroyd mentioned earlier. The failure to
relate the rich verbal textures of *Under Milk Wood* to Thomas's
radio prose or even to his literary prose usually led to the belief
that he was writing a form of poetry, although in his brilliant
review of the work Gene Baro recognised the error of this
approach:

Now, I must say that the language of this play, though vibrant, musical,
and apt, is yet rather the masterful juggling and fooling of a language
genius than the full issue of his creative effort. All in all, the language is
appropriate to the cast and temper of the play, and certainly contributes
to its life; but it is the quick, impressionistic language of Dylan Thomas'
stories and not the prismatic language of his poetry.[41]

Yet even in one of the best scholarly articles about it, Laurence
Lerner sometimes uses 'poem', without quotation marks, as an
alternative to 'play' and claims that '*Under Milk Wood* is certainly
part of English poetry'.[42] Lerner's emphasis is understandable
considering his illuminating view of *Under Milk Wood* as a modern
version of pastoral having affinities with such famous Renaissance works as Tasso's *Aminta* and Guarini's *Il Pastor Fido*, but
talk of 'poetry' confuses matters just as much as Kenneth Tynan's
totally different emphasis on 'theatre', when he relates it to a
number of stage plays and places Thomas in a line of playwrights
stemming from Ibsen and Chekhov and including Giraudoux,
Synge, and O'Casey.[43]

Discussion of *Under Milk Wood* as drama has led to completely opposed and equally misguided positions: on the one hand, the view mentioned earlier that the play was the work of a potentially great poetic dramatist; and on the other, the view expounded most strongly by Holbrook that it is a failure because it is not dramatic. The word 'play' certainly raises expectations that *Under Milk Wood* fails to fulfil, but as Val Gielgud's comments about the difficulty early radio dramatists had in thinking in terms of the microphone rather than the stage make clear, it is the terminology that is unsatisfactory:

I believe that it is the use of the word 'play' which is the cause of so much misunderstanding, if not of definite error. To begin with, we are all accustomed, in everyday phraseology, to going 'to see' plays, as opposed to going 'to hear' them. In consequence the mere juxtaposition of the words 'radio' and 'play' must imply for many people a contradiction in terms. To go on with, the word 'play' implies a number of conventions – of length, of construction, of unities, and so forth – which, if accepted by the radio dramatist, serve only to hamper his freedom and cramp his style.[44]

In a letter to Marguerite Caetani about his work in progress, Thomas himself struggled with a definition when he said that he was trying to

write a piece, a play, an impression for voices, an entertainment out of the darkness, of the town I live in, and to write it simply and warmly and comically with lots of movement and varieties of moods, so that, at many levels, through sight and speech, description and dialogue, evocation and parody, you came to know the town as an inhabitant of it.[45]

Once *Under Milk Wood* is considered as a piece for radio, a 'play for voices' rather than a 'play', the problems that arise when it is discussed as 'drama' or 'poetry' evaporate, although Henry Treece succeeded in liberating it from these categories without referring explicitly to radio, in a remarkably perceptive paragraph in his tribute to Thomas after the poet's death:

Under Milk Wood can give no possible support to any belief that Dylan Thomas might have become a playwright. It is a series of labyrinthine, microscopic insights, magnificently moving, emotionally, in its separate units, but blurred and static when seen as a whole. Nothing seems to happen (which makes it so true a picture of a small town, of course) apart from the varied beating of the hearts in the hundred rooms. It bears no more relation to a play than does a clock-maker's shop, where the many machines tick out their day at speeds and tones dictated by their individual mechanisms. Or, to use another metaphor, *Under Milk Wood* is an ant-hill, which is quite static from a distance of ten yards and only comes to life when observed from ten inches. It is a pointilliste technique too refined for the theatre.[46]

Treece's description, with its emphasis on Thomas's atomistic method, fits certain kinds of radio features very well, although what he had in mind was Thomas's famous statement, actually made in a letter to Treece, about each of his poems needing 'a host of images because its centre is a host of images'.[47] It was the feature form that Thomas resorted to after commencing with and eventually rejecting an orthodox dramatic structure for his extended work for radio. The long gestation of *Under Milk Wood* and its various embryonic transformations have frequently been discussed, notably by Daniel Jones[48] and Douglas Cleverdon,[49] and some writers, including his friend John Davenport, believe that Thomas only dropped his elaborate dramatic framework 'because he was incapable of dramatic structure' and was therefore 'unable to carry out the original scheme from which it had sprung',[50] much to his own dissatisfaction. In the letter that Thomas sent to Marguerite Caetani accompanying his submission of *Llareggub* to her as editor of *Botteghe Oscure,* he says that 'I have reluctantly, and, I hope, only temporarily, abandoned' *The Town Was Mad,*[51] but his ensuing detailed description of *Llareggub* indicates considerable enthusiasm for his revised project rather than dissatisfaction about the change of direction. Even if one agrees with Raymond Williams that 'the loss of *The Town Was Mad* is a thing to regret',[52] Thomas was probably following his intuition as a broadcaster and an experienced creative writer for radio, as well as Cleverdon's advice, in jettisoning an essentially theatrical conception, which he initially must have felt he needed in order to shape a large-scale work, in favour of a loose form more suited to original writing for the medium. Cleverdon claims that when he suggested cutting out the plot, Thomas 'seemed relieved at this proposal, and accepted it without demur'.[53] Henry Hewes's article about the New York stage-readings in May 1953 has been almost totally neglected by embryologists of the work, but it is extremely important because it contains Thomas's own account of the gestation; and although this could be interpreted as a confession that 'he was incapable of dramatic structure' as Davenport suggests, it supports Cleverdon's view that Thomas was doing the right thing in following his radio nose instead of confining himself within a preconceived scheme:

[*Under Milk Wood*] has no plot and no crisis, and the slight revelation which might indicate a growth on the part of Captain Cat tends to get buried in Llareggub's multicolored assortment of citizens.

Mr Thomas is the first to admit all this. 'When I began eighteen months ago', he says, 'I had a very simple plot. I thought I'd make all the characters even more eccentric than they are now. Then I'd have a new nationalist Government taking over Wales. One of the new Government's inspectors comes to Llareggub and says to the mayor, "We're taking charge of affairs here now, and we've decided to declare this disgraceful town an open-air lunatic asylum." The townspeople scream with rage and each person defends himself, and his seemingly insane actions. In the end they accept, preferring to remain "mad", because their insanity appears to them healthier than the sanity of the Government.'

However, Mr Thomas soon found this plot too restricting. He found himself hacking the plot out instead of writing what he wanted to say. 'You know,' he adds, 'if you feel you're hacking it out, you're either incompetent or doing something wrong.'

Drawing the most charitable of these two deductions, the poet decided to abandon the plot. For a time he toyed with the idea of having one of the characters die, to give a feeling of the passage of time, but he even gave that up. 'I guess I just got boozed up on the language', he admits with the not unhappy look of a man who has learned to face and live with his compulsions.

'I also did another unpardonable thing,' confesses the poet, 'I fell in love with one of my characters, so that Polly Garter gets too much attention at the expense of the others.'[54]

Thomas's adoption and adaptation of the feature form solved his problem of how to present an entire community on radio, and as he explained to Marguerite Caetani he 'wanted to make the town alive through a new medium'.[55] Radio plays with an orthodox dramatic form and therefore without a narrator are usually most successful with a small cast, for the simple reason that identification of characters by voice alone is much harder than in the theatre. Without constant explanations of who new arrivals are, a large cast can be most confusing, but such explanations are themselves counter-productive since they disrupt the dramatic illusion. In order to encompass the living and the dead, voices from the present and the past, about forty adult villagers and their memories, not to mention a number of school-children, Thomas had no option but to employ a narrator as a unifying and connecting device. The script calls for seventy-four individual voices as well as the chorus of children, and in a work lasting about ninety minutes there are between 610 and 620 vocal entries (since many consist of only a word or a phrase, 'speeches' seems inappropriate), depending on which text you use and whether you count repeated speech-prefixes. Yet in employing narration, Thomas makes a virtue of necessity, transforming what could have been no more than a device, and a cumbersome one, into an omniscient consciousness approximating to Thomas's own, that embraces the entire village and can lead us to any part of it, even its dreams and fantasies – in his letter to Marguerite Caetani he calls it 'a kind of conscience, a guardian angel'.[56] This is why Donald McWhinnie, in his severe remarks about the abuse of the narrator in radio drama as an easy way out of difficulties ('his is the most misused role in radio'), exempts *Under Milk Wood* from his strictures:

I never heard *Under Milk Wood* criticized for its use of narration – though its role here is gigantic – because Thomas knew how to use it: as an integral part of the script; not an intrusion, but an element which is always part of the total logic and whose poetic overtones constantly reveal fresh facets of the theme.[57]

Even though Raymond Williams argues that the narration is the weakest part of the work on stylistic grounds, he too defends Thomas's extensive use of narration as one way of breaking out of the confines of both domestic drama and naturalism:

In terms of recent stage drama, narrative can be called undramatic, but in fact, on a longer view, it can be seen that in some of the most satisfactory dramatic forms ever achieved – in Athenian tragic drama in particular – narrative has had an important place. The rehabilitation of narrative, in broadcast drama, was a sound instinct, and *Under Milk Wood*, in spite of the crudity of its narrative structure, is the most successful example we have of its dramatic usefulness.[58]

Unlike the Narrator in *Return Journey*, the two Voices in *Under Milk Wood* remain entirely aloof from the characters in that they do not communicate with them, one of the results being that dramatic encounters are more limited than in the earlier work. The Voices are never absent for long, and on one occasion when they are relatively silent it is because blind Captain Cat takes over the narrative, though in a more personal and speculative way, describing the morning activities of the village not from an omniscient perspective but from his position as a privileged eavesdropper as he responds to what he hears around him. Furthermore, the most extended passages without interruption from the narrators are not of ordinary dialogue but are the complex montage of voices constituting Mr Waldo's dream, the montage of rapidly intercut gossip from the women in Mrs Organ Morgan's shop, and the children's kissing game. There are, in fact, no really sustained passages of dialogue in the play, the unmarried characters usually being presented alone, while the married ones are seldom encountered except in the company of their spouses. The characters observe and even overhear each other, but rarely meet; on his postal round Willy Nilly speaks to only four people, while the Sailors Arms is less of a social centre than Mrs Organ Morgan's shop, since Sinbad communicates with only two characters there, Mr Waldo and Cherry Owen. Yet in spite of this apparent fragmentation, the effect Thomas generates is not of isolated individuals but of a community, and he achieves this partly, of course, by the comprehensive overview provided by the Voices but also by juxtaposing and interweaving the voices of the characters throughout, thus creating an aural totality, a community of voices.

In an orthodox theatrical production, the characters appear much more isolated than they do on radio, because we *see* them, and this alters the work significantly. It is in the nature of radio to establish connections that do not exist in space: such connections are entirely aural and not in the least visual, since they depend on a contiguity of voices, not of speakers. When the First Voice introduces the voices of the dreaming Dai Bread, Polly Garter, Nogood Boyo, and Lord Cut-Glass, who say in turn 'Harems', 'Babies', 'Nothing', and 'Tick tock tick tock tick tock tick tock'[59] without any interspersed comment, the characters are linked aurally although physically they are quite separate. The same is true of the daytime, as when Mrs Pugh says, 'I will say this for her, she never makes a mistake', immediately after Mary Ann Sailors's 'I'm eighty-five years three months and a day!'; or when Eli Jenkins comments in his disingenuous way, 'Praise the Lord! We are a musical nation', after Polly Garter's song, 'I loved a man whose name was Tom.' The most audacious example of connections being established in this way is the cross-cutting between the children's Shakespearean song about love just before their kissing game ('When birds do sing hey ding a ding a ding/Sweet lovers love the Spring') and Polly's song about her lovers:

POLLY GARTER. Tom, Dick and Harry were three fine men.
                And I'll never have such
CHILDREN.   ding a ding
POLLY GARTER. again.

The juxtapositions arising from what Treece calls Thomas's pointillism do not make for drama in the ordinary sense, but what *Under Milk Wood* lacks in the way of drama, it more than makes up for in variety. Because it is without a visual dimension, radio is an extraordinarily versatile medium, being able to make rapid transitions in time and space, between speech and unspoken thoughts, and from consciousness to subconsciousness or dream, in an effortless way. In this respect it is totally unlike theatre, having more in common with another visual medium, film; and although it is dangerous to press an analogy between a purely aural medium and a predominantly visual one, the two Voices do behave like movie cameras and might even be called 'verbal cameras'. They move through the village, observing but unobserved, tracking along or panning around the streets, now giving an overall view in long shot, now focusing on details in close-up, sometimes even zooming in on particulars, as in the lists of goods for sale in Mrs Organ Morgan's general store or of confectionery in Miss Price's sweet shop. The whole of the opening description by the First Voice, with its direct appeal to the listener ('Hush... You can hear the dew falling... Only *your* eyes are unclosed to see the black and folded town... And you alone can hear... Listen... Listen... Look... Only you can hear ... Only you can see... Only you can hear and see...') and its slow movement from long shot to close-up ('Come closer now... From where you are, you can hear their dreams'), leading to the superimposed flashbacks of Captain Cat's dream, is cinematic in method. Equally cinematic and completely untheatrical are the facility and speed with which changes can be effected between scenes by the narrators, who sometimes introduce characters to speak only a word or a phrase before cutting to someone and somewhere else. By describing what a character sees, the Voices can also provide an aural equivalent of a cinematic point-of-view shot, as when Mrs Pugh's words 'I want to look *out*. I want to see' are followed by the Second Voice's 'Lily Smalls

the treasure down on her red knees washing the front step', then
cutting back to Mrs Pugh's outraged reaction, 'She's tucked her
dress in her bloomers – oh, the baggage!' This episode continues
with some more 'shots' from Mrs Pugh's point of view, including
one of Attila Rees that is actually interrupted in mid-sentence to
permit a brief exchange between the Pughs about the policeman's
intentions:

SECOND VOICE. P.C. Attila Rees, ox-broad, barge-booted, stamping out
   of Handcuff House in a heavy beef-red huff, black-browed under his
   damp helmet...
MRS PUGH. He's going to arrest Polly Garter, mark my words.
MR PUGH. What for, dear?
MRS PUGH. For having babies.
SECOND VOICE. . . . and lumbering down towards the strand to see that the
   sea is still there.

This closely resembles cinematic cross-cutting.

As a collage of voices *Under Milk Wood* could have settled into a
monotonous pattern of narrative alternating with dialogue or
soliloquy, but Thomas rings the changes of vocal presentation to
avoid this danger. Prose is the principal medium of both narration and non-narrative speech, although the idiom of the two
Voices is Thomas's characteristic radio prose at its most heightened and therefore very different from the colloquial dialogue;
but he also incorporates verse (Eli Jenkins's 'morning service' and
'sunset poem', for example, or Captain Cat and Rosie Probert's
dream conversation in the afternoon) and song (mainly the children and Polly Garter, but also Mr Waldo's pub ballad near the
end). The dialogue itself varies from the naturalistic to the
extremely stylised, as in the gossip of the women in Mrs Organ
Morgan's shop, which is superb radio writing, fast and fluid, but
completely untheatrical:

THIRD WOMAN. Seen Mrs Butcher Beynon?
SECOND WOMAN. She said Butcher Beynon put dogs in the mincer
FIRST WOMAN. go on, he's pulling her leg
THIRD WOMAN. now don't you dare tell her that, there's a dear
SECOND WOMAN. or she'll think he's trying to pull it off and eat it.
FOURTH WOMAN. There's a nasty lot live here when you come to think.

Sometimes, as in this case, the narrators present an episode
which proceeds entirely in dialogue, but on other occasions narrative and dialogue are interwoven, so that a situation is simul-

taneously described and presented dramatically, in a way that is novelistic rather than theatrical. During the meal-times of the Pughs and the Organ Morgans, this technique is used to brilliant comic effect:

MR PUGH. You know best, dear,

FIRST VOICE. says Mr Pugh, and quick as a flash he ducks her in rat soup.

MRS PUGH. What's that book by your trough, Mr Pugh?

MR PUGH. It's a theological work, me dear. *Lives of the Great Saints.*

FIRST VOICE. Mrs Pugh smiles. An icicle forms in the cold air of the dining-vault.

MRS PUGH. I saw you talking to a saint this morning. Saint Polly Garter. She was martyred again last night. Mrs Organ Morgan saw her with Mr Waldo.

MRS ORGAN MORGAN. And when they saw me they pretended they were looking for nests,

SECOND VOICE. said Mrs Organ Morgan to her husband, with her mouth full of fish as a pelican's.

MRS ORGAN MORGAN. But you don't go nesting in long combinations, I said to myself, like Mr Waldo was wearing, and your dress nearly over your head like Polly Garter's. Oh, they didn't fool me.

SECOND VOICE. One big bird gulp, and the flounder's gone. She licks her lips and goes stabbing again.

This episode also contains the equivalent of a cinematic jump-cut, by which Thomas moves from one set of characters to another without intervening narration, and this again illustrates his variety of technique. A variant of this 'jump-cut' transition is the non-naturalistic introduction of a speaker who is not physically present in the scene, as when 'Mrs Willy Nilly steams open Mr Mog Edwards' letter to Miss Myfanwy Price and reads it aloud to Willy Nilly' but with Mog's voice entering to do almost all the reading; or when Nogood Boyo, alone in his boat, fantasises about Mrs Dai Bread Two 'dressed only in a bangle' and pleads with this product of his imagination to accept the 'nice wet corset' he has caught, only to be rebuffed by her voice, 'No, I *won't!*'

Thomas handles soliloquy or interior monologue just as flexibly as dialogue, often allowing it to proceed without narrative intrusion, as in Lily Smalls's extended dialogue with herself in front of a mirror first thing in the morning, but sometimes intertwining it with narrative as when Gossamer Beynon reveals her suppressed sexual self and gives vent to her erotic fantasies about Sinbad:

GOSSAMER BEYNON. I don't care if he *is* common,

SECOND VOICE. she whispers to her salad-day deep self,
GOSSAMER BEYNON. I want to gobble him up. I don't care if he *does* drop his aitches,
SECOND VOICE. she tells the stripped and mother-of-the-world big-beamed and Eve-hipped spring of her self,
GOSSAMER BEYNON. so long as he's all cucumber and hooves.

Monologue is also welded with dialogue, something that radio can accomplish without any of the awkwardness encountered in the theatre. Lily Smalls's aside, 'Where d'you think? In the cat-box?', before her proper reply to Mrs Beynon's question, 'Where's my tea, girl?', illustrates the ease with which radio moves from one level of reality to another, an ability best exemplified by the amusing shift, achieved by means of a simple sound effect, from Mr Pugh's murderous fantasy as he takes his wife her morning tea to their subsequent conversation:

MR PUGH. Here's your arsenic, dear.
     And your weedkiller biscuit.
     I've throttled your parakeet.
     I've spat in the vases.
     I've put cheese in the mouseholes.
     Here's your...
          [*Door creaks open*]
     ...nice tea, dear.

On other occasions, characters speak without soliloquising, as in the breakfast section, where the First Voice introduces various villagers who assume the role of narrator to describe themselves from the outside:

FIRST VOICE. Mr Pugh
MR PUGH. remembers ground glass as he juggles his omelet.
FIRST VOICE. Mrs Pugh
MRS PUGH. nags the salt-cellar.
FIRST VOICE. Willy Nilly postman
WILLY NILLY. downs his last bucket of black brackish tea.

The section preceding this one is particularly interesting, since the juxtaposed speeches of the characters are neither pure narration nor interior monologue but a blend of different modes. After the First Voice provides a bird's-eye view of the village ('the morning fishwife gulls...observe'), the eye picks out seven characters who speak quasi-soliloquies in succession with no interruption by the Voices. These speeches all begin with 'Me' and a name, continue with narrator-like objective description, and in some cases then shift into direct speech – Mrs Dai Bread One's side only of a conversation with a neighbour, for example, and Polly Garter's maternal chatter to the baby she is feeding.

During the long night sequence Thomas orchestrates the numerous voices with at least as much variety as in the daytime episodes. In some cases the dreamers and their dreams are simply described by the two Voices, perhaps very briefly (Cherry Owen) or perhaps at greater length (Evans the Death). In other cases, such as Eli Jenkins's and Mr Pugh's, the dreamers themselves reveal something of their dreams, if only one word. Then again, two characters, Organ Morgan and Mary Ann Sailors, take over the narrative function from the Voices and actually expound their dreams. And four dreams, those of Captain Cat, Myfanwy Price, Mr Waldo, and Mrs Ogmore-Pritchard, are dramatically realised, although Miss Price's dream might also be seen as Mog Edwards's, since he is the only other participant in it and is not mentioned elsewhere in the night sequence. Her straightforward dream, which contains the only complex sound effect ('Noise of money-tills and chapel bells') in a script with remarkably few sound effects anyway, differs from the other three in that it concerns the living and looks forward to the future, however improbable the marriage of these two characters is. Technically Captain Cat's and Mr Waldo's dreams are the most interesting, Captain Cat's being a montage of seven rapidly intercut voices, his own and those of six dead people from his seafaring days, while Mr Waldo's is even more complex, being a montage of sixteen even more rapidly intercut voices from different stages of his past, including childhood, love-affairs, and marriage.

What this analysis establishes is the sheer virtuosity of Thomas's writing for radio in *Under Milk Wood*, something that after twenty-five years still remains most impressive, but that is usually not taken into account by critics. Only a writer with a very sure grasp of the medium, of what would work and what would not, could have orchestrated the voices with such extraordinary flexibility, handling them with total disregard of orthodox theatrical assumptions and varying the method of presentation very skilfully to avoid monotony in an extended work without normal dramatic momentum. On the face of it, a play for voices consisting of sustained narration and a host of characters, none of whom is in focus for long, seems like a recipe for disaster, likely to result in a scrappy, disjointed, and confusing shambles. The enormous popularity of *Under Milk Wood* is the best evidence that Thomas triumphed over the difficulties he created for himself in attempting a feature-like portrait of Llareggub. The village itself comes alive as a whole, not just in fragments; and instead of being shadowy figures, most of the characters are extremely vivid and memorable, though each of them occupies only a small part of the play and has little or no psychological depth. This is because Thomas draws them with a few broad strokes as universal comic types, although he manages to give some of them, notably Captain Cat and Polly Garter, a depth of emotion that occasionally produces moments of pathos. It is very easy to agree with John Davenport when he says of *Under Milk Wood* that 'as a radio play it is marvellously successful; it is gay, it is tender; it sparkles', yet his ensuing remark that 'it remains a radio play, no more',[60] with its condescending view of the genre, is more controversial, since it implies that the radio play cannot aspire to the condition of literature. G. S. Fraser, almost the only literary critic to acknowledge the relationship between *Under Milk Wood* and the feature – 'It derives not from any literary model, but from the radio form of the "feature", in narrative and dialogue, evoking the spirit of a place' – puts the other case when he says that 'it turns that form into literature'.[61]

The critical debate about *Under Milk Wood* has really been about its literary value and has been conducted with little or no reference to radio. This is rather like the debate about Restoration comedy, which so often seems to ignore the facts that the plays were written for the stage, not the page, and that dialogue is not the same as prose. If it is remembered that *Under Milk Wood* is a radio work first and a literary work second, it is possible to approach it without the exalted expectations and standards that critics, both for and against, have misguidedly brought to bear. In radio terms *Under Milk Wood* is very ambitious, but it differs from Thomas's poetry in not being a self-conscious attempt to write Literature with a capital L, and its literary ambitions are indeed modest.

If the feature is the clue to an understanding of *Under Milk Wood* as radio, then a synthesis of Tynan's view of it as 'a true comedy of humours' – 'We are gripped, as in comedy, we have immemorially been gripped, by a bunch of characters with one-track minds'[62] – and of Lerner's view of it as a version of pastoral[63] is the most helpful literary and dramatic approach. I have discussed these aspects elsewhere, but what is important about both views is that they completely undermine the bogus issue of realism. Considered realistically, Llareggub would be a place of psychosis, not 'a place of love', and the inhabitants would really be 'a nasty lot', but Thomas's comic–pastoral mode redeems both place and characters from such charges; it is 'a place of love', of Thomas's 'love for Man' as he put it in his prefatory note to his *Collected Poems*.[64] Even so, Llareggub is often equated with Laugharne, its inhabitants with actual people, and Thomas has been condemned in Wales for presenting a grotesque falsification of Welsh village life, as though he had created a distasteful documentary. Thomas's letter to Marguerite Caetani about *Llareggub* makes it clear that he knew exactly what he was doing, and that the romance world he creates approximates to Mary Ann Sailors's view of it as Paradise Regained, the Garden of Eden, the Chosen Land, the Peaceable Kingdom. In this imaginary world, Mog Edwards and Myfanwy Price are not frustrated lovers who can never make contact, which they would be in a realistic mode:

Every day of the week they write love letters to each other, he from the top, she from the bottom, of the town: all their lives they have known of each other's existence, and of their mutual love: they have seen each other a thousand times, and never spoken: easily they could have been together, married, had children: but that is not the life for them: their passionate love, at just this distance, is all they need.[65]

Dai Bread's bigamy is no crime since 'all three enjoy it',[66] and Polly Garter's promiscuity is condoned 'because she loves babies but does not want only one man's'.[67] Even the Pughs are perfectly matched:

She likes nagging; he likes plotting, in supposed secrecy, against her. He would always like plotting, whoever he lived with; she would always like nagging, whoever she lived with. How lucky they are to be married... And so with all of them, all the eccentrics whose eccentricities, in these first pages, are but briefly and impressionistically noted: all, by their own rights, are ordinary and good; and the First Voice, and the poet preacher, never judge nor condemn but explain and make strangely simple and simply strange.[68]

Under Milk Wood is literature, though not great literature, but it is great radio, and as such, to borrow Tynan's words about the Edinburgh Festival production, 'it lights up the sky'.[69]

4 Telling the story: Susan Hill and Dorothy L. Sayers

DONALD A. LOW

When we go to Heaven, all I ask is that we shall be given some interesting job & allowed to get on with it. No management; no box-office; no dramatic critics; & an audience of cheerful angels who don't mind laughing. (Dorothy L. Sayers to Val Gielgud, 13 January 1942)[1]

RADIO IS AS RICH a story-telling medium as any in the twentieth century. Given its appeal to the ear through speech – and also by means of music, silence, and sound – this is easy to understand. The novel and short story developed largely as forms for the printed word, and silent reading is a sophisticated activity with its own conventions and assumptions. But turn to young children anywhere: the first way in which most of us come across stories is by hearing them read aloud. 'Acting out' or drama is the next stage. What is more, all story-writing carries some echo and implication of human speech, most obviously in the form of dialogue. It follows that radio offers to the skilled writer a medium in which stories and drama belong naturally, and the chance to recover an old dimension while finding a new. The writer's passport into radio drama is a trained ear for dialogue.

There is a wry and truthful BBC boast that radio drama in Britain has launched on their careers a number of writers who have gone on to realise their dreams by working subsequently for the theatre, playwrights of the calibre of Harold Pinter and Tom Stoppard. But a quite different group of successful radio dramatists consists of writers who, before supplying scripts for radio, had already made their mark in the novel. Radio drama provides an additional outlet and resource for these writers, who do not necessarily ever aim for the kind of mastery of visual presentation which the stage requires. Some of the best of all British radio plays have been created by storytellers of long professional experience, novelists who possess narrative energy and a subtle auditory imagination.

111

The truth of this is borne out by the radio work of two novelists of different generations and different types, Susan Hill and Dorothy L. Sayers. Born in 1942, Susan Hill grew up an avid radio listener, familiar with *Under Milk Wood* and *The Dark Tower*. She published several novels before beginning to write for radio, but when she did, it was to find that 'I slipped into the medium as into an old glove, which seemed to have moulded itself long ago to the shape of my own hand, and I am still surprised that I did not make use of it much earlier.'[2] In *The Cold Country and Other Plays for Radio* (1975), she reveals the sharp psychological intelligence of a novelist of the seventies adept in exploring the inner fears and loneliness, as well as the hopes, of her characters. Her special flair is for hinting at comedy and even beauty amidst insecurity and mounting anguish. No Beckett, she is nevertheless an 'endgame' writer, or what Denis Donoghue has called a 'connoisseur of chaos'; thus her work belongs to a mainstream twentieth-century tradition. The formula which she adopts to express this vision in her radio plays is essentially a simple one. Something which begins by being low-key and apparently trivial gradually gathers pace, is felt to be thoroughly ominous, and moves towards a desperate and painful ending. This sound-drama technique can be compared with her approach in fiction: in both media she makes use of a popular narrative type, the tale of doom or story with a horrifying crisis, and invests it with depth and unexpected meaning. As she has noted, the radio dramatist 'may do anything – except *bore*'. Susan Hill's radio Gothic spine-chillers are never boring.

Elwyn Evans has described the spare style of modern radio writing as 'essentially conversation, tightened, sharpened, made (often in the most literal sense) killingly funny; the phrases, the interruptions, the pauses all chosen and subtly counterpointed to make contact with the listener on a disconcerting variety of levels'.[3] The context shows that he has in mind especially Stan Barstow and Giles Cooper in making this comment, but it might equally serve as a description of *The Cold Country*. In this play, four explorers are snowed up somewhere near the South Pole with no hope of getting away and nobody at hand to rescue them. Not even the radio is working any more, although it takes a long time for Jo, the most naive and trusting member of the group, to accept this. As the days pass, they all get on each other's nerves, and the resulting dissolution is grim: a hopeless walk undertaken by Jo out of guilt and ending in his death; a murder; a second, truly guilty exit into the icebound waste; and aimless guitar-playing by the sole survivor in the tent, merging into the Lyke-Wake Dirge. Susan Hill explains in her Introduction to the printed version of the play that ever since the news of man's conquest of Everest in 1953 she has been fascinated by 'cold white desolate worlds'. *The Cold Country* is anti-heroic, a study of defeat, and perhaps significantly of man's defeat – in her other plays, where there are female characters as well as male, the emphasis seems not quite so stark. The adroitness with which she handles phrases, interruptions, and pauses to communicate the tensions and faltering interaction of Ossie, Chip, Barney, and Jo is extremely sensitive. Chip, for instance, who is to end by killing his friend Barney in a moment of hysteria, begins by telling bright jokes in the teeth of adversity. Ingeniously, Susan Hill disturbs her listeners with words made familiar by Brian Cant's television programme for children, *Playaway*:

CHIP. That's right, troops, keep up the old morale.
JO. It's Ossie. Making all sorts of snap judgements. We don't get on, he says, we're driving one another mad. Well I think we're doing all right. As well as anyone else would do under the circumstances. I think...
BARNEY. Oh, spare us the sermon.
OSSIE. O.K., O.K., forget it, I only said...
CHIP [*interrupting quickly*]. I say, I say, I say, my aunt's gone to the West Indies.
OSSIE. Jamaica?
CHIP. No, she went of her own accord. [*Pause*] Well come on!... All right, try again. I say, I say, I say, my aunt's gone to the *East* Indies.
OSSIE. Jakarta?
CHIP. No, she went by plane.
JO. Oh, for God's sake!
CHIP. Barney, why do cows wear cow-bells?
BARNEY. I don't know, Chip, why do cows wear cow-bells?
CHIP. Because their horns won't work. Da-da-dee-da-da-DA! [*Silence*] Oh, I give up, I do really.
JO. Good.
CHIP. What's on your mind anyway, Jo?
JO. Oh, nothing, nothing. How to make you lot get off your backsides. Whether we're going to let ourselves live or die. Because it's up to us, you know. What we're doing here, what it's all about. What went wrong.[4]

The trouble with Chip is that he does not wear motley consistently enough – in *King Lear* neither the Fool nor Edgar says, 'Oh, I give up, I do really.' But Susan Hill pays some kind of tribute to Chip for trying. Only Ossie lasts longer, it may be because he has the superior consolation of art. He wears the rest down by playing 'Roses of Picardy' on the mouth-organ, then moves on to the guitar. Even as a time-killer, Susan Hill appears to imply, music-making has value, keeping alive the imagination and the will to live in harsh places.

Ossie has said with vindictiveness, 'When I get home, I'll write a book like they've never read before, I'll tell them how it really is.' Presumably at the end he somehow survives, and so gains the chance to write about his experiences; *The Cold Country* deliberately runs counter to what is held to be the false glamour of *Scott of the Antarctic*. Elsewhere, Susan Hill develops the theme of the solitary and apparently antisocial individual's imagination as the only way through hell, the single positive force worth holding on to in a welter of destructiveness all around. The radio play is particularly well suited to express such a theme. Words about solitude which are listened to in solitude communicate strongly the idea of human separateness.

Lizard in the Grass (1971) presents the extraordinary experiences of an intensely imaginative adolescent girl, an orphan, caught by unhappy chance in an uncongenial convent school where she rubs up both staff and pupils the wrong way. There are overtones of Joyce's *Portrait of the Artist as a Young Man* here in the way phrases of the institution are loaded with hostile feeling. It is hard to say which is worse, the taunts of Jane's classmates, or the inflexible lovelessness of Sister Patrick, but both are brought home to us in jingling words:

CLARE. [*Sharp whisper, very close*]. Jane Pace...
JANE [*startled*]. What? What is it?
CLARE. What have you done?
    [*Other girls in the taunting chorus*]
  Now what have you done?
  You've been sent for.
  You're to see Sister Superior.
  Jane Pace.
  You got an order mark.
  Three.
  In one week.
  You're for it.
  Again.

What have you done? What have you done? Jane Pace, in disgrace,
Jane Pace, in disgrace, Jane, Jane, Jane...
   [*A desk bangs suddenly. Scurrying. Silence. Scraping of chairs.*]
SISTER PATRICK. Good morning, Four A.
CLASS [*sing-song unison*]. Good morning, Sister Patrick.
   [*Pause. Then Sister imitates sarcastically*]
SISTER P. Good-*mor*-ning-*Sister-Pat*-rick.
   [*A murmur*]
Listen to you. Listen! What do you sound like? Stand up straight.
Stand up as girls should stand first thing each morning. Bright, Alert,
Attentive. Jane Pace...
JANE. I didn't...[5]

Sister Patrick treats poor dreamy Jane as a deviant needing to be
straightened out, and very nearly succeeds in breaking her spirit.
However, the girl receives a crumb of affection from an eccentric
old nun, Imelda, who is barely tolerated by the rest of the community, and Jane's love of unorthodox reading sees her through,
after a fashion, so that she ends up holding conversations with
the ghost of John Skelton, spirited out of a bone which she finds
on the beach. He, it turns out, was treated somewhat shabbily in
his lifetime, and he is glad to have the chance to share his troubles
with Jane. His words 'come to me' form a distinctly sinister
refrain towards the close. Susan Hill brings off the difficult feat of
controlling her invention, so that the play does not topple over
either into 'lonely-hearts' sentimentality or into that other trap
for radio dramatists, 'twangling instruments' metaphysics.
Unlike, say, Bruce Stewart's *The Tor Sands Experience* (BBC *Hi-Fi
Theatre*, 1979), in which ingenious but finally tedious stereophonic effects failed to lift a weak philosophical idea, *Lizard
in the Grass* develops a fantasy in words powerful enough to be
believed in. 'There should be no time', says Sister Patrick, 'for a
head full of peculiar imaginings. "This is the weather the cuckoo
likes." That is what I have set her to learn.' But Jane's head is her
own, and she chooses to learn much less comfortable verses, with
the result that she is accused of harbouring simultaneously
immodest and morbid thoughts 'about skeletons and wombs'.
Susan Hill weaves in cleverly selected quotations at will, using
them to distinguish her introspective heroine from everyone else
in the play:

MEGAN. Clare Boothright, just you get on, you stop talking to Jane Pace,
   it's forbidden, it's not allowed.

CLARE. Well I can't shut my case
    [*A sudden screech of laughter goes up somewhere else.*]
    I can't take anything out, I need everything.
JANE [*very quietly*].
    'That when ye think all danger for to pass,
    Ware of the lizard lieth lurking in the grass.'
CLARE. What?
MEGAN [*calls*]. It's twenty past. Just gone twenty past.[6]

Such words from the past are at once teasing and poetic in their suggestiveness, adding notably to the linguistic texture of the play.

    Susan Hill is able to capture in *Lizard in the Grass* the apparently random effect of different trains of thoughts cutting into each other because she has learned as a novelist to listen to people talking and to highlight moments of spoken interplay. This is common ground between fiction and the radio play, but there was much to learn about creating drama for the airwaves, and she gives full credit for vital encouragement to Guy Vaesen, the BBC producer of all but one of her plays, and also to Geoffrey Burgon, who wrote music for three of them. In the 1973 stereo play *Consider the Lilies*, Guy Vaesen's role as constructive critic was especially important, and the dramatist states that 'it ought to bear his name, as co-author'.[7] *Consider the Lilies* breaks new ground in combining Susan Hill's characteristic honesty about suffering – in the course of the action a young girl dies of a wasting illness – with visionary optimism. A main source of inspiration this time is Blake. The central figure, a middle-aged botanist called Bowman, has intense moments of apprehension of heaven on earth very much in the manner of the revolutionary poet–artist; then he and Susannah, the girl who dies, commune with each other partly in allusive fashion.

SUSANNAH. My nurse gets bored. 'All those trees', she says. 'All those trees.' I suppose it's tiring for her, pushing me everywhere. She likes a 'nice sit-down'. I look at the trees.
BOWMAN. 'The tree which moves some to tears of joy is, in the eyes of others, only a green thing which stands in the way.'
SUSANNAH. But I'm lucky. I haven't any troubles. They don't know when I'll die... I'd like to wait until the winter. Everything else will die then. But people look after me. I have every day to look at things. Everyone else has to work and worry. I learned something, too. I read a lot of books. I can always read.
BOWMAN. What did you learn?

SUSANNAH. 'The stars reflect the visions of holiness and the trees are uttering prophecies and speaking instructive words to the sons of men.'

BOWMAN. That's the truth. That's what I see. Oh, Susannah, don't die. You mustn't die.

SUSANNAH. I shall. I don't seem to belong here now. It's a nuisance. I feel like a shot bird. Heavy.

BOWMAN. We've reached the edge of the lake.

SUSANNAH. 'Every night and every morn
   Some to misery are born.
   Every morn and every night
   Some are born to sweet delight.'[8]

There is a danger that such exchanges may seem flat, failing to move the listener in the manner that the writer intends; Susan Hill's sensibility is really very different from Blake's. To counterpoint the visionary theme, she develops a comic sub-plot, in which Lesage, Bowman's statistically minded second-in-command, schemes with his garrulous mother about how to pension off the admirer of lilies so that he can get his job. This layer of the play works very well indeed, so characterful is the dialogue:

LESAGE. Plants, flowers, the whole botanical gardens, the whole organisation... I could talk to him about my plans for a research programme in carnivorous plants. I could... I don't know. I can't seem to find a way through. We never meet. He lives in another world.

MRS L. It's not right, you're young, you're ambitious. You always liked plants, even from a little boy. You made a beautiful garden in a kitchen saucer when you were only three, the afternoon before those four houses in Albany Street got a direct hit, and not so much as a warning, not a peep were we given out of that siren, crash-bang, while I was peeling the potatoes, I thought the world was coming to an end.

LESAGE. I still have dreams about that. The noise.

MRS L. You were too young to remember. And there you'd been, making that lovely garden, all neat it was, all orderly, little paths marked out in rows of pebbles, bits of twigs and so on, just like a proper laid-out public park.[9]

What impresses most is that the different elements of *Consider the Lilies* blend together to operate successfully on the 'disconcerting variety of levels' noted by Elwyn Evans as characteristic of recent radio writing at its best. Bowman is no less a man of truth for being seen through the eyes of Lesage as culpably vague and absent-minded – their collision is genuinely funny, part of the price of Blakean change. And Susannah loses none of her vulnerability or dignity because of the ironies which attend Bowman's progress: 'you must tell your visions', she tells him. Affirmation and playful satire both have a place in the drama, just as they do, quite differently, in *The Marriage of Heaven and Hell*. Moreover, the work is genuinely stereophonic, as there is music and a chorus of plants, 'a male and a female chorus, set on either speaker... they are separate at the beginning, and join together towards the end, when the music becomes reminiscent of the music which will later "blossom out" into the visionary theme'. Few radio plays to date have exploited the full resources of the medium with such assurance and tact.

What are the proper boundaries of the radio dramatist's role? Should he or she stay away from rehearsal, or is a place to be specially reserved in the studio? Susan Hill is clear about a lesson of experience gained during rehearsal of *Consider the Lilies*:

> I had never gone into the studio during the recording of any of my plays; I felt that the presence of the author (even when sitting mute in the background of the control room) would inhibit producer and cast. But I was persuaded to go down for the production of 'Consider the Lilies', only to find that, especially in the final scenes, the actors were having great problems with the interpretation of their parts, because of faulty writing. After long talks with Tony Britton, Helen Worth and, again Guy Vaesen, several scenes were rearranged, cut, or rewritten entirely in the margins of scripts, during lunch and coffee breaks. I still adhere to my rule that the author must not interfere in any way with the work of producer, actors or technicians, but I shall not be absent from studio during any future recordings, if only because a radio playwright's education is a continuous one, and a day spent listening and observing, in silence, can teach one more than weeks in the study with a script-in-progress.[10]

This is an admirably frank and well-defined position. Only an outsider ignorant of production schedules would want to see writers continuously present among broadcasting staff, interfering in their work; yet the dogmatism which would exclude the radio dramatist from the studio is equally short-sighted. Much depends, clearly, on the quality of the relationship between writer and producer. Where there is trust, a constructive studio partnership involving writer, actors, and producer is possible.

In the matter of the relationship between writer, producer, and actors there is a striking resemblance between Susan Hill and Dorothy L. Sayers. *Consider the Lilies and Other Plays for Radio* is dedicated to Guy Vaesen. More than thirty years earlier, Dorothy L. Sayers had dedicated the printed version of *A Man Born To Be King* to her producer with the words 'These plays are for Val Gielgud who has made them his already'. As we shall see, Dorothy L. Sayers insisted on being allowed to attend rehearsals, but she too was well aware of the practical limits placed upon her authority by radio; and like Susan Hill she listed the names of actors and actresses opposite their parts when the chance of publication offered itself.

At this point, it is worth considering briefly *Voices at Play*, a collection of short stories and radio plays published in 1961 by Muriel Spark. Muriel Spark has as sure an ear for idiosyncrasies of speech as anyone in modern fiction, and there is little doubt that with the kind of commitment to radio she has brought to the novel she could have become an outstandingly successful radio dramatist – perhaps she may yet choose to do so. As it is, a radio version of her early satirical novel *The Ballad of Peckham Rye*, with music by Tristram Cary, has been listed by Douglas Cleverdon among notable achievements of the BBC Features Department,[11] while *Voices at Play* offers further tantalising proof of one radio playwright who got away.

In her Author's Note in *Voices at Play* Muriel Spark draws attention to a common 'creative wavelength' shared by her short stories and radio plays, despite the difference in form between the two kinds. She also writes amusingly about the hallowed BBC term 'feature' and shows the professional writer's quickness to turn its generous scope to advantage:

This book contains two different forms of writing: short stories and radio plays. The excuse for both sorts being put together is that all were written on the same creative wavelength. The plays were written for the out-ward, and the stories for the inward ear. But one form of writing was very much affected by the other, and so I hope they show a consistent mood.

The plays were written at the suggestion of Mr. Rayner Heppenstall for the Third Programme. By definition they were supposed to be 'fea-tures' rather than proper plays. I never quite grasped the distinction between dramatic features and plays except to discern what was in my favour, namely the freedom to do as I pleased with characters and voices without thought of conforming to a settled category. I turned my mind into a wireless set and let the characters play on my ear. Sometimes Mr. Heppenstall clamoured for more visual bits to be written in, so that the listener's imagination could be supplied with what was wanting to the eye.

> And so if the plays have turned out to be plays, that is by accident; and
> if it comes to that, in many ways the same could be said of the stories[12].

Insitutional orthodoxy and the writer's viewpoint seldom coin-
cide. The theory was that a radio play differed from a dramatic
feature in having a dramatic plot and structure. In practice at this
date numerous examples of what would now be called radio
plays were still being categorised by the BBC as 'features', largely
because of the way in which production departments were organised. Muriel Spark's directness in publicly minimising the difference between the two may conceivably have seemed a little
daring in some quarters in 1961, but by 1975 a former Head of
Radio Training at the BBC could comment on 'dramatised features' by Dylan Thomas, Bill Naughton, and Henry Reed, 'Ideas
as to what constitutes a play have undergone a revolution, and all
these productions would now be unhesitatingly classified as
drama.'[13] These words apply equally well to the radio material
included in *Voices at Play*.

The distinction of Muriel Spark's radio plays lies in their combination of the zany with a subtle sense of menace. It is rather as if
the Goon Show – surely a potent influence on radio dramatists –
had moved into suburbia among pot plants and fading gentilities,
and become disconcertingly acid. *The Interview* is a *tour de force* of
subversive fantasy. Dame Lettice Chatterton, 'well known in
political circles in the twenties', now shares a Knightsbridge flat
with her secretary–companion, Miss Bone ('Tiggy'), and, when
he is at home, with her nephew Roy, a theological student. Roy is
away a lot, and in his absence the two women find each other's
company intolerable – the play opens with Dame Lettice casually
asking, 'Why don't you get your teeth seen to, Tiggy? They look
terrible.' Dame Lettice is in process of dictating her memoirs – 'It
has therefore always been difficult for me comma with so many
sides to my personality comma to present only one of those sides
at any one time to the world full stop. If these memoirs (underline
memoirs) prove anything at all comma they prove... they
prove...'[14] She keeps losing track in mid-sentence as she finds
fault with Tiggy, or recalls her unedited past, or wonders what
Roy is up to. Tiggy, who is equally malicious but apparently less
muddled, fills in the gaps by swotting for a General Knowledge
Quiz in which she hopes to win a large prize. As she does so, she
feeds her employer 'clues' about Roy, some of which are deliber-

ately misleading. These cause Dame Lettice to imagine Roy's return in circumstances of varying degrees of weirdness. The 'interview' of the title describes not only the ritualistic exchanges between memoir-writer and secretary, but a succession of little conversations between Roy and Dame Lettice which take place in the mind of the latter. Only the radio play could accommodate this kind of freewheeling comedy of associations, the secret of which lies in the quality of the writing:

LETTICE. There is an ashtray in Roy's room; Tiggy, go and fetch it.
TIGGY. Oh-oh-oh. I don't like going in there. All those water colours, they remind me of poor Roy. Suppose something has happened to him? But never mind, Dame Lettice, he will explain on his return.
LETTICE. What does he mean, he will explain on his return? I only hope his theological studies have not gone to his head.
TIGGY. I think they must have. I expect he has gone chasing Sylvia Tree.
LETTICE. Who is Sylvia?
TIGGY. Friend of Trevor. Roy said she was a witch.
LETTICE. Did he? What did he mean, a witch? Why should a theological student run after a witch?
TIGGY. To catch her, I suppose. And he will explain on his return. Hengist and Horsa were the reputed leaders of the first Anglo-Saxon invasion...
    [*Fade*]
LETTICE. What can he mean, he will explain on his return? I shall keep him waiting, of course. And then I shall say to him, 'Oh, hallo, Roy, enjoy your trip?' And he will say to me, 'Enjoy it, if only you knew...'
ROY. If only you knew the difficulties I have been facing. Do you remember Sylvia Tree?
LETTICE. Of course. A dark girl, a friend of Trevor what's-his-name.
TIGGY [*from a distance*]. Don't start imagining things, Dame Lettice. You know it doesn't do any good.
LETTICE. A dark girl, a friend of Trevor what's-his-name.
ROY. A very dark girl. She's a witch.[15]

Such a passage illustrates vividly what Muriel Spark meant in claiming that she had let the characters play upon her ear, and also some of her reasons for welcoming the freedom offered by the dramatic feature on radio. She creates entertainment out of the riotous imaginative life of an anxious woman's mind, and it is entertainment designed specifically for the ear. Parody and unexpected echoes come in, with almost farcical effect: it is easy to imagine Dame Lettice delivering her question 'Who is Sylvia?' in a tone of affronted dignity, perhaps with an Edith Evans vibrato. This delightfully random, seemingly undisciplined dialogue has the economy of true baroque. The single direction *'Fade'* is enough to denote a perfectly timed cut to the next sequence, and similarly Tiggy's voice heard *'from a distance'* lets the listener grasp that Tiggy is going through the motions of checking Dame Lettice's fertility of invention. But Muriel Spark's is never for long a wholly comfortable, even if it is a hilarious, sort of comedy. Before long, we are wondering if indeed there is a 'witch' in the play – could it perhaps be Tiggy? – and if Roy's metaphysical concerns have gone to his head, as his aunt suspects, to the extent of turning him into a ghost. The boundaries between reality and illusion have been expertly dissolved.

In certain moods, Muriel Spark mixes into her potent brew more than a trace of *Doppelgänger* fear. It is a technique she handles with authoritative sleight of hand. Variations on the theme are played in her 'elemental drama', *The Danger Zone*, in which her accuracy of hearing is brought to bear on a Welsh community persistently troubled by the 'generation gap'; in *The Dry River Bed*, a sort of *Passage to India* in miniature for radio with grotesquely funny overtones (the plot concerns 'the sort of thing that happens at the end of the dry season'); and in *The Party through the Wall*, a macabre fable of bed-sitter land in which she subverts from within the idea of the reliable narrator – a convention in radio drama no less than in fiction – by peeling off the layers of respectability and, in the end, revealing that he is a murderer and a lunatic. In each of her radio plays she uses her command of unexpected juxtaposition to manipulate the listener's responses. Sudden transitions from one level of association to another are what she is best at.

The circumstances in which Dorothy L. Sayers wrote *The Man Born To Be King*, her play-cycle on the life of Christ, were very different from those of the post-war period in which first Muriel Spark and then Susan Hill were to contribute to BBC radio. The nation was in the throes of the struggle with Hitler's Germany, and this affected everything from the outlook of the writer and her public – Dorothy L. Sayers frankly admitted that the theme of contrasting kinds of kingdom running through the plays was suggested partly by the political background of the time – to practical problems of radio production. When the twelve plays making up *The Man Born To Be King* were published, Val Gielgud wrote in a Production Note:

Not one made use of a cast of less than thirty-five, and not one of them could be allowed more than forty-eight hours within which to be rehearsed and produced. Before the war I would not have dreamed of undertaking plays of their calibre with less than a week's rehearsal, with all the advantages of a dramatic control panel and a suite of studios in which such disturbing elements as crowds and effects could have been isolated from and very simply balanced against the main scenes and characters.[16]

Not only the war, however, but also the tensions of the creative temperament and – notably – the intricacies of BBC internal organisation complicated the work of writer, producer, and actors. The original proposal for a series of plays on religious subjects came from the Director of Religious Broadcasting, who remained intelligently involved in the project throughout; but the actual programme chosen to broadcast the plays was *Children's Hour*, controlled from Bristol by another department; and it was only after a shattering row with the senior staff of *Children's Hour* that Dorothy L. Sayers was allowed something she had asked for all along, namely the presence of Val Gielgud, Director of Drama and Features, as producer. She had worked with him before, and explained that he enjoyed a reputation in the BBC as a 'Sayers-tamer' quite simply because he knew his job and respected hers as writer. The *Children's Hour* crisis remained unknown to the listening audience; but then a second and very public controversy flared up over press allegations that the dialogue of the plays would contain offensive modern slang. This led to questions in Parliament and hurried consultations at very high level. The play-cycle when broadcast was at once recognised as a quite exceptional achievement from every point of view, but only its author and one or two members of BBC staff knew just how much it had cost in terms of sheer tenacity and professionalism.

Luckily, a large number of letters written by Dorothy L. Sayers during the making of *The Man Born To Be King* are on file in the Written Archives Centre of the BBC. These offer a particularly trenchant and well-informed commentary from a writer's point of view on a major radio dramatic undertaking, and show why Janet Hitchman, her biographer, has described Dorothy L. Sayers as 'the last of the great letter-writers'. From the moment when the idea was first put to her, Dorothy L. Sayers seems to have sensed that the challenge to create a religious play-cycle for radio was at once uniquely demanding – apart from anything else, since the Middle Ages dramatic representation of Christ had been exposed to veto or censorship – and one to which she must respond. Without ever compromising either her theological principles or her integrity as a writer, she proceeded to ensure that what she called 'the most difficult and delicate job I have ever struck' would not fail either because of artistic timidity on her part or through bureaucratic interference. In the Peter Wimsey books, one of her strongest points had been her plotting. Faced with a different kind of task now, she set about identifying where the main obstacles were likely to arise, and devised a strategy for overcoming them. This ability showed itself both in the construction of the plays and in her highly individual way of dealing with the BBC. She saw at once that the series must have overall unity and coherence but that each play must nevertheless stand on its own as a self-contained whole. This was perhaps her main dramatic objective, and in the end it was fully, even triumphantly, realised. She did not behave graciously towards the highly experienced producers of *Children's Hour* who wanted to tell her how to make things simple for children ('a blazing impertinence'); but in obeying her strong instinct to fight clear of such tinkering she made excellence possible. It was certainly not tactful of her to read to the assembled radio reviewers of the country passages of dialogue which they could brand as 'slang'. On the other hand, it was not for nothing that the author of *Murder Must Advertise* had served as an advertising copywriter. The ensuing furore resulted in *The Man Born To Be King* attracting more attention than any other BBC radio plays before or since.

The daughter of a Church of England vicar, Dorothy L. Sayers had been interested in writing on Christian themes nearly all her life. As early as 1918 she had brought out a book of verse called *Catholic Tales and Christian Songs;* and while, in the twenties and early thirties, she threw herself wholeheartedly into the writing of detective fiction it was always with the knowledge that in time weightier subjects than the exploits of Harriet Vane and Lord Peter Wimsey – which included a memorable ecclesiastical foray in *The Nine Tailors* (1934) – were likely to claim her attention. In the later 1930s, influenced partly by Muriel St Clare Byrne, a specialist in the Tudor period, she became increasingly involved with the live theatre. *Busman's Honeymoon* (1938), the last of her novels, was in its first form written collaboratively with Muriel St Clare Byrne two years earlier as a play. In the same year the

Friends of Canterbury Cathedral asked Dorothy L. Sayers to write a play for their festival. She responded with a blank verse drama, *The Zeal of Thy House*, about William of Sens, the twelfth-century architect of Canterbury – an exploration of pride which anticipates the subject of William Golding's novel *The Spire*. *The Zeal of Thy House* was first performed in the Chapter House of Canterbury Cathedral in June 1937, and the play was so well received that in 1938 it was acted by an entirely professional cast in three London theatres, the Westminster, the Duke of York's, and the Garrick. With characteristic energy and *brio*, Dorothy L. Sayers took an active interest in everything to do with each production, from costumes to the subsequent dramatic careers of the actors. In the process she learned a good deal about plays, those who perform them, and audiences.

As a result of the success of *The Zeal of Thy House*, F. A. Iremonger, BBC 'Director of Religion', wrote to invite Dorothy L. Sayers to write a play for broadcasting. 'Of all the programmes put out by this Department of the BBC', he remarked, 'there is none more important than those in which we attempt to broadcast "Religious Drama". I write "attempt" deliberately, for the art of writing religious radio-plays is hardly yet in its infancy – it is just struggling to be born!'[17] At first Dorothy L. Sayers was unwilling to fall in with this suggestion, replying through her agent that the BBC might care instead to broadcast *The Zeal of Thy House*, subject to certain conditions. (In an internal memorandum, Val Gielgud wrote to Iremonger, 'The lady is very exigeante! Insists on choice of cast and things like that which I really can't cope with! To say nothing of the money! I quite like the play.')[18] But then she heard further details from a mutual friend about Iremonger's 'scheme with regard to a Nativity play for broadcasting'. This led her to write to him on 3 May from her home at Witham in Essex:

As you may know, I always embark with some reluctance on work for the BBC because there is a perpetual feud between them and me in the matter of fees. It is very difficult to get from them adequate payment for the author's work and the time taken up in rehearsals and so forth. [Had she known her correspondent better, she might have added that another of her objections to the BBC was their maddening habit of dropping from publicity material the initial of her middle name. Leigh was both her mother's name and that of her grand-uncle Percival Leigh, a founder of *Punch* and well-known amateur actor of his day.] Also, I have only lately begun to acquire theatrical technique, and it is going to be another big job to discover a technique for broadcasting. However, I promised to Mr. McCormick that I would think about the matter, and should be glad to see you...[19]

Ten days later they met, and found common ground in what Iremonger described to his Controller of Programmes as 'an informal and tentative talk'. The latter agreed that an adequate fee must be paid and that Dorothy L. Sayers should work with Val Gielgud, who had impressed her as producer of radio adaptations of her novels. By the autumn of 1938 a draft of the Nativity play was complete, and Dorothy L. Sayers sent Gielgud instructions about music which would be required 'if, by any chance, we succeed in getting the play through' – she feared that Iremonger might reject the play because it contained moments of comedy. Her notes on songs show the quality of close attention to detail which she was to bring to all of her radio dramatic work:

(1) Melchior's song, 'High upon the holy tree'; this should be written in ballad style. (2) Song of the Legionaires: this is a marching song with one of those refrains, 'Bread and cheese', which go on and on in march till 'time ready'. (3) Greek Gentleman's song 'Golden Apollo'; this should be in the manner of an Elizabethan madrigal. (4) Jewish Gentleman's song, 'Adam and Eve': this is one of those cumulative songs in the folk-song manner after the fashion of 'The tree in the wood', in which two lines are added in every verse...[20]

Gielgud was enthusiastic about the script, and Robert Chignell was commissioned to supply music.

The *Radio Times* of 23 December 1938 carried an article by Dorothy L. Sayers in which she explained that she had departed from the 'twiddling triviality' of unrealistic Nativity plays in favour of a bolder approach:

Jesus and Mary and Joseph, the Shepherds, King Herod, the Pharisees, the people of the Jews – we are accustomed to think of them all, good and bad alike, as 'sacred personages' living a remote symbolical life 'in the Bible'. But they did not live 'in the Bible'; they lived in this confused and passionate world, amid social and political conditions curiously like those of the present day. Unless we can recapture a strong apprehension of that plain fact, they will for ever remain for us an assemblage of wraiths and shadows... It is especially the social and political background that I have tried to sketch in my Nativity play for broadcasting, *He That Should Come.*

The editor of the *Radio Times* was short of space, and, perhaps anticipating an adverse reaction on the part of the public, he cut

out a few sentences, including the characteristically uncom-
promising remark that 'Christmas card prettiness' has 'the false
simplicity which is the lazy mind's escape from problems too
complicated for solution' and the claim that a listener to a Nativity
play of the traditional type 'is apt to come to it in that drowsily
acquiescent mood in which one hears a distant barrel-organ
playing over an old tune familiar in childhood; a little sentimental
recollection may be pleasantly stirred, but neither mind nor emotions are startled into alertness'.[21] The hour-long broadcast of *He
That Should Come* went out on Christmas Day, 'under Mr. Gielgud's personal supervision'. Soon, Dorothy L. Sayers and the
BBC received a large number of letters about the play, and nearly
all of them were full of praise. Mrs Winston Churchill wrote that
she, her husband, and family had 'never enjoyed anything
more'; while Dorothy L. Sayers's fellow crime-writer John Rhode
informed her that the play had gone down well with his 'pub
audience', the older generation of the village – 'As one of them
put it "it is nice to think that people in the Bible were folks like
us". Queer, isn't it, that the mediaeval intimate conception of
Bible history has faded away?' These tributes pleased her, for she
had wanted to appeal to all sorts and conditions of men, but
perhaps none amused her more than the response of a Mr
Graham of Sutherland. He wrote that he had listened to the play
in a snow-bound Roxburghshire farmhouse, 'in a company of the
unco guid, don't-believe-in-wireless-on-Sundays variety and we
loved it, every bit of it'. For his part, Val Gielgud acknowledged
that the production 'certainly rang the bell' in the BBC and the
press. He added that he hoped it would not be long before he had
the pleasure of working with her again.[22]

The fresh idiom and historical realism of *He That Should Come*
made for direct communication. In February 1940 the play was
broadcast again, this time for Manchester, and Dorothy L. Sayers
wrote to Gielgud that she had listened and missed 'his touch,
especially in the background noises'. But a new project had
already been mooted. On the fifth of that month Dr James Welch,
F. A. Iremonger's successor, wrote to invite her to help 'in the
work of religious broadcasting to the children'. What he had in
mind, he explained, was 'a series of thirty minute plays on the
Life of our Lord', about twelve in all. The plays would be broadcast during Sunday *Children's Hour*, for which his department
shared responsibility with the programme's regular full-time

staff. Audience Research figures showed that *Children's Hour* had a large listening public, including more than five million adults. He added, 'I feel that we might rightly and reverently use direct speech but my mind is not quite made up about this yet.'[23]

Dorothy L. Sayers replied on 18 February that the sort of series Welch had proposed of 'little dramas from the New Testament' was something she had often thought she would like to undertake. The idea was 'exceedingly tempting', but much careful thought would be required, and she could not supply such plays in a hurry. She then drew attention to an outstanding difficulty, the traditional prohibition against dramatic representations of Christ. Might not the radio play be a means of getting round this and the 'convention of unreality' which followed from it?

It seems to me that in broadcasting we are freed of any of the obvious objections which attend the visual representation of Christ by an actor, and are protected from the vulgarities and incongruities which the ordinary theatrical or film producer might import into a stage or screen representation. Radio plays, therefore, seem to present an admirable medium through which to break down the convention of unreality surrounding Our Lord's person and might very well pave the way to a more vivid conception of the Divine Humanity which, at present, threatens to be lost in a kind of Apollinarian mist.

She then went on to discuss the obvious difficulty of the right choice of language:

It would not, of course, be suitable to give to Christ any speeches which do not appear in the Scriptures, but if all the other characters 'talk Bible', the realism will be lost, whereas if they talk modern English we may get a patchwork effect. However, the difficulty is not really insuperable; it is just a question of choosing language which is neither slangy on the one hand, nor Wardour Street on the other. This difficulty did not, of course, arise in the mediaeval mystery plays whose authors were quite prepared to let Christ say anything that seemed natural and appropriate, but we could not go so far as this without arousing roars of disapproval among the pious.[24]

James Welch was delighted to learn that her first response was so favourable. In answering this letter on 1 March, he showed that he fully shared her belief in the need for a bold new approach. One great asset was that the plays would be broadcast to children, who were free from crippling prejudices:

Not only does the radio enjoy a freedom which is denied the films and stage, but also in a 'Children's Hour' broadcast we can rightly ignore to a great extent the prejudices of adult listeners, which are absent from the minds and feelings of children. To make the Gospel story live for these children is our object... I believe it may be right for us to put our Lord's words into modern language.[25]

Welch also contacted Derek McCulloch, Director of *Children's Hour*, pointing out that in their own way the dramatisations which were under discussion might well make radio history and passing on Val Gielgud's tip that Dorothy L. Sayers was a 'tower of strength' to any producer with whom she saw eye to eye. 'She is not prepared', he warned, 'merely to write and hand the stuff over to a producer; and for that who can blame her?'[26]

Not long before this there had been a shocked correspondence in the press about allegations that children were growing up ignorant of the Bible and Christianity. In an article entitled 'Divine Comedy' in the *Manchester Guardian* of 15 March 1940 Dorothy L. Sayers joined the debate. She did not refer to her invitation from the BBC, but the way in which she tackled the question of religious education reflected her excitement and growing conviction that the project must be carried through:

At the name of Jesus, every voice goes plummy, every gesture becomes pontifical, and a fearful creeping paralysis slows down the pace of the dialogue. You've got to translate the thing in terms of life and action – what would the double nature feel like, look like... are we offering [the Christ-story to children] as dramatic reality? or shall we merely succeed in making each of them as stereotyped and dull as ourselves? It is very difficult to recognize opportunity when it comes in the guise of disaster; but if we are going to offend these little ones by the contamination of our own unimaginative lethargy, it would be better that a millstone were hanged about our necks, and that we were cast into the sea. Are we so shocked at ignorance? There are times when ignorance is a welcome bliss; – what would it be like to go and see *Hamlet* with a perfectly virgin mind?

By the summer, she had decided on a unifying theme, that of the kingship of Christ. 'At this moment', she wrote to Welch on 23 July 1940, 'even children can't help knowing that there is a great dispute going on about how the world should be governed, and to what end.' If it was put to them in a simple and vivid way, they would readily grasp the meaning of the quarrel which led to the Crucifixion. For that reason she intended to 'make this business of the Kingdom the framework of the series'. Thinking in dramatic terms was forcing her to make up her mind about Judas and the other characters in the Christ story. She was particularly anxious to interpret the character of Judas, who in the New Testament 'comes on with his mind all made up and villainous', for she had the detective novelist's instinctive sense of plot. Drama, she confessed, confronted the writer more directly with problems of characterisation than did fiction: 'one can often get on quite well with a narration without precisely defining one's attitude to one's characters; but one can't do it in a play, because the actor has a tiresome way of coming along and demanding to know what sort of person one intends him to be'.[27] Welch had meanwhile been active in trying to obtain the necessary permission for a series of radio plays about the life of Christ. On 28 August, the Earl of Clarendon, Censor of Plays at the Lord Chamberlain's Office, wrote to the Director-General of the BBC, F. W. Ogilvie, confirming that there would be no objection as no one would appear publicly taking the part of Christ. He emphasised that the position with regard to television was different, for this would involve a visible physical impersonation as well as the use of the voice.

Although Dorothy L. Sayers had told Welch that she was 'stubbornly set' on Val Gielgud as her producer, it seemed at first as if the arrangements, preferred by the BBC hierarchy, whereby Derek McCulloch's *Children's Hour* department were going to handle the plays might work well. It was to McCulloch that she sent the first play, *Kings in Judaea*, on 5 November 1940, along with a long and friendly letter in which she defined the theme of the series: 'The thing one wants to put against the *idea* of the Kingdom of Heaven is the *idea* of the political kingdom, not the caprice of one wicked man.' She explained that she had two 'things' or strong preferences about broadcast drama. First, plays should explain themselves within their own dialogue. It might be a prejudice inherited from stage practice, but she did not like to hear a narrator expounding the situation, and therefore she had cut down the part of the narrator in *Kings in Judaea* to four brief Bible texts. Next, each play should be as far as possible a complete and self-explanatory play in itself, with a beginning, a middle, and an end of its own 'and not just a slice out of a long narrative'. This added considerably to her troubles because it meant 'constructing each play at the same time as a self-contained unit and *also* as a structural unit within the series', but she was determined to avoid bittiness. It was at least in her favour that the BBC had decided the plays should last forty-five minutes rather than thirty. She had used part of the extra time to enliven *Kings in Judaea* with 'a bit of crowdage and shoutery'.[28]

McCulloch believed in BBC departmental democracy. He replied to Dorothy L. Sayers that no sooner was the play received than his staff had 'torn it from him'. Her comment in return, 'I hope they have now supplied you with a copy', should have checked his zeal; but by then all members of the *Children's Hour* staff had been invited to comment on the play. Without exception, they greatly liked *Kings in Judaea*, but a minority were concerned that in parts it might be above the heads of children. On 19 November May Jenkin, *Children's Hour* Assistant Director, wrote to Dorothy L. Sayers expressing this criticism and asking for permission 'discreetly to edit'. Dorothy L. Sayers, recognising as she put it later that to cede an inch was to cede the whole territory, declined to let May Jenkin alter a word. Angrily, she wrote on 22 November,

You are supposed to be playing to children – the only audience, perhaps, in the country whose minds are still open and sensitive to the spell of poetic speech... The thing *they* react to and remember is not logical argument, but mystery and the queer beauty of melodious words... I knew how *you* would react to those passages; it is my business to know. It is also my business to know how my real audience will react; and yours to trust me to know it.[29]

Derek McCulloch took up the cause of his aggrieved deputy, writing to Dorothy L. Sayers of his staff's long experience of producing suitable material for the entertainment of children through the medium of the microphone, complaining, 'you have wielded a huge bludgeon', and pleading with her to come to discuss things in Bristol. But by this time the fat was in the fire. In a letter of 28 November Dorothy L. Sayers refused to yield to McCulloch's cajolery and proceeded to outline her case as a writer against BBC committee proceduralism:

Oh, no, you don't, my poppet. You won't get me to do three days of exhausting travel to Bristol in order to argue about my plays with a committee. What goes into the play, and the language in which it is written, is the author's business. If the Management don't like it, they reject the play, and there is an end of the contract... If I am asked to write a play for you, it is because I have the reputation of being able to write. Do you think I should have that reputation if I had allowed my style to be dictated to me by little bodies of unliterary critics?[30]

The same day she wrote to James Welch about the need for a much clearer definition of roles and responsibilities on the part of BBC staff. She was not prepared to accept the judgement of a committee upon her English style, although she was always ready to alter *in rehearsal* any phrase which presented difficulty to the actor. McCulloch did not seem to know 'where a producer's job begins and ends': 'The producer's job is to deal with the play in rehearsal, and not to act as the Management. In his own sphere the producer is God – but he is not God in the author's sphere. The author is God there; and the producer's business is to produce the play.' A 'trail of amateurishness' in BBC departments resulted in interference by everybody in everybody else's job, 'and that I cannot put up with', she warned. What had happened was in no way Welch's fault, but she had had enough of the *Children's Hour* attitude:

Theatre, you see, is theatre. It is because these little committees of the Children's Hour have no experience of the theatre that they never succeed in producing theatre, but only school lessons... Get me Val. I must have a producer who is a professional producer and nothing else, and who can talk the language of the theatre.[31]

As it happened, Welch was on sick leave with a broken collarbone, but he immediately returned to work to deal with Dorothy L. Sayers's request, while contending at the same time with memoranda generated by the irate staff of *Children's Hour*. ('I am so boiling', noted McCulloch, 'that I could write a thesis on the whole question.') All might have been patched up quickly had it not been for the BBC habit of circulating documents from one department to another. Dorothy L. Sayers's letter to Welch was passed to Bristol, where May Jenkin read it. She was particularly incensed by the suggestion that nobody at *Children's Hour* understood theatre, and on 19 December wrote to inform Dorothy L. Sayers that 'we cannot possibly delegate to any author, however distinguished, the right to say what shall or shall not be broadcast in a Children's Hour play'.[32] The result of this was that the playwright tore up her contract into tiny pieces and sent it back to the BBC.

For a time it now looked as though everything was at an end. McCulloch fulminated to Welch and to the Controller of Programmes, B. E. Nicolls, about Dorothy L. Sayers's 'lack of insight and human understanding'. The Controller sympathised, commenting, 'I never have believed that we do much good by encouraging temperament.' But James Welch was determined not to lose his series. He observed accurately to McCulloch that 'she is an artist who writes out of great artistic travail when inspiration visits her' and set about the difficult task of arranging for the plays to be produced by the Head of Features and Drama while remaining part of the Sunday output of *Children's Hour*. 'I am not the only person', Dorothy L. Sayers had written to him, 'to whom BBC work is sheer nightmare, because of the amateur-ishness, the confusion, and the preposterous over-lapping of control.' In his reply on 7 January 1941, he mildly observed that his own complaint against the BBC was that it fell between the stools of Civil Service traditions and limitations and Fleet Street commercial efficiency. He met her request for a clarification of roles by adding that if he got the permission he sought, he would have to be 'management', Gielgud the producer, and BBC Programme Contracts the contracting party.[33]

To the playwright's considerable relief, Welch got his way. What had taken place, she informed him, was an instance of the process known in the theatre as 'throwing a fit' – after which everybody bursts into tears and kisses everybody, and they all behave like lambs'. Before long, she was back at work on the series and writing to Val Gielgud about the trickiness of devising a colloquial rendering of Christ's sayings which was at once dignified and in keeping with the idiom of the rest of the characters. As she explained to him, the difficulty of translating into modern terms was not merely linguistic:

You think that 'leaven' is old-fashioned, and you substitute 'yeast' – and then you suddenly become aware that *not one town child in 500* has ever seen bread made – it's just something that comes from the baker. They may know the effect of baking-powder on pastry – but they've never seen a lump of heavy dough rise up silently and swell to the top of the pan all by itself with no hand touching it.[34]

The excellent relationships which she enjoyed with both Gielgud and Welch made it possible for her to concentrate on such matters now. No detail was too small to take trouble over. In dealing with crowd-conversation in the second play, *The King's Herald*, for example, she supplied a number a 'suitable exclamations' because, as she wrote to Gielgud, this seemed 'better than leaving the actors to say "burble-burble" on their own'. She consistently tried to imagine the effect of her lines on two quite different groups, the actors who would speak them at the microphone and the children who would listen at home. In this way, she sought to avoid the error of 'a Children's Hour thing about Absalom . . . which sounded as if everybody was in the pulpit (Miaou! Miaou!)'. Very much on her mind, too, was the need to give *The Man Born To Be King* dramatic unity and connectedness. *The Heirs to the Kingdom*, the fourth play, she pointed out to Gielgud, was 'a most frightful travelling pantechnicon, full of odds and ends', but that was only because she was already preparing the way for the latter part of the play-cycle. She continued to throw the weight of the series on its dialogue, doing 'as little as possible with noises off'.

Gielgud shared her sense of humour, which allowed her to comment freely on difficulties and key decisions. There were too many parts for men and too few for women, although she did her best to provide a balance. 'I wish most of Christ's female friends had been rather more respectable', she observed in mock exasperation. Then there was the question of where to bring down the final curtain. The series would end, she wrote on 3 March 1941, with the Resurrection, and for good reason:

I know that we are leaving out the Ascension and Pentecost. But I don't really see how anybody is to go up into Heaven by wireless. I could do it in a film – or even Drury Lane; but in my opinion – my umble but fixed opinion – the thing that speech-without-sight is least capable of conveying is physical movement of an abrupt and unlikely kind, and I fear the general affect would be that of the ascent of Montgolfier's balloon and the running commentary of a bunch of sight-seers. Nor do I feel that the 'speaking with tongues' would sound like anything but a cross between a row at the League of Nations and the Zoo at feeding time.[35]

Fortunately, Gielgud did not pass on these letters for perusal by the staff of *Children's Hour*, or there might have been renewed misunderstanding.

There was much discussion in the BBC about who should take the part of Christ in what was already being thought of as the 'radio Oberammergau'. In the end, the actor chosen was Robert Speaight; but the intention was that the cast should not be named in the *Radio Times* or elsewhere. The first play was due to be broadcast on 21 December. On the tenth of the month, Dorothy L. Sayers came up to town for 'Dr Welch's bunfight', a press conference at the Berners Hotel. 'Bunfight' turned out to be prophetic. She had seldom got on well with the press, and on this occasion she alienated some of those present by choosing to read from the new work passages which made use of modern colloquial idiom. Among the next day's headlines were 'BBC "Life of Christ" in Slang' in the *Daily Mail* – Dorothy L. Sayers subsequently threatened the *Mail* with a libel action and received an apology – and 'Gangsterisms in Bible Play' in the *Daily Herald*.

In the fracas which followed, the BBC appeared for a time to get cold feet. Alan Thomas, editor of *The Listener*, was ordered to withdraw from the issue of 18 December an article in which he had written, 'In this country the story of Jesus has not been directly presented on the stage since the Middle Ages; for the purpose of this radio version there are, therefore, no traditional lines to follow.'[36] There was talk of cancelling the series altogether. Dozens of complaints were directed at Broadcasting House, many of them organised by H. H. Martin, Secretary of the Lord's Day Observance Society, who opposed the idea of the BBC's broadcasting any plays on the life of Christ, let alone plays making use of slang; before long there came into being a Committee Co-Ordinating Protests Against Broadcasts Representing Our Lord as Speaking in His Own Person. In the House of Commons, Sir Percy Hurd, Conservative MP for Devizes, asked the Minister of Information to take steps to revise the scripts so as to avoid giving offence to Christian feeling. For the Government, a Parliamentary Secretary replied that the problem was a delicate one of good taste, and made the point that a special meeting of the BBC's Religious Advisory Committee had been called. Ogilvie, the Director-General of the BBC, was told that a religious controversy should be avoided; but it was too late for that. A meeting of the BBC Governors was summoned.

Once again, James Welch found himself faced with hostile criticism from different sides. He could cope easily enough with the grumble of Gordon Stowell, editor of the *Radio Times*, that Speaight's name had been given to the dailies, whereas no details of the cast list could be printed in the BBC's own journal; later, this particular policy was to be relaxed. It was impossible, however, to placate the Lord's Day Observance Society. Moreover, the Bishop of Winchester had written ominously to the Director-General about the first script, which he had been asked to read on behalf of the Religious Advisory Committee, 'there are phrases which jar, and I can quite understand large numbers of

people being deeply disturbed by some of the phrases used'.[37]
Dorothy L. Sayers had tried to protect her work from interference
by writing to Welch on 15 December, 'If there is to be any tinkering with the general presentment, or with the isolated passages,
in order to appease outside interests, I shall be regretfully obliged
to withdraw the scripts, under the terms of the contract.'[38] But the
pressure now being brought to bear upon both was intense, and
they had to agree to submit all the scripts to the Religious Advisory Committee before the plays were broadcast. As Christmas
drew near, the future looked far from certain.

What saved *The Man Born To Be King* was the success of the first
play when it was broadcast on the evening of 21 December. Both
children and adults found their attention caught and held. *Kings
in Judaea* had the same kind of positive reception as Dorothy L.
Sayers's first Nativity play for broadcasting three years before.
The presentation of Biblical characters as human beings with
familiar real-life qualities was immediately welcomed as something fresh and down-to-earth. Critics who listened without
prejudice discovered that the dramatic treatment was free from
sensationalism, while the language of the play was not slang but
direct and lively modern English. The *Manchester Guardian*'s radio
reviewer thought there was too much dialogue, but Jonah
Barrington summed up the prevailing reaction in the *Daily Express*
of 22 December, noting that 'Dorothy Sayers' radio play had no
shocks...it was reverent and sincere'. Many people got in touch
with the BBC to say that they looked forward keenly to the
continuation of the series; and voices were now raised against the
Lord's Day Observance Society for trying to have the plays ban-
ned without giving them a hearing. The fierce criticism which
had threatened the entire venture gave way to the kind of discussion which guarantees a large audience.

Every generation of radio dramatists, producers, and listeners
discovers afresh that radio plays succeed most readily with
limited casts and few main characters. The ear finds it hard to
identify and keep separate many different voices, so that the best
course for the writer is usually to select and delimit. However,
certain subjects require that there be many actors. *The Man Born
To Be King* was innovatory in recreating the varied human world
of the Gospels, for radio, using a generous range of voices to
enact cultural history.

Dorothy L. Sayers was quick to give credit where it was due.

James Welch had 'fought a courageous fight', she wrote to Giel-gud on 13 January 1942, in a letter congratulating the latter on the award of an OBE in the New Years Honours list. The letters could stand for 'Order of the Blasphemous Enterprise', quipped Giel-gud in return. As the series went on, with a new play being broadcast every fourth Sunday, Dorothy L. Sayers came to know the actors and actresses who performed *The Man Born To Be King* almost as well as she knew the producer, for she was present at rehearsals, and was always willing to answer questions from the cast. The quality of her writing, and superb team-work, ensured that the initial public interest was maintained and strengthened. She left nothing to chance when it was possible to help her colleagues, the actors, interpret exactly what she had in mind creating their roles. It is very doubtful if any radio dramatist anywhere has ever supplied such witty and detailed notes, so rich in broadcasting intelligence, as she prepared on twelve sep-arate occasions for use during production by Gielgud, Speaight, the brilliantly gifted James McKechnie who played the part of John, and the rest of the company. Ranging from incisive theolo-gical comment to discrimination of character types, these notes are included, in the form in which they were transmitted to the producer and actors, in the printed version of *The Man Born To Be King*.

'Oh, gosh, I should like some peace about this show!' Dorothy L. Sayers exclaimed in true theatrical fashion to Gielgud at one point, but the only let-up in tension came immediately after each play was broadcast. On 1 July 1942, after the eighth play, *Royal Progress*, the producer wrote to her, 'with a cast of thirty-seven, to say nothing of the donkey, it was as tough an assignment as I can remember'.[39] *King of Sorrows*, the eleventh play, dealt with the Crucifixion, and Dorothy L. Sayers had been aware all along that this presented the greatest challenge, especially as children and their parents would react differently to the subject. She wrote to Gielgud on 26 September 1942, 'So you were scared, were you?... I was scared, too – not so much about the Bishops or the listeners, but because howling crowds always scare me, & this one was alarmingly "actual". '[40]

The Man Born To Be King won great praise for the BBC. It was, unquestionably, a triumph of artistic daring and integrity on the writer's part. At the end of the undertaking, she was presented with a set of recordings of the broadcasts, and B. E. Nicolls, the

Controller of Programmes, who not so long before had com-
plained of her 'abominable rudeness', thanked her for making
possible 'a landmark in the history of broadcasting'.[41] Ideas of
religious drama, of radio drama, and of children's broadcasting
had all been changed. Genius is unrepeatable, but there may
possibly be a lesson of permanent value in Dorothy L. Sayers's
comment in a letter of 27 May 1947 to Noel Iliff, who was responsible for the first complete post-war production of *The Man Born
To Be King*:

it's all a question of experience – learning what can and can't be done on
the mike, and what traps actors are most likely to fall into, and what
particular routine each producer prefers. But unless the author is
allowed to come and make himself an interfering nuisance in the studio,
he can never get the experience, and so never learn *not* to be a nuisance –
which is why authors must always be grateful to the producer who
charitably puts up with them.[42]

Behind the accomplished radio dramatic story-telling of *The Man
Born To Be King* lay another kind of story altogether. But for the
single-minded determination of the playwright and of certain
individuals within the BBC, including Val Gielgud, the creativity
which led to *The Man Born To Be King* would have stood little
chance.

5   Giles Cooper: the medium as moralist

FRANCES GRAY

> I have no text. No chain of words to keep my thoughts from floating too
> far from the rock of faith. If I had there would be nothing to fasten them
> with. Nothing, nothing. There is no rock, there never has been and there
> never will be. I know that now. I have known it all my life, but it seemed
> such a terrible thing to admit that I denied it. Well now the cock has
> crowed for me and if there were a hell I should be well qualified to hold
> the keys...[1]

IT MIGHT SEEM PARADOXICAL to begin a study of a radio playwright with a quotation from a television play; but *Kittens Are
Brave*, written towards the end of Cooper's life, is in itself something of a paradox. Its form gave Cooper a rare opportunity to
make a direct statement of something like a personal moral vision, one implied in most of his plays but which the characters
rarely attain to or articulate. This makes the play a fair starting-
point for a retrospective study; but the very clarity of the vision in
it is, in a TV context, surprising; for what it states is, I believe,
what made Cooper a great writer for radio.

Kittens Are Brave is a duel between two men: Wensley Grafton,
the trendy media man, and the disillusioned priest, Gordon
Shiplake; on the surface the voice of 'telly-truth' wins hands
down. Grafton prosecutes Shiplake for writing obscene letters,
reveals the degraded nature of his family, and strips him of
family, living, and self-respect. He loses little in the process
except the already fading love of his wife. But what Shiplake
achieves through all the humiliations heaped on him in the name
of truth is the integrity to face himself and his beliefs and to state
them publicly in a last sermon: that there is nothing between us
and the darkness of our own souls, and that this must be faced
and not obfuscated by the petty evils around us. It is, for Cooper,
an optimistic conclusion, in that Shiplake visibly learns and
gains stature; but the cost of that learning is also faced. He is
shown, after his moment of truth, in a new job as downtrodden

companion to a rich eccentric; looking back, he comments that his
sermon passed unheard: 'I used my priestly voice.' Nevertheless,
he has spoken. He recognises the central fact of nothingness, the
absence of a 'rock', and still finds it worth while to set the record
straight. He affirms what Heidegger called the *Dasein*: that he has
an existence which he is responsible for and with reference to
which he can make a stand.[2]

Grafton himself has no personality to assert, involved as he is
with his screen image, an involvement which he, like many
Cooper heroes, can disguise even to himself as a preoccupation
with real values. He sees television as a way of presenting what
he calls 'truth'; but, as he tells his wife when she objects to some
image-oriented improvements to the studio set which represents
their home, 'True isn't the same as real.' Shiplake, in order to
speak the truth, has to reject his medium, the Church. One of the
unspoken questions at the end of *Kittens Are Brave* is whether
television is a way to speak the truth, whether it has corrupted
Grafton or he has corrupted it. It is interesting to speculate
whether Cooper would have looked at the question in later plays
– and in what medium.

He might well have resorted to radio. Cooper, for most of his
life, was examining the experience on the near side of nothingness, characters who reject the *Dasein* and lock on to problems
which distract them from the problem of existence itself. Sometimes they grasp Shiplake's truth, but they cannot cope with it; if
their evasive strategies are demolished, they set up new ones;
and the twentieth century provides them with plenty. Their
universe is peculiarly fit for radio to express; yet Cooper was the
first to translate it into radio terms adequately and precisely. This
was his unique contribution to radio; it provided him with a
language capable of depicting the twilight zones between illusion
and disillusion.

Much of the grammar of that language had been laid down by
the time Cooper came to the medium in the fifties. It is interesting, however, to see how single-minded radio drama's development had been up to that point. Its pioneers wanted to find its
strengths, and these they rightly located in two qualities – intimacy and flexibility. 'A rush through time and space'[3] was
Tyrone Guthrie's description of one of his own radio plays,
among the first ever performed, and every radio writer since has
been aware of the medium's temporal and spatial capabilities. In

radio, the author can set his play in Ancient Greece or on Mars without the need for sets or costumes; he can move between the two in seconds; his characters can age years in minutes; there is nothing, in fact, that words can do which he cannot, swiftly and cheaply. He has only to feed the imagination and the listener will act as designer and even scene-shifter. This creative role is positively demanded of him by a medium that works by, as it were, whispering in his ear. The microphone was for many writers the fastest possible route into the mind of an audience. 'Remember,' said Guthrie in the twenties, 'you are overhearing her thoughts.'[4] 'Come closer now,' said Dylan Thomas in the fifties. These two qualities are always present in good radio; when one looks at Cooper's most talented predecessors, it seems as if radio had settled for exploiting these qualities to the full rather than uncovering others. Perhaps the classic example of the form in the forties is Louis MacNeice's *The Dark Tower*.[5] It is a record of a spiritual journey, using all the technical resources of radio to paint a series of fantastic landscapes forming an objective correlative to the hero's state of mind. The microphone keeps us with Roland, gives us a share in his conciousness. We experience the Dark Tower as he does. MacNeice makes him and his journey real to us.

It is an indication of the play's quality that they *are* real; but it is also an indication of the radio possibilities that MacNeice's generation left undeveloped. In concentrating on radio's strengths, they gave their creations something of the solidity of the stage and stage-settings; they ignored the fact that radio has a stage of its own – and that the nature of a stage dictates to a great extent what can be shown upon it. When, for instance, we sit in a proscenium-arch theatre and see a criminal arrested in the library at Styles, we make a great many assumptions. We assume that somewhere spatially related to the library are a police station, a court, a jail; in doing so we assent to the reality of the law, the state, and the class system; we also assume that everything that happens on the stage is literally true, that the criminal is not a figment of Hercule Poirot's imagination.

In watching the Shakespearean stage in action we come closer to the experience offered by MacNeice. *Antony and Cleopatra* asks us to accept that the bare stage is sometimes Rome, sometimes Egypt; there is a spiritual rather than a spatial link. *Macbeth* asks us to accept the reality of hell, because the dead rise out of it. This is not unlike the *Dark Tower* world, but in giving it that

Shakespearean reality MacNeice lost sight of something radio could do which Shakespeare could not. What we see on stage at any one moment has to have some kind of objective reality for us. Egypt is there in the person of Cleopatra; she cannot suddenly tell us in mid-scene that she is in Rome. We believe in hell if an actor dressed as a demon tells us he is in hell; hell will go on being real while he stands before us. But in the stage of radio we lack this visual solidity. The stage of radio is the darkness and silence of the listener's skull. A sound is heard. Then it is gone. We have no confirmation that it ever existed. Only our ears testify to the fact – and hearsay evidence, as the law knows, is not reliable. Mac-Neice and his contemporaries worked, often brilliantly, against this lack of consistent reality by constantly supporting the imagination:

NEAERA. The sea today is adagios of doves.
ROLAND. The sea today is gulls and dolphins.
NEAERA. The sea today is noughts and crosses.[6]

This exploits the need to keep the location constantly before us by using it to illuminate character and emotion; but it still assumes that that need exists. But in some ways, as Cooper himself discovered when he came to radio, the apparent weakness of a purely aural medium can be a positive strength, a richer dimension of its flexibility. The radio writer can transcend the spatial and temporal agility of the Elizabethan stage and allow the places, people, and events he describes to change their very nature as he chooses; he can move from the real to the unreal and back again; he can leave us unsure whether we are hearing illusion or reality; he can even, in seconds, change our perception of what has already happened. Here are the closing moments of Cooper's play The Disagreeable Oyster:[7]

BUNDY. It was a spiteful joke. They left me naked on the pavement and a man called Sid took me to a nudist colony...or did he?
...
BAKER. The bread's baked. Here's your loaf.
BUNDY. How much?
BAKER. Nothing to pay. Share it between the two of you.
BUNDY. Thank you.
BAKER. If you want to catch your train, you'd better run.
BUNDY MINOR. I'm tired.
BAKER. That's right, you want to go home.
BUNDY MINOR. Oh yes!

BUNDY. Goodbye!
   [*Running feet. They stop.*]
BUNDY MINOR. What did he mean by 'The two of you'? [*Distant train
   whistle*]
BUNDY. No idea.[8]

Cooper here demands a radical shift in the way we have perceived the whole action. Our assent to it is concealed from us by
the deceptively relaxed pace; despite those running feet, the
action is here at its slowest, a point of rest in a hectic play.
Nonetheless, a demand is made. Throughout, we have accepted
a certain way of experiencing Bundy; he is split into two parts,
Major and Minor, played by different actors. Major is the public
face, Minor the inner and more anarchic spirit, at once the temp-
ter who gets Major into trouble and the frightened child who
wishes he hadn't. We are accustomed to every situation being
seen in double focus:

BUNDY MINOR. Yes, women. Passionate Bundy, crammed to the gorge
   with primeval urges. I'm a gorilla, I beat my breast in the jungle, I
   snort and paw the ground.
BUNDY. That's all very well, but actually well, there's nobody suitable,
   not really.[9]

We are used too to the fact that Bundy presents a single visible
front. Suddenly, Cooper makes both Bundies visible, to the
Baker at least. At the same time he questions the reality of experiences which we and the Bundies have already accepted. And
because we have, now, only the memory of hearsay, Cooper can
alter our perception. The Baker, perceiving Bundy's duality, is
the voice of truth, the voice of the child who points out the
nakedness of the Emperor in his new clothes; and this makes us
trust what is said and done in his shop. His gentle questioning (in
production he was given a Scottish accent which combined with
the Sunday bells to suggest the Manse) makes Bundy perform the
unprecedented act of thinking. The effect is to make us re-
examine the past with Bundy and to accept the indisputable
reality of certain events recollected in tranquillity. He rejects the
nudist colony as panicky nightmare, and we do too. But this
episode comes at the end of the day and involves all the characters we have previously encountered, only slightly more
unpleasant when stark naked. If it is nightmare, we must accept
that it is grounded in reality. The snobbery and callousness

Bundy has endured all day are now implied to be true; the nightmare merely reflects them. We have to look again, soberly, at the events leading up to the nudist colony and see as reality what seemed to be farce:

EM. Never a moment to ourselves.
VI. Not to mention that.
AG. And then carry them round for nine months.
EM. And the awful time we have.
VI. Not only in hospital, what about after?
AG. Yes, the nappies and the potties and the feeds and the nights kept up.
EM. With the housework on top of it.
VI. Not to mention that.
AG. And there he sits and says we're a lot of sluts.
BUNDY. I'm sorry, I only wanted my hat back.
VI. Anybody want a hat?
WOMEN. [Derisive cheer]
EM. Chuck it here.
AG. Kick it around.
VI. Fill it full of coffee.
BUNDY. No!
AG. Tomato ketchup. Make him eat it.
EM. Come on girls.
VI. Hold him down.
BUNDY. No, no, no!
AG. Take his shoes off, he's kicking.
VI. And his trousers...[10]

At first it seems stylised, lines ritually allotted and building up to a calculated crescendo as Vi's reminders of female mysteries lash the women into Bacchic fury – archetypal hags participating in that archetypal orgy, a charabanc outing, as ritually permissive as the Feast of Fools. We laugh because it seems to have no foot in reality; the tone has been set by Bundy's visit to a cartoon film; but the self-inflicted sufferings of Donald Duck closely parallel his day's experience; the lines of the Ditch Hamlet Mothers may be ritualistic in effect, but the rhythm of each line is that of ordinary speech. The scene is ambiguous enough for reassessment of its basis in truth; and we accept with it a new view of the world. We accept that people are as savage as a cartoon film in their dealings with one another – a point Cooper does not labour, but it is there, even in this lightest of comedies.

It is plain from the shifting universe of *The Disagreeable Oyster* that Cooper has something in common with the Absurdists, and

the richness of his radio development in the middle fifties coin-
cides with the impact of Beckett and Ionesco in the British theatre.
The Absurdists, however, tended to treat their stage in one of two
ways: they showed a world where nothing was certain, using sets
and structures as consistent with nineteenth-century certainty as
anything by Pinero – for instance, some of Sartre's plays set in
naturalistic backgrounds; or they tried to reflect the condition of
Absurdity in sets and actions full of fantasy – *Rhinoceros*, for
example, or *Victims of Duty*. Even these excursions into non-
naturalism occasionally barked their shins against the sheer solidity of properties and the obstinately real bodies of the actors. It
is not surprising that many Absurdist plays adapted very successfully to radio – witness Martin Esslin's continuing patronage
of Mrozek and Havel, for instance, or the fruitful relationship
between Broadcasting House and Samuel Beckett.

Cooper differs from the Absurdists in that he wants – and in
radio certainly gets – the freedom to move between the apparently ordered world implied in a box set and the free-ranging
fantasy of Ionesco. He moves with breathtaking virtuosity, but it
is not simply a matter of technique; for Cooper the human condition cannot be divorced from an immediate *Gestalt*. His characters
stand on the edge of chaos but surrounded with the concrete
realities that brought them there; their desperation is spiritual but
grounded in a recognisable world. It is a moral universe which
the still prevalently naturalistic stage of the forties and fifties
could not easily express, and Cooper's stage plays often betray a
frustration at its lack of existential mobility; one of his earliest and
deservedly unperformed attempts demanded that the set itself
transform itself from bed-sit to oriental palace,[11] basically in order
to permit the hero to explore himself; Cooper's late and in many
ways accomplished stage plays still bear traces of the same frustration; *Everything in the Garden* is a brilliantly savage comedy
using the metaphor of prostitution for an acquisitive society; but
in order to show its full implications Cooper demanded that an
actor towards the end of the play step out of character and refuse
to go on with his hypocritical part.[12] It was an unsatisfying device
which called attention to itself rather than to the moral universe
behind it; Cooper abandoned it and allowed the play to tail off. It
is interesting to speculate whether he would eventually have
written a completely satisfying stage play; in order to do so he
would have had to find a shape and style that gave him the

freedom he found in radio. As it is, it is to radio that we must turn to find Cooper's special vision clearly articulated.

So confident was he in the mobility of this medium that his plays often had a deceptive simplicity. They lack entirely the 'literary' flavour of MacNeice's experiments or the pretentiousness of, say, the New Apocalyptics, and often confused the BBC administration by appearing too straightforward for the Third and too avant-garde for the Home Service. *Pig in the Middle,* for instance, looks like a naturalistic play about a family holiday and all the attendant inconveniences – the rain, the lack of privacy, an irritating relative.[13] The action swings into nightmare as elderly Uncle Arthur dies and Frank and Susan's small son Angus claims that his last act was to plant the beach with abandoned mines during a war game. We never learn the truth about the mines, but their possible presence is a fit symbol for the unspoken unhappiness of the family. Cooper creates a dreamlike atmosphere by exploiting the liberating aspects of a beach holiday; he makes absurd contrasts between solitary self-revelation and family reticence:

FRANK [*at the top of his voice letting it quaver up and down*]. AaaaaaaaaaaaaaaaaaaH!
  [*Silence except for the lapping of waves*]
  Oh glory all alone and sea and sand. But sad. Erosion, yes and bells beneath the water, yes and every year a little more of this, a little less of the other. The end would be a shallow, shallow sea, the whole world drowned. There'd be no tides, of course, no in and out, just surges following the moon, our bones would drift and lift and lapse upon the bed. [*Fading*] Upon the bed, upon the bed, upon the bed . . .
  [*Fade in Susan reading to Angus*]
SUSAN. You're an old lazy-bones, squeaked Roger the Roller to Margaret Motor-Mower.[14]

The puncturing of a speech so charged with symbolism (incidentally with a more apt, if more downbeat, symbol of Frank's sexual frustration in the person of a rusty motor-mower) preserves the smooth domestic surface but ensures we see the despair beneath it. The mixture of comedy and agonised fantasy prepares us for the incident of the mines; real or not, they are the incarnation of the frustrations and mutual hatreds of the four characters. Susan and Frank have treated Uncle Arthur like a naughty child, sending him to bed for telling an offensive story; now they find he has power beyond the grave; he has bored them with war stories;

suddenly the war is made real. Family quarrels are transformed into the very essence of despair as they discover their impotence in the face of a violent and implacable world: Angus is helpless, like all children, and resents the fact; Uncle Arthur admits before his death that his obsession with war has hidden a real memory of terror rather than heroism; Frank's desire for his wife, his longing for something more that 'fifteen years in bitumen', is frustrated, and the articulation of that frustration in the possible minefield has upset the balance of day-to-day living. He is now faced with a spiritual abyss which cannot be ignored, but in the face of it he still has to continue his mundane existence. Here again, Cooper provides a symbol rich in absurdity and matter-of-factness. The ice-cream man arrives, late:

FRANK. But oh, why can't I do something, cry and kick and scream like Angus does or weep like Susan did or die like Uncle Arthur? All I can do is stand between the lot of them and wait and hold my Bumper Block, my Bumper Party Block, which, oh, my God, is melting! [*The last on a shout of despair. Then quietly*] I suppose I'll have to eat it.[15]

Frank's impotence is shared by most of Cooper's heroes, and most of them come in the end to realise that they have no choice but to eat the Bumper Party Block. *Pig in the Middle* restricts the sphere of choicelessness and despair to the area of relationships, and it is perhaps significant that it adapted extremely well to television,[16] the sixties' chosen instrument for intimate dissection, Naomi Capon wisely resisting any temptation to clarify the existence of the mines and keeping the focus firmly upon the characters. But *Before the Monday* traces the cause of the feeling of Absurdity back to very specific aspects of the twentieth century and explores them in a way only an existentially mobile medium can do. The hero, Desmond, has a typically twentieth-century job which in itself represents a kind of living death for the *Dasein*: 'Assistant personnel manager with Guglipp's. Office machinery . . . all those personnel working away to make machines which have been made by other machines which have been made by . . . no.'[17] He makes nothing, he is no use, and he is totally dependent on a system which creates industries out of making nothing. Divorced from it, he has even less capacity for choice and self-definition. His decision to opt out by suicide is undercut by his chosen method of self-neglect. He can't even choose whether or not to be saved, for a piece of the system, the flower-

shop girl Jane, turns up because of a yearly arrangement about
his wife's birthday, made in the days when he could still cope,
and sets about saving him.

Desmond's helplessness springs from his realisation of how he
relates to the world; he has become all perception and no action, a
condition which Aldous Huxley described as 'Mind at Large':
'Each person is at each moment capable of remembering all that
has ever happened to him and of perceiving everything that is
happening everywhere in the universe. The function of the brain
and nervous system is to protect us from being overwhelmed and
confused by this mass of wholly useless and irrelevant knowledge.'[18] 'Mind at Large' enjoys an unfiltered perception, which
Huxley, attaining it through mescalin, could describe in glowing
terms; he never suggested that it should do anything but enjoy its
own state. In the mundane world, however, it is an agony
because one is required to act in the face of this total knowledge.
Desmond cannot bear even to eat, because the full sociological,
political, and metaphysical implications of the act crush him:

Agony thinking of it. Just a tin of sardines. Sheet metal rolled out thin
and covered with tin which comes from Peru in boats and men have
made machines to mould it into shape and then the fishermen sail out
and they have nets and smelly engines and a thousand other things, and
olives grow on desiccated hills – and on the tin a picture in *two* colours.
No![19]

It seems, at first, as if this is to be a romantic comedy of a
Superfluous Man, a Byronic hero, saved – or not – by a good
woman. When Jane first enters it seems that two opposing forces
have been marshalled, easily distinguished by the difference in
vocabulary. Desmond speaks of death, illness, and personnel
management; Jane in more concrete terms about holidays,
cinemas, flowers, and cups of tea. She represents life in all its
physicality, cutting off Desmond's abstract nouns by rubbing a
cool flannel across his face. But the play is not simply a study of an
individual with a particular attitude to life; its structure is
designed to focus our attention on a situation, a condition, not
the characters experiencing it. Cooper exploits the ambiguities of
radio to place the action in a dream world which precludes our
searching for psychological plausibility but which allows the real
world to intrude when it illuminates the play. The short prelude
establishes its territory:

JANE. Saturday before...
DESMOND. August.
JANE. Before the Monday. Hot.
DESMOND. Quiet.
JANE. Holiday, holiday, holidee.
DESMOND. All gone away.
JANE. Gone away.
DESMOND. Left it all to me.
JANE. Climbing up...
DESMOND. On the stairs.
JANE. Oh hot, oh Hottentot...
      [*Gurgle of water tank*]
DESMOND. The water tank.
JANE [*relieved*]. The water tank.
DESMOND. On the stairs.
JANE. Ninety-six, ninety-seven, ninety-eight, they ought to have a
      hundred. Flat six, Harrison D.
DESMOND. That's me.[20]

This places the play on two simultaneous levels. First, in a precise
time and place, solid reality. At the same time, it undermines that
reality. It is neither holiday, holy day, nor working day; Sunday
can define itself with church bells, but Saturday is only 'before'.
Nothing will be achieved in this limbo of inactivity; like Osborne
in *Look Back in Anger*, like Tony Hancock, Cooper uses the British
weekend as a symbol of joyless self-exploration.

The prelude also implies that the mental state to be explored is
somehow common to Desmond and Jane, by almost telepathic
exchanges such as 'The water tank...the water tank'. Desmond
throughout the play performs this service for Jane, putting into
words thoughts that she cannot articulate and showing that
things are not always what they seem; but the speed with which
they pick up each other's cues implies closer links than teacher
and pupil; stichomythia presupposes some sort of relationship
or common ground, for within it no exposition is possible, no
ambiguities can be resolved. These implied links mean that we
are not surprised by any developments of that relationship
within the play – we do not ask, for instance, why Jane does not
send for a doctor when she finds Desmond dying on the mat, and
it does not strain our credulity when she drifts into bed with
Desmond, although she is shown as a rather priggish girl. The
links, however, transcend personal psychology, a fact Cooper
can make clear in his blind, ambiguous medium; he can make the

characters speak as if face to face, while demonstrating a different spatial relationship altogether. Jane is located 'on the stairs', but it is not 'on the stairs' that her dialogue with Desmond is taking place. The focus, then, is placed on the feeling rather than on either of the persons sharing it.

'I think there's a pain somewhere in the room', said Mrs Gradgrind in *Hard Times*. 'But I couldn't positively say that I have got it.' In *Before the Monday* there is an existential pain somewhere in the flat, but it's not always possible to say who has it. Response to existence has become so intimately associated with things like cups of tea and tins of sardines (equally invisible, of course, in radio terms) that its existence is almost as concrete as theirs; and a tragic corollary of this seems to be that there is not enough *Dasein* to go round. At the beginning of the play, Jane knows who she is and what she is for; Desmond is losing his sense of self in the face of the demands life makes. At the end of the play, the position is reversed. The implication seems to be that one way to solve the loss of self is to steal another's. The transition is presumably made when Jane and Desmond sleep together. Cooper does not depict the sexual encounter itself, perhaps because it would inevitably have overtones of warmth and humanity. Instead, he surrounds the act with an aura of violence: Desmond obtains the energy to do something as definite as an act of seduction by threatening with a knife the one-man band they have invited to come up and entertain them. We expect, as he claims to feel 'miles better', that the inevitable embrace will happen now, but Cooper precedes it with a scene of both violence and deception. Jane is curious about a locked room and Desmond plies her with circumstantial evidence as to what it might conceal: 'You're thinking . . . oh, of Sunday papers and black headlines. How some men to save their children and their wives from all the dreadful truth of life . . . failure and disease and hunger and the death of innocence and trust . . . some men kill . . .'[21] When the room is opened and flies are heard buzzing out in a cloud, it proves to contain nothing more than piles of accumulated washing-up – an excellent aural joke, but one with frightening implications. The verbal violence is an apparent substitute for a seduction speech, for Jane falls into Desmond's arms in relief when the door is opened; the link between sex and violence makes us uneasy. It implies a threat to Jane's personality, the assumptions on which her life is grounded; for what Desmond is doing is putting thoughts of despair into her mind; like radio, he is dropping pictures into her head; and, while the pictures turn out not to be literal truth, they do not cease to be valid, especially as Desmond presents the 'murder' in the third person, something any man might do. It is a hearsay account of a confrontation with nothingness. Cooper has been accused by Martin Shuttleworth of skirting the real implications of that locked room: 'This is a writer capable of a *Crime and Punishment* – but no, he withdraws with an urbane little *mou*.'[22] But this is to treat the play as if it were a stage or TV work which would demand that we *see* the corpses or the washing-up; in this case Cooper would have had to make a choice as to which we did see – and if he took the latter course the balance of the play would shift; Jane would inevitably become the victim of a physical attack, or she would escape; and this would turn the play into a study of Desmond as murderer. As it is, the 'murder' remains as a telling image of the cost of attaining selfhood: and the room where non-being is is never without an occupant.

The intimacy of radio means that the shifting universe, the nothingness at its heart, is invariably perceived through the experience of an individual or individuals, as it is in *Before the Monday*. This might at first appear to preclude political analysis, which demands a broad canvas. But in fact Cooper deals with politics in a unique way. He shows, not ideas in action, but ideas transmuted by the brain. History and theories of history exist not only in themselves but as they are perceived; and they may be altered by the way in which they are perceived and even misinterpreted. The relationship between political myth and political reality is the theme of a late television play, *To the Frontier*:[23]

FINN. All things are as true as each other. The Gorgon's head, the Norman Conquest, the Repeal of the Corn Laws.
JOHN. Nonsense! Rubbish! Some are facts, some are myths.
FINN. Nothing is a fact unless it's happening to you at the moment. When it's happened, it's a myth.
JOHN. But a myth can have no result!
FINN. Upstairs there is a very fine picture of Moses receiving the ten commandments on Mount Sinai.

As in *Kittens Are Brave*, Cooper makes an explicit statement of an idea which underlies much of his radio work. It might be worth examining the increasing tendency of his television plays in the mid-sixties to engineer a point – a discussion, a sermon, a key speech – in which a definite statement is made. It is possible that his work in television might have taken very different directions. In radio, however, he rarely made statements, but in his directly political plays looked without comment at the interplay between myth and reality. It is an area of course that radio was particularly well equipped to deal with, as it can, as I have tried to show, make the abstract concrete or even the concrete abstract.

Cooper's favourite political myth was, significantly, the favourite of another major radio talent of the fifties, the Goons. Both the Goons and Cooper returned again and again to a theme which was rarely discussed on stage, even at the height of the post-1956 New Wave – the decline and fall of the British Empire. Sometimes Cooper treated it naturalistically, as in his study of a colony collapsing in its own decay, *Dangerous Word.* [24] More often, however, he looked at the spectre of Empire as it appears in the minds of Empire-builders themselves, the displaced and unwanted soldiers and the dislocated flag-wavers who cannot accept that their time is past. He switches with dazzling authority from nostalgia-inspired chimeras to the appalling realities they can generate. In, for instance, *The Return of General Forefinger* [25] he employs a plot which is pure Goon; in fact, George Forefinger Brady's attempt to bring back the statue of his Uncle Forefinger from India so that his Aunt Augusta can enshrine it safely in her Irish castle has a possible source in Neddy Seagoon's efforts to capture Napoleon's piano. [26] But Cooper mixes the cartoon humour with an unnerving element of reality. Two facts tended to soften even the most violent Goon episodes. One was the fact that it was a regular team production and the characters were constants. The violence experienced by Eccles and Bluebottle often bordered on the horrific, but the audience was always aware that they were part of a pattern of lunacy and that suffering was their function within it:

SEAGOON. There! I've sawn all four legs off.
EIDELBURGER. Strange – first time I've known of a piano with four legs.
ECCLES. Hey – I keep falling down... [27]

The audience anticipates the joke as soon as the saw is produced – given that the piano legs must go, so must Eccles's – but because the leglessness exists only in the structure of the joke, the legs are restored a moment later with 'the wonder leg-grower recommended by all good centipedes'. But when Quentin, George's reluctant side-kick, dies in jail through George's own incompetence, he cannot be resurrected. We hear him suffering in a monologue intercut with scenes of caste-ridden Indians shifting the statue and recalling the good old days of the juggernaut; he speaks, as he dies of thirst, in naturalistic tones which force us to see the whole farcical action in the cold light of reality, to appreciate the full implications of George's Empire-building ambitions. Quentin's death also highlights the second major difference between Cooper's surrealist portrayal of the fall of Empire and that of the Goons. It is caused by George's sheer administrative stupidity; on the surface, this is a quality he shares with Major Bloodnok and Grytpype-Thynne. But, although their mistakes were often disastrous, there was a kind of ontological perfection about Goonhood; the idiocy proceeded from consistent beings with consistent beliefs and consistent *raisons d'être*. Bloodnok may be a Blimp and a fool, but he is a whole fool. George's incompetence is as much spiritual as practical. He sets out on his quest in a Buchanesque spirit, seizing the opportunity to prove his initiative and idealism; he fails at his Richard Hannay imitation – there is a ludicrous sequence in which he attempts the classic 'follow that car' manoeuvre with an uncomprehending taxi-driver – because he lacks the true driving force behind it; he sees the White Man's Burden not as something to be borne but to be flaunted; he drags the statue halfway across the Orient even though the news of Aunt Augusta's death has already reached him; it has ceased to be a symbol of Empire and become a tool of personal fantasy. Aunt Augusta, perspicacious in her senility, has never recognised George as her relation and thinks he is the son of her butcher; she is more or less right; he is not a gentleman in the old sense of the word, but he clings so tightly to that old sense and its symbols that he cannot redefine and exemplify a new gentility. The difference between George and the older generation lies in their differing responses to the myth of Empire. Aunt Augusta accepts that the reality is past and spends her days tending its symbols, desiring no more power to be generated by those symbols than that required to bring them home and prevent a repetition of what happened outside the public convenience in Cairo. Forefinger himself, in his statue persona, is a touching symbol of the past, no more; but when the myth he represents corrupts the young, in the person of George, he becomes lethal, crushing one of the statue-movers beneath his weight. Memory can be made terrifyingly concrete.

While *The Return of General Forefinger* moves from cartoon to reality, myth to the realisation of myth in terms of physical pain, *Without the Grail*[28] begins in reality which apparently contrasts with myth; then it shows the myth becoming reality. Here again, we are not always sure where reality ends and nightmare begins, but the framework of the play forbids the comforting option that all is fantasy. It begins with the pragmatic hero, Innes Corrie, preparing to go on business to a tea plantation in India and tying up the loose ends of his life, such as brushing off his socially unsuitable girl friend. The fact that we experience subsequent events through Innes, already established as toughly cynical, tends to mean that we believe those events. At first we see the plantation as a strange outpost of Empire; the owner, Felix Barrington, drills the servants in the etiquette of calling-cards and organises port after dinner and tea on the lawn. Cooper gradually exposes the façade: monkeys throw dung at the tea parties, the port is coloured water, and Barrington's children reject his myths for their own: his son Derek for dreams of an England as false as anything at the plantation, his daughter Leila for Communism, his protégé Siri for his own Naga heritage. At first it seems that the trappings have simply been ridiculed; but then Cooper uncovers a complex relationship between icon and reality. Felix outlines his beliefs in a style which bypasses political vocabulary and deals in symbol: he sees himself as a latter-day Arthur – not the chivalric king of Malory or Tennyson, but the Briton who kept the ideals of Rome alive in the Dark Ages when the legions had gone home:

FELIX. The garrisons went and the flags came down; then the traders began to go, and after them the engineers and the builders of bridges, the makers of roads. All of them, all of them are giving up and going home. My family came out for the Company two hundred years ago. England's an ideal but we're planted in this earth. We've lost the taste for fog. And now we have a duty. 'Stern daughter of the Voice of God', you know, while India sits waiting for her conqueror.[29]

His contempt for Tennyson is ironic in view of this essentially Victorian dream of benevolent rule over lesser breeds without the Law, a view Tennyson himself was far too sophisticated to uphold without question; as is his attitude to Malory; Derek tries to help Innes escape from the plantation where he is a virtual prisoner; he is murdered with his father's possible connivance, or at least his knowledge, a moment in which Barrington chooses to read an account of the death of Mordred; but in identifying Derek with Mordred he thinks only of the betrayer, not of Mordred who is the product of an unlawful union, who fits nowhere and has a genuine grudge, just as Derek, the son of what Leila realistically calls a 'pillow-dictionary', fits neither into the Naga culture or the English ideal he has built up. The sounds of the play – the tigers, the monkeys, the Indian voices – clash violently with the vocabulary of chivalry and stress the point finally articulated by Innes, the absence of the Grail, both as word and as concept. It is typical of Cooper's irony that it should be the tough Innes who first speaks the word. At the start of the play, he despises the abstract:

HAZEL. And when you've found a girl whose face will look right behind those long green candles, I suppose you'll order yourself to fall in love with her.
INNES. What's love got to do with it? Love's a word. This is life.[30]

What launches the play into nightmare is precisely this clash between 'words' and 'life'. Felix clings to myths, chivalric, Victorian, and Roman; but he ignores their guiding principles and confuses them until they are powerless to convince his children any more than the pink water can convince Innes that it is port. But the myths have results because Felix is prepared to kill for them; he outlines his ideals to Innes with a gun in one hand, a copy of the *Morte D'Arthur* in the other. And myth gives rise to myth; Siri reacts against the Empire dream by creating his own about the Nagas; when Innes explodes one of the symbols of Barrington's dream by revealing that his private arsenal is largely useless, Siri sets off a Naga revolt; the Nagas cut off Barrington's head – there is magic in a head. Leila, the Communist, has clung to her own myth, that she is fostering the corrupt world of the plantation as a weak link in the capitalist chain; confronted with the reality of revolution, she can make no sense of it. Innes himself, the man with no belief in 'words', suddenly finds that his own foundations are rocking, that his self-sufficiency is also a myth; when he tells Leila how he grew to believe in himself alone he does it through a story, an image of himself lost and crying as a child in a fun fair – an image as vivid to us, and as remote to Leila, as that of Arthur and Mordred. Confronted with the body of Felix, Innes has no beliefs, no words, nothing that can make him more than basic inarticulate man crying 'no head...no head...'

When he recovers his poise he tries to find a focus for his life in Leila, but too late:

LEILA. ...For a moment I thought perhaps there might be something else, that all my father's tales were true.

INNES. Love?

LEILA. A word, like all his other words. Now this is life. You taught me that.

INNES. I never said it, not to you.

LEILA. You didn't have to say it. There you were.[31]

This describes the political situation as well as the emotional one. The words have all become flesh – love, revolution, Empire, death-or-glory – and the flesh is so unlike the word that the connection between them is eroded. The scene plainly shows the nature of Cooper's political imagination. Radio for him is not the epic stage which looks directly at ideas, at history, but the stage of the monad, which looks at the distortions and dreams spun out of history by the experience of the individual. When *Without the Grail* was televised,[32] it dwindled into a somewhat frustrating adventure story. Here was a plantation, a piece of India, whose fate was undecided. Beyond visible hills were the Nagas, the Chinese; the territory had several possible futures, and the territory demanded our attention; to look solely at two characters seemed self-indulgent. On radio, we remained with the microphone and with Innes; and through Innes, with the complex array of myths and the results of myths created by the characters: a confusion which produces nothing but the agonised need voiced by Innes for a Grail, an overriding myth to cling to, a way of making sense of experience.

Few characters in Cooper's work possess anything like a Grail; the Cooper hero stands, invariably, on chaos; he feels values shifting under his feet; and for him values are so closely linked to the physical world that the very ground shifts and changes, too; his confused ideas turn into realities and rend him; he puts his faith in half-digested political notions, in material goods, in his own barely explored personality. The faith is always tested and found wanting; the physical and mental universe rocks, and the hero is faced with darkness and nothingness. Often, he disintegrates; often, he scuttles back into his regimented and mindless existence and pretends nothing has happened. Just occasionally, he learns enough to acknowledge the absence of a rock of faith, a Grail, the reality of nothing. It is not an optimistic vision of man or his prospects; yet a Cooper play is rarely depressing. This is partly a function of his sheer wit – few radio writers, after all, exploit large-scale nudity, as in *The Disagreeable Oyster*, or use a bathroom to contain an entire moral universe, as in *Under the Loofah Tree*. [33] But the real excitement generated by a Cooper play is that of watching a medium and a moral view in pefect harmony. Radio in Cooper's hands can take the foggy beliefs and desires of his heroes and give them the same solidity for the listener that they have in the minds which originated them – often a greater solidity than the apprehensible universe. Radio is the quickest way to draw a map of a mind. The minds depicted by Cooper may be horrifying in their limitations; and these limitations may make existence a nightmare; but the physical realisation of that nightmare and of the nothingness behind it is brilliantly achieved, in the darkness and silence of the listener's head that is the true stage of radio.

6 The radio plays of Henry Reed

ROGER SAVAGE

> Love . . . art . . . scholarship . . . the classical heritage: even a Third
> Programme that has recently been (as our dear, dear Janet would say)
> so rudely castrated, must find a place, a brief moment, to honour them.
> (Herbert Reeve, in *The Primal Scene, As It Were...*)

AT ONE TIME OR ANOTHER, Henry Reed has been celebrated in
three different roles: as the radio dramatist who created the
memorable 'composeress' Hilda Tablet, as the translator who in a
single season had three of his translations (all from the same
playwright) running in the West End, and as the poet whose
'Naming of Parts' is 'probably the most widely quoted and
anthologised single poem written in the Second World War'.
(The opinion is Vernon Scannell's, in his book on the poetry of
that war, which takes its title *Not Without Glory* from Horace *via*
another of Reed's war-poems.)[1] The roles are various enough for
some of his admirers in one of them not to be quite sure whether
the others were played by the same man. Could there be two
Henry Reeds perhaps, or even three? Certainty on the point has
been made harder by Reed's never having had more than a
handful of his books in print at any one time and by his keeping a
low profile in the London literary circus. For instance, born in the
same year as Dylan Thomas, he appears only rarely in the
memoirs of the forties, fifties and sixties (though he can be found
as 10557689 Pte Reed, H. in John Lehmann's autobiography *I Am
My Brother*, as 'the most elusive of my friends' in Sir Arthur
Bliss's *As I Remember*, and as an admired colleague in the *Letters* of
J. R. Ackerley, who was literary editor of *The Listener* from 1935 to
1959). Again, certainty about his identity has not been helped by
his all but sharing a name with Sir Herbert Read, in his day a
much more public man. Henry Reed must have suffered too
many confusions for comfort, though he does get a wry revenge
in his cycle of radio plays about the eccentric circle of an imagi-

nary literary lion by giving the lion's much-put-upon biographer the name 'Herbert Reeve' and making a running joke of people getting it slightly wrong. Rest assured, however, that it is one indivisible Reed who plays all the roles. 'Poet, radio-dramatist, translator' is how his style runs in editions of *Who's Who* since 1977, and the fact that it ran 'poet, critic, and radio-dramatist' in earlier editions suggests that any serious account of his work must take some notice of the mass of his reviews, articles, essays, and talks, even if very few of them have found their way into hard covers. Any account of Reed's work must also be provisional, since he is – as his *alter ego* Reeve would say – 'happily still with us'. He celebrated his sixty-fifth birthday in 1979, and so presumably did Reeve, since he too was born on 22 February 1914.[2]

It is typical of Reed's taste in literature that he should have included passages from the *Agamemnon* of Aeschylus and Sophocles' *Antigone* in a *Personal Anthology* he compiled for the BBC in 1970; and it is a pointer to the formation of that taste that the translations he used in the broadcast were by Louis MacNeice and E. R. Dodds, since both men were teaching at Birmingham University when he graduated BA with a First there in 1934. Around this time Reed was writing verse and travelling, notably in Italy, and after taking his MA he went into journalism, freelancing on literature and travel for the *Birmingham Post* and *Manchester Guardian*, among others. He has said that he was glad at Birmingham to have been 'one of a group of people which included Auden and MacNeice, John Hampson and Walter Allen, the painter John Melville, the critic Robert Melville and the sculptor Gordon Herrick';[3] and one fruit of this connection is the painting of Reed by John Melville which is reproduced in the twenty-seventh *Penguin New Writing*. His poems were beginning to be published in national journals when the Second World War broke out, and in 1941, after he had taught for a year at his old school, King Edward VI's in Birmingham, he was conscripted into the Royal Army Ordnance Corps before being transferred to the Foreign Office to work in Naval Intelligence. Though his first book of verse, *A Map of Verona*, did not come out until after peace had been declared, there are at least three poems in it – making up the celebrated 'Lessons of the War' sequence – which grew out of Reed's experiences as an RAOC trainee; and even 'Chard Whitlow', the delightful T. S. Eliot parody in the same collection, is a document of the war. It was written as an entry in a *New Statesman*

competition calling for speculations as to what contributions
certain modern poets would make to *The Postscript*, the wartime
BBC's regular uplift talk after the *Nine O'Clock News* on Sunday
evenings. It may seem odd that a pastiche Eliot *Quartet*-
movement about the London Blitz which bristles with allusions
to Eliot's earlier verse should have no clear echoes of the Blitz
sections of 'Little Gidding'; but in fact 'Chard Whitlow' is prophetic of 'Little Gidding'. Reed's poem first appeared in May 1941,
and Eliot did not finish a preliminary draft of his last *Quartet* until
the June of that year.[4] As a miniature parody BBC programme,
'Chard Whitlow' is of course also prophetic of Reed's later radio
work:

> Oh, listeners,
> And you especially who have switched off the wireless,
> And sit in Stoke or Basingstoke, listening appreciatively to
>   the silence
> (Which is also the silence of hell), pray not for yourselves
>   but your souls.[5]

As the war came to an end, Reed was publishing poems, book
reviews, and a few longer critical essays such as the piece on
Thomas Hardy's *Dynasts* in the eighteenth *Penguin New Writing*.
Eventually he was able to leave Naval Intelligence *et hoc genus
omne*, or as *Who's Who* puts it: 'Released VJ day, 1945; recalled to
Army, 1945; did not go, 1945; matter silently dropped, 1945.'
From then on he lived (mainly in London and Dorset) as a Man of
Letters, one of the literate intelligentsia – often quite aggressively
so. He could for instance stress in the Introduction to his little
book on the wartime novel that 'I have written as an intellectual
addressing other intellectuals', could begin a *New Statesman*
review with 'Everybody will remember that encouraging
moment on page 108 of *Finnegans Wake* when', could publish a
sixteen-line poem in *The Listener* with the tag 'From the French of
Arnauld and the Italian of Leopardi', and could roundly declare
in the *B.B.C. Quarterly* that the launching of the Third Programme
was to be welcomed because it acknowledged 'the fact that some
listeners are fools and some are not, and that we cannot wait for
the fools to catch up with their betters'.[6] He published the *Verona*
collection in 1946, an enlarged New York edition of it in 1947, and
individual poems spasmodically up to 1950. Meanwhile he
brought out two other books which were not much more than the
tips of two icebergs in his post-war activity.

One of the books was *The Novel since 1939*. It was published for the British Council in 1946, and the Reed who wrote it was kept busy at the time as a reviewer, mainly but not exclusively of new fiction, mainly signing his pieces but also contributing extensively to the anonymous Book Chronicle in *The Listener*. As a reviewer he was not easy to please. The style was urbane but the approach highly serious; so it is interesting that the few books which he welcomed with real warmth between 1945 and 1950 should include *Brideshead Revisited, Dangling Man, The Shrimp and the Anemone* and *Titus Groan* ('I do not think I have ever so much enjoyed a novel sent me for review').[7] It is also interesting that his inwardness with the novel seems not to have led to his writing novels himself, especially when a later play of his, *Return to Naples*, has a 'wholly autobiographical' hero ambitious to be a great novelist.[8] Perhaps too much reviewing sapped the impulse, or perhaps the answer lies in Reed's profound admiration for James Joyce:

It is my tentative belief that *Ulysses* has completed the history of the novel, at all events for a time; and that there has been no great novelist to emerge since *Ulysses* appeared in 1922. There is a good deal of readable fiction still being written; as a reviewer one may praise and welcome it, for we do welcome pictures of ourselves in our own time pinned down and wriggling under competent and intelligent pens, of whom there are no fewer, probably, than at any other time. As a reviewer, one praises them, I have said; if one is able intermittently to attain to any critical sense, which it is very difficult for a reviewer to do, one is forced to disregard them. I think *Ulysses* stands as a barrier, which our novelists have not yet surmounted... I remember that Mr T. S. Eliot, writing of Virgil, suggested that he realised to the full, for the first time, the possibilities of a great language; and thereby finished it off. Can it be that James Joyce has done as much for English prose?[9]

This obituary comes from a radio talk which Reed gave in 1950, and radio was of course his other major sphere of activity in these years, as critic (on both sides of the microphone), arranger, and creative writer. He wrote the radio column for the *New Statesman and Nation* from October 1947 to February 1948, and as a broadcaster was involved in much reviewing and discussion of the arts, notably in the Sunday lunchtime programme *The Critics*. He also read his own poems on the air, selected extracts from other authors (Defoe for example) to provide interludes between Third Programme broadcasts, and in 1946 made a radio piece of his own, first in a fifteen-minute and then in a half-hour version. It was called *Noises*, and a friendly review described it as 'a short essay on the psychology of noises in which noises were used to play, wittily and suggestively, on the imagination of the listener'.[10] But the most spectacular radio project to involve him at this time was Stephen Potter's production of *Moby Dick* in January 1947, with Ralph Richardson as Captain Ahab and an ambitious orchestral score by Antony Hopkins. Reed made the adaptation, and the printing of this was his other book for the late 1940s. *Moby Dick: A Play for Radio from Herman Melville's Novel* is dedicated to Edward Sackville-West, Reed's colleague as radio critic on the *New Statesman* and the author of *The Rescue*, another radio version of a sea-dog epic – this time Homer's – which had itself been published in 1945. Like the radio scripts which Reed's friend MacNeice published about that time (*Christopher Columbus* and *The Dark Tower*), *The Rescue* and *Moby Dick* have pioneering Prefaces. The creative radio writers clearly felt the need to get a solid body of theory and practice into print. Reed himself stressed this a few years later in a combative essay in the *B.B.C. Quarterly* for 1949 called 'What the Wireless Can Do for Literature':

So far, I believe, when the radio faces us with a work of art created specially by and for it, we do not quite know what to expect from it nor quite how much of ourselves to give it. We do not know how much weight to put on our own end of the rope. Nor, usually, does the script-writer at the other end... The radio is, so far, a part of only the passive intellectual life of our time, not of the active or donative. We need not despair over this fact: it must have been equally so during the time of pre-Elizabethan drama... When all is said, the best service that the B.B.C. can do for literature – and indeed the only way in which serious radio can, in the end, keep alive – is by creating literature of its own, and by aiming not merely to create in it a specialised and separate body of eccentric and quickly fading works, but to add to the general corpus of English literature... Radio must realise that though it too [like the stage] may be the immediate medium through which a literature comes into being, even this literature will aim at a permanence beyond performance. In the last resort, the printed page must become the easily available repository of all good talk and writing... If the B.B.C. is to lose its sense of being concerned only with ephemera, its authors must be encouraged to feel that their radio-writings may have a permanent value on the printed page... I think that one of the most notable steps forward towards maturity in radio-drama is the fact that an increasing number of radio-plays are finding their way into print ... Only when an author's radio-drama is to be observed as being a part of his seriously developing *oeuvre* will radio show signs of being reliable: *then* indeed shall we know what to expect, how much to 'give' to it as we listen.[11]

On a physical level one *could* observe Reed's *Moby Dick* of 1947 as being part of his developing *oeuvre*: Jonathan Cape printed it in the same format and with the same green cover as the *Map of Verona* of 1946. But after that, no radio play of Reed's (translations apart) saw print until 1971, and this in spite of the fact that over a dozen were broadcast, of which it could be argued that several – I would venture *The Streets of Pompeii*, *The Great Desire I Had*, *A Very Great Man Indeed*, and *Vincenzo* – are radio literature of real importance.

That Reed soldiered on with them – writing, often extensively revising between broadcasts, taking a major role himself in the broadcasting of at least one of them (*The Great Desire I Had*), and winning an Italia Prize for another (*The Streets of Pompeii*) – must in part have been due to the buoyant state of the medium. Unlike the novel, it had not just been killed by a James Joyce. Significant creative talents, MacNeice and Sackville-West among them, were keeping it very much alive, and other such talents were always very welcome. Indeed, perhaps the BBC was too welcoming. For many years Reed was to give by far the greater part of his creativity to radio, so much so that, in the period between the summer of 1950 and the autumn of 1969, he published hardly any new poems, except for a free adaptation of Theocritus ('The Enchantress') made in 1951 for Arthur Bliss to set, an Aubade also set by Bliss as one of a group of modern madrigals for the 1953 Coronation, and 'The Auction Sale', a narrative poem which appeared in *Encounter* in 1958. In the same period he wrote, adapted or translated no fewer than three dozen dramatic works and feature programmes for the BBC.

His first full-length original play, *Pytheas: A Dramatic Speculation*, dates from May 1947, only four months after the *Moby Dick* adaptation, and like *Moby Dick* it has the form of a sea-quest. Pytheas, the hero, is the contemporary of Aristotle who sailed from Marseilles through the Pillars of Hercules to discover 'Ultima Thule' in the northern ocean. Two years later speculation was followed by biography in the two parts of a play about the Italian romantic poet Giacomo Leopardi: *The Unblest* of 1949, dealing with his adolescence, and *The Monument* of 1950, leading from his young manhood to his early death. Later in 1950 came

Canterbury Cathedral, whose sub-title *An Exploration in Sound* describes it well, provided 'sound' is taken to mean music and evocative studio voices rather than radiophonics and documentary material on tape. In the same year Reed contributed a piece to a series of programmes with the group title *Return Journey*: his *Return to Naples* is an autobiographical play tracing sixteen years of his relationship with a vivid and endearing Neapolitan family. In 1952 two more plays of his were given which deal with Britons and Italians in Italy, *The Streets of Pompeii* and *The Great Desire I Had*. *Pompeii* is another exploration in sound, this time of the Roman city before and after the fatal eruption and of the reactions to it of various twentieth-century tourists. *The Great Desire* is another dramatic speculation, which sends William Shakespeare to Ferrara, Verona, Padua, Venice, and Mantua in the early 1590s and has him involved there with a brilliant *commedia dell'arte* troup, the Gelosi, as vivid and endearing in their way as the family in *Return to Naples*. One more play has Mantua Castle and environs as its setting, *Vincenzo*, first broadcast in 1955 and billed in *Radio Times* as a tragi-comedy. Like the Leopardi diptych it is a dramatic biography: we follow the hero's life from his eighteenth year till his death. And like *The Great Desire I Had* the period is Late Renaissance: the hero is the Gonzaga duke Vincenzo I, patron of Claudio Monteverdi and murderer of the Admirable Crichton.

These plays of 1947 to 1955 form a group, which is overlapped in time by another and seemingly very different group of pieces written between 1951 and 1959: *A By-Election in the Nineties, A Very Great Man Indeed, The Private Life of Hilda Tablet, Emily Butter, A Hedge, Backwards, The Primal Scene, As It Were..., Not A Drum Was Heard*, and *Musique Discrète. A By-Election in the Nineties*, a study of *Realpolitik* in Victorian Wessex, has an impish mood in common with the others, but is set apart from them by its period. The others, from *A Very Great Man Indeed* to *Musique Discrète*, form a cycle – dramatic *roman fleuve* cum highbrow soap opera – although they were not at first planned as such.[12] The cycle is set in the 1950s, presupposes a great late-lamented novelist Richard Shewin (rhyming with 'go in'), and presents the circle of his surviving friends and relations. The relations comprise a widowed sister-in-law Nancy (mother to a large brood of pop-musical sons and one *Scrutiny*-reading daughter), a hugely self-pitying and Freud-fancying brother Stephen, Stephen's cat-fixated wife Connie, and Connie's brother and sister: the dotty, bell-fixated General Arthur Gland and Miss Alice Gland (who practises creative sleep). The friends range from the demi-mondaine to the very blue-blooded, but the most formidable of them is the composer Hilda Tablet, who has a memorable circle of her own: Viennese soprano companion (manic-depressive and food-fixated), very gay young secretary, tame music critic, rather less tame librettist, lachrymose Greek multi-millionaire patron, and so on. Into this singular world comes the earnest scholar Herbert Reeve, prim, proper, and very wet behind the ears; and to the extent that the series of plays has a plot at all, Reeve is at the centre of it. He has plans to write Richard Shewin's biography; but he is soon hijacked into undertaking a twelve-volume life of Hilda Tablet. He is released from this in the long run, however (while he and most of the friends and relations are enjoying a Mediterranean cruise on the millionaire's yacht), by Miss Tablet's giving the task to General Gland. *En route* to this happy outcome, and to Herbert's engagement to Nancy Shewin's daughter (who has by now deserted Dr Leavis for Melanie Klein), we are present at the premières of two masterworks: Miss Tablet's all-female opera *Emily Butter* and a posthumous play by Richard Shewin which seems to be cousin to E. M. Forster's *Maurice* and which has to be drastically rewritten before it is made safe for the Shaftes-bury Avenue of the 1950s. Then, as epilogues to the plot proper, the BBC itself is shown interviewing General Gland in an attempt to secure his war memoirs and mounting a request programme of the music of Miss Tablet, by now Dame Hilda. (Her music, and the pop-songs of Owen Shewin, were pastiched for the series by Donald Swann.)

In addition to writing his own plays, Reed was in these years involved with adapting and interpreting the work of other English-speaking writers for radio audiences. The writers ranged from Ruth Draper (four selections from her monologues) through William Plomer and Walt Whitman to Thomas Hardy. There were programmes of and about Hardy's verse, an arrangement of *The Dynasts* in six ninety-minute episodes epically transmitted by the combined forces of the BBC Features and Drama departments in one week of June 1951, and *Thomas Hardy: A Radio Portrait by His Friends*. Reed was also making a name in the 1950s as a translator and adapter for radio from the French and Italian. Notable here was his dramatisation in 1954 of Jules Laforgue's 'moral legend' *Hamlet, or The Consequences of Filial Piety*. But more often he was concerned with plays of the twentieth century, and his versions included Henry de Montherlant's *Malatesta* and *The Land Where the King Is a Child*, Luigi Pirandello's *All for the Best*, Jacques Audiberti's *Alarica* (from *Le Mal Court)* and Silvio Giovaninetti's *One Flesh*. However, the writer most closely associated with him in this respect was the Italian dramatist Ugo Betti. Betti died in 1953, and in the next eight years the BBC broadcast seven of his plays in Reed translations: *Crime on Goat Island, Irene, The House on the Water, Corruption in the Palace of Justice, Holiday Land, The Queen and the Rebels* and *The Burnt Flower-Bed*. The translations of the last three (with *Holiday Land* renamed *Summertime)* were published in 1956 as *Three Plays by Ugo Betti*. In his Foreword, Reed asserts that 'the series of thirteen plays which Betti produced between 1941 and his death in 1953 must be among the greatest creative outbursts in dramatic literature', and it seems that, for a few years at least, the theatrical impresarios were inclined to agree. Several of Reed's translations were taken over by the conventional theatre, notably in the autumn of 1955, when stage premières of 'his' *Queen and the Rebels, Summertime*, and *Burnt Flower-Bed* were given in London.

Reed's career as a translator continued through the sixties and seventies, embracing several novels (Balzac's *Père Goriot* and *Eugénie Grandet* among them) and a quantity of nineteenth- and twentieth-century Italian drama, especially works by Giacosa, Pirandello, Dino Buzzati, and Natalia Ginzburg. And though this period saw a reduction in the quantity of his written criticism, his spoken criticism must have flourished during the several academic terms of the mid-1960s he taught in Seattle as professor at the University of Washington. However, by that time he had stopped writing creatively for radio, and to date – with the exception of a reworked, more Melvillian finale to his *Moby Dick* adaption for a new production in 1979 – he has not started again. The reasons for this silence are doubtless complex, but they may well include the vexed matter of publication, and the matter of finance too. After all, he had written in 'What the Wireless Can Do for Literature' that serious radio dramatists have problems

because they are not certain of receiving the permanence of print afterwards; and the radio's rewards to the dramatic writer are almost always bound to remain, both presentationally and financially, meagre. I had hoped not to mention the finances; but they are of basic importance: a serious work of art takes much time to compose; the fees for the regulation three performances of a long radio-play are not great.[13]

Then there was possibly the matter of television: the leap to prominence of TV drama and the feeling among pioneer radio dramatists that the new, less imaginatively rewarding medium was blighting their own before radio – like pre-Virgilian Latin or the pre-Shakespearean stage – had been realised to the full. ('It is melancholy to reflect', wrote W. H. Auden in his introduction to a posthumous collection of MacNeice's plays, 'that, since the advent of television, radio drama is probably a dying art.')[14] A photograph has been published of writers at a BBC television course in 1952 grouped round the fateful screen, but it is difficult to penetrate Reed's sphinx-like expression.[15] It is easier to interpret his attitude ten years later when introducing one of his programmes of Ruth Draper's monologues. He quotes Draper as saying that it is her audience that 'must supply the imagination. All I can do myself is to make the audience give it to me. I suppose my work needs more of this than most acting does, for I give people no help in the way of scenery, lighting or stage effects.' He goes on to contrast Draper's art with cinema and television, which impoverish active imagination, and the implications for his own radio art are clear.

However, whatever the causes of his silence as original dramatist from 1959 until the present, it is ironic that he should have had to wait a dozen years before the BBC published two collections of his plays in 1971: *Hilda Tablet and Others: Four Pieces for Radio* (comprising four of the seven parts of the Shewin sequence) and *The Streets of Pompeii and Other Plays for Radio*, the other plays being the Leopardi pair, *Return to Naples*, *The Great Desire I Had*, and *Vincenzo*.[16] The *Tablet* collection is dedicated to George Painter in return for the dedication of the first volume of Painter's life of Proust (the two men had first read Proust together when schoolboys at Birmingham), and the Dedicatory Letter talks rather darkly of a biography on which Reed himself had been working for some years. The Foreword to the *Pompeii* collection discusses the difference in status between a radio script and a theatrical one, reminding the reader that 'these scripts were all written a long time ago'. Still, it was perhaps as a result of his long-time withdrawal from creative radio that Reed began to publish poems frequently again in the late sixties, mainly in *The*

Listener. The 'Lessons of the War' sequence, which stood at three poems in *A Map of Verona* and had a fourth ('Movement of Bodies') added in 1950, was completed with 'Returning of Issue' in 1970, when the five were published together in a limited edition. Seven years later, a further collection was mooted, to be called *The Auction Sale and Other Poems*. However, though mentioned in the 1977 *Who's Who*, it has yet to see print.

Reed's four careers – as poet, critic, translator, and dramatist – have something of that 'faculty of sudden appearance and sudden disappearance, with long periods of invisibility between' which Arthur Bliss in his autobiography found in Reed the man.[17] But one feels that he now might take up or extend any of them in combination with any other. And, of course, however much the four careers go their own way and have their own active and latent phases, they are the careers of one individual and cannot be wholly compartmentalised. There are overlaps, common preoccupations, shared methods. Thus the poet who hides quite a long translated Rimbaud quotation (from 'Villes') in the title poem of the *Verona* collection is the dramatist who hides even longer translated Leopardi quotations (notably from 'La Ginestra') in the Sibyl's speeches of *The Streets of Pompeii*. The lover of Greek drama who requires a decent knowledge of Sophocles from his readers if they are going to a get a great deal from poems like 'Philoctetes', 'The Interval', 'Antigone', or 'Chrysothemis' is the lover of Elizabethan drama who requires considerable knowledge of half a dozen Shakespeare plays in his listeners if they are fully to savour *The Great Desire I Had*. The writer of a British Council booklet on the English novel 1939–45 primarily so that foreigners can be helped to catch up with the best of the native product after the breakdown in communications in the 1940s is the translator from foreign tongues who communicates recent work of Audiberti, Montherlant, Giovaninetti, Paride Bombi, Samy Fayad, and Virginio Puecher to the English in the 1950s. The translator of Dino Buzzati's novel *Il Grande Ritratto* as *Larger than Life* in 1962 is also its radio dramatiser as *Zone 36* in 1965. The regular reviewer of fiction in *The Listener* and *New Statesman and Nation* is himself the creator of the novels of Richard Shewin, whose styles glance roguishly at James, Lawrence, Graham Greene *et al.*, and whose titles (*The Hot and the Cold, The Floor and the Ceiling, The Arse and the Elbow*, and so on) tap a rich vein of thirties and forties titling (*The Root and*

the Flower, The Light and the Dark, The Ballad and the Source, and so
forth). The presenter of Hardy's life, poetry, and epic-drama to
the radio audience also contributes a series of learned reviews of
Hardiana to the book pages of *The Listener,* [18] appears among the
two dozen acknowledgements in R. L. Purdy's weighty bibliographical study of Hardy, and is reliably rumoured to have made
Hardy the subject of the biography-in-progress mentioned in the
Tablet dedication. The critic who in his journalistic work so often
cites Joyce and Eliot as the true touchstones of excellence in
modern literature not only gives lengthy and searching radio
talks about them as well,[19] but also works unattributed quotations from the first part of 'The Dry Salvages' and the last part of
Finnegans Wake into the final section of his first radio piece, *Noises.*
Not content with which, he pays homage to *The Rock* and *Murder
in the Cathedral* in his Canterbury exploration and to 'The Hollow
Men' in the title of Richard Shewin's most often quoted novel,
The Bang and the Whimper, while giving a stream of consciousness
à la Molly Bloom to the feather-headed opera-singer in *Vincenzo*
and centring *The Great Desire I Had* on a Finneganesque pun on a
line from *Twelfth Night*: 'This is the heir, that is the glorious son'.
  On this fairly superficial level, Reed's work is all of a piece
throughout. But the consistency goes deeper and can perhaps tell
us something useful about the achievement of the original radio
plays which are at the centre of that work. 'His three volumes of
lyric poetry, his three collections of short stories, and his single
short novel have a distinction of their own; but they can fairly be
regarded as the marginalia to the succession of twenty-five
dramatic works which they accompanied, and whose thought
and preoccupation they echo, underline and occasionally antici-
pate.'[20] *Mutatis mutandis,* this remark of Reed's about Ugo Betti
can be applied to his own poetry, criticism, and translations as
they relate to his radio drama. And it is the plays' relationship
with the poetry which is of course the most important. For one
thing, one can only assert that Reed 'began as a poet, went on as a
dramatist and then became a poet again' if one defines 'poet'
simply as a publisher of individual poems; and even then the
assertion is not wholly accurate. With a broader definition of
poetry, it is arguable that he is as much a poet in *The Streets of
Pompeii* as in *A Map of Verona*. ('Though most of it is in prose,' he
writes in a *Radio Times* introduction to *Pompeii*, 'it has worked out
as a sort of dramatic poem.')[21] And with the narrower definition

'poetry equals verse', no one could deny that Reed the poet is in evidence in almost all the plays, since almost all are either in or contain verse.

The two Leopardi pieces are the most consistently versified. They are written in a very flexible 'sprung' pentameter throughout, and it is surely not accidental that they were first given in May 1949 and March 1950 and so flank the first performances of Eliot's *Cocktail Party* in August 1949. Significantly, when Reed gave a couple of penetrating radio talks soon afterwards on the functions of verse and prose in the theatre (especially the Shakespearean and modern theatre), he called them 'Towards *The Cocktail Party*'. 'What I want', he says in the first talk,

is the restoration of verse to its dominant position on the stage, because only thereby can the drama, I think, regain a position where it will command the respect we normally accord to the novel or to the poetry printed in books... In English, only the use of verse on the stage can elevate the drama... This elevation has been achieved with illuminating certainty and success only once in the last two hundred years, in Mr Eliot's *The Cocktail Party*. [22]

Though the sound of the Leopardi plays is only occasionally Eliotesque (since, among other things, the metre is different), Reed is clearly attempting to write them throughout in the sort of verse he describes Eliot as achieving, 'a verse equidistant between prose and poetry [which] can with equal consistency move towards the state of either'. [23] But such a verse is not the norm of Reed's drama as a whole. This is possibly because he felt that, since the radio audience's mode of listening and degree of imaginative participation are (or should be) more intense than those of a conventional theatre audience, a high degree of concentration and a proper emphasis on the spoken word can be achieved in radio without verse predominating. Be this as it may, verse is largely saved in his other plays for choric sequences or for scenes of exaltation and celebration. Thus in *Moby Dick* Reed takes away the reporting role which Melville gives young Ishmael and instead presents the action of the novel directly through an adaptation of such parts of Melville's prose as he has radio space for; but at the same time he creates an observing, reflecting choric group out of Ishmael and the godly Father Mapple and writes a series of very telling poems for them which punctuate the action and encapsulate Melville's expansive reflections on the nature of whaling, the whiteness of Moby Dick, the immensity of the

Pacific, and so on. Again, in *The Streets of Pompeii*, where ideas of fecundity and sterility, imagination and pedantry, love and death are woven together through the patterning of the experiences of a dozen Pompeian natives and visitors, several modes of speech are woven and patterned too; and they include, along with colloquial and heightened prose, a formal verse for the elegies of the Cumaean Sibyl and a more relaxed pentameter for the young lovers, Attilio and Francesca. (The lovers are even given a full-dress sonnet apiece as a soliloquy at their moment of most intense feeling.) Then in the Richard Shewin sequence, celebration almost always involves verse set to music, songs which are generally the original creations of Nancy Shewin's boys. This allows Reed the *pasticheur* to produce some memorably awful pop lyrics for Donald Swann to set, their awfulness only partly disguising the fact that they deal with subjects close to Reed's heart. Even in a play for which Reed's words are wholly in prose, intensification and crystallisation come from verse and music. The scene in *Vincenzo* where the Duke talks *sotto voce* with his illegitimate son Silvio during a court performance of the opera *Arianna* is not only a comic image of the fine flower of Renaissance civilisation growing from some pretty twisted roots. It is also a tragic image of the play as a whole. Passionate woman deserted by a lord of creation is portrayed definitively in Rinuccini's verse and Monteverdi's music; and in Reed's prose the play at large probes the feelings of a succession of such women, dazzled and deserted by Duke Vincenzo.

But it is not only the craft of verse which Reed the poet lends Reed the dramatist. The interests and attitudes of the poetry are in the drama too. Take a group of the plays in relation to a single poem, the fine narrative piece 'The Auction Sale', in which a Paduan *Mars and Venus* is sold at an English country auction to a London dealer at a higher price than a captivated young farmer can afford. The poem is set in Dorset, as – fictionalised as 'Mulset' – are the whole of *A By-Election in the Nineties* and the rural scenes of the Richard Shewin plays. The subject of the poem is a thwarted quest, which relates it (matters of scale and intensity apart) to the *Moby Dick* adaptation. It celebrates Italian Renaissance painting, as do the Giulio Romano scenes in *Vincenzo* and *The Great Desire I Had*. It is concerned, like *The Streets of Pompeii*, with the holiness of the heart's affections. It juxtaposes hard cash and high art as ironically (if not as farcically) as does Aeschylus

Aphanisis in *The Primal Scene, As It Were* . . ., planning to buy up the Elgin marbles and re-erect them in Florida. And its final section raises the characteristic Reedian lump in the throat of the ends of several of the plays, notably *The Monument*.

Again, take a group of poems in relation to a single play: the *Verona* collection of 1946 and the 'dramatic speculation' *Pytheas* of 1947. The subject of the play, Reed's first full-length original radio piece, seems at first as recherché as the substance of many of the poems seems obscure: a Greek scientist disinterred from a classical dictionary. But the play soon clarifies into what promises to be a Romantic Tale of Ships and the Sea, and so shares an ambience with several of the *Verona* poems, especially 'Sailors' Harbour', 'The Captain', and 'The Return'. Pytheas himself is a Mediterranean voyager lured northward by curiosity and imagi-nation, much as the northern voyager in the *Verona* title poem is lured southward to the Mediterranean. The evocation of the northern seas when Pytheas reaches them is similar to the sea-scapes in the 'Tintagel' sequence; and when Pytheas' companion Ctesiphon builds fantasies round the classical names of the crew members during the voyage, he is only following the example of his creator in such poems as 'Chrysothemis' and 'Philoctetes' (though his intentions are certainly different). Pytheas and Ctesiphon themselves – the one all questing idealism, the other all pragmatic immediacy – have a yin–yang relationship as polar as that of the dreamy private soldier and the RAOC instructor in 'Naming of Parts'. At the end of their journey they come, not to the tin-mines which Pytheas' commercial backers in Massilia have sent him to find, but to Thule, the ultimate place, a 'sharp black rock in the ice' which has a twin in Reed's Antarctic explora-tion poem 'South'. So, instead of tin, Pytheas will take the image of Ultima Thule back to his countrymen as a symbol:

> At the end of a hill-road; and at the end of a life;
> And at the end of a love; and at the end of youth;
> And at the end of evening. Here can be there for them.
> In taking report of this place, I only take them
> A name for a place which they have always known.[24]

In its highly circumstantial build-up to a climax of pure symbol-ism, the play is of a piece with Reed's long poem, 'The Place and the Person', with its very detailed narrative of a sinister dance and phantom ship which turn out to be essentially symbolic.

However, in *Pytheas* the solemn symbolic climax is preceded by comic antimasque: Pytheas and his crew land in a pantomime Ancient Britain and encounter (among other even wilder anachronisms) a shaggy chieftain who greets them with a Beowulfese harangue, a parodic *tour de force* from the ghost-writer of 'Mr Eliot's Sunday Evening Postscript'. Finally, the whole play is framed and interrupted by the choric conversations of a twentieth-century brother and sister who speculate freely in rhyming hexameters about Pytheas' experiences; and this way of mediating between legend and audience is akin to the presentation of the myth in 'Antigone', a poem Reed published in a 1947 *Penguin New Writing*, where one anonymous witness interrogates another about the martyrdom of the princess.

However, if *Pytheas* echoes Reed's earlier poetry, it also foreshadows aspects of his later drama. For instance, it has (in common with the *Moby Dick* adaptation of the same year) a questing voyager for a hero and a narrative chorus of two voices to give it a graspable shape. In almost all of his later plays Reed again uses choric narration in one form or another, and as for voyaging, he is a most assiduous courier. In *The Great Desire I Had* he escorts Shakespeare to five different Italian cities, and in *Return to Naples* takes 'H', his younger self, to the same city five times. He guides us with great care round the cathedral at Canterbury (outside first, then in) and round the ruins at Pompeii too, counterpointing plausible itineraries for four different groups of tourists and a resident lizard. At the climax of *The Monument* he gives the two selves of Giacomo Leopardi, man and boy, a vision of the cities which have meant so much to him in his two plays –

GIACOMO. My birthdays have all slipped from me.
LEOPARDI. And all the cities are silent under the sun,
          Florence and Pisa, Rome and Bologna, peaceful.
GIACOMO. And Recanati and Naples are here in the sun!

– and in *The Primal Scene, As It Were* ... he reverses the route of Pytheas to Ultima Thule, geographically, symbolically, and in dramatic tone, as most of the notables of the Richard Shewin cycle make their way back by yacht to the ruins of Ancient Greece. *Pytheas* also casts a forward shadow psychologically. In his voyage up the Atlantic coast, Pytheas is able to spy on the wild mysteries of an island of naked Bacchantes:

> Amnis, that small mysterious isle
> Wholly forbidden to men, and echoing through the night
> To the shrieks of maddened women in a secret mystical rite.

It is perhaps from their tribe that the variously formidable women of the later plays come: the monstrously repressive Countess Adelaide Leopardi, the gusty, domineering, mannish Hilda Tablet, and the stupendous Bianca Cappello, the only woman publicly to get the better of Vincenzo Gonzaga. More certainly the Quixote–Sancho relationship between Pytheas and Ctesiphon, questing intellectual and cheerful sensualist, announces a theme on which several later works play variations: the anxious Shakespeare and his 'dear transcendent child of the morning', Thomas Shewin; the tormented hunchback genius Leopardi and the sunny, straightforward man of the world Ranieri; the buttoned-up scholar Herbert Reeve and Miss Tablet's cheerfully homosexual secretary Evelyn –

REEVE. Don't . . . don't lean on my shoulder, Evelyn, there's a good chap.
EVELYN [*gently*]. Ticklish?

– and 'H' in *Return to Naples* earnestly reading Freud in a bookshop while one of the Neapolitan boys he is staying with couples uncomplicatedly with an Austrian girl friend ('twice'). In the brown-limbed Pytheas' discovery of a harmonious peace in remotest England, we may even find the beginnings of the idea of a happy adoption by a group of strangers which recurs in Reed's work: Shakespeare being drawn into the world of the Gelosi; Leopardi and 'H' each gaining a Neapolitan family; Herbert Reeve being absorbed into the Shewin–Tablet clan and eventually marrying Janet, the great novelist's niece.

Generically speaking, however, *Pytheas* is not so typical of Reed's other radio work. It is too volatile in tone. The realistic, the symbolic, the parodic, the introverted, the ancient, the modern, the grave, and the gay are there in fairly equal proportions. The other plays tend either to be predominantly funny (*A By-Election in the Nineties*, the Shewin cycle) or to be predominantly straight-faced (*Canterbury Cathedral*, the Melville and Hardy adaptations, the plays set in Italy). This is not to say that the predominantly straight-faced plays do not have some very funny scenes. Even the gravest of them, the Leopardi diptych, has room for a delightful pastiche of bad Italian translations of Shakespeare. Nor is it to claim that 'straight-faced' and 'funny' are particularly imposing

critical terms. 'Tragic' and 'comic' would certainly be more reson-
ant, and if only because Reed's own criticism so often returns to
concepts of tragedy and comedy, it is tempting to use them.
'Tragic' especially is a term of highest praise from Reed the
reviewer; but he is aware of the rarity of the truly tragic, and so we
should not assume that we shall find it in his own original work.
As a dramatist, his own most direct investment in tragedy is
probably through his adaptations and translations: *Moby Dick*,
The Dynasts, some of the Betti pieces. Indeed, he describes Betti in
his Foreword to *Three Plays* as 'a dramatist whose unusual maturity of vision gives us pity and terror, where we normally find only
their modern substitutes, pathos and hysteria'; and he extends
the idea in a soliloquy he gives the Shakespeare of *The Great
Desire I Had* as he ponders the writing of tragedy: 'One is alone
with it, as one is alone with it in life. Not, I suspect, that it ever
happens in life. We confuse it with grief and loss and exile, with
the breaking of the heart and the death or departure of the
beloved... which are only minor ailments.' Pathos, hysteria,
grief, loss, exile, and heartbreak are powerfully present in *The
Unblest* and *The Monument*, in the eruption scenes of *The Streets of
Pompeii*, and in the experiences of Margherita Farnese and the
choric ladies of *Vincenzo*. The presentation is compassionate,
elegiac, humane, touching, rather than grandly tragic. And as for
the grandly comic, several of Reed's plays have all the wit, satiric
zest, and/or underlying warmth for the form, yet are not in the
high comic league because of their episodic nature, their lack of
ambitious intrigue. It is significant that Reed himself calls the
published selections from the Shewin cycle not plays at all, but
rather *pieces* for radio.

So perhaps 'straight-faced' and 'funny' will be allowed to serve
to designate what clearly are two distinct streams of Reed's
dramatic work, the work (in Roy Walker's phrase) of the Thinking Reed and the Winking Reed.[25] What determines the difference between the streams is Reed's characterisation of his choric
narrators, which is why *Pytheas* is generically untypical. There the
brother and sister who narrate may at any moment be roguish:

> SHE. It is said they landed in Cornwall.
> HE.   It is said they landed in Kent.
> SHE. There are many conflicting reports of the places to
>   which they went.
> HE. It is said they wintered in England;

SHE.   That they also summered there.
HE. It is said that the weather was filthy;
SHE.   It is said that the weather was fair.
HE. One can imagine the wild rough hills, the roadless
    plains, the bogs.
SHE. One can imagine no end of bogus dialogues.

Or they may be high-Eliotesque:

HE. And there at last he stood, Pytheas at the world's end.
    Was it Orkney?
SHE.   Was it Norway?
HE.   It does not matter. The end
    Has various places to be; and this was the world's end.
SHE. Pytheas, the brown-limbed Greek; Pytheas at the
    world's end.
HE. And an end from which one returns is nevertheless an
    end.

The later plays, on the other hand, are either hosted chorically by
figures of consistent fun (the orotund narrator of *A By-Election*,
Herbert Reeve and sundry BBC personnel in the Richard Shewin
cycle) or by figures we take quite seriously: the eloquent, not to
say aureate, narrators of *Canterbury Cathedral* and *The Great
Desire*, Reed's mature self in *Return to Naples*, the Sibyl and the
Traveller in *Pompeii*, the soliloquising poet in the Leopardi plays,
and some of the Duke's ladies in *Vincenzo*.

The plays of the Thinking Reed – those included in the *Pompeii*
collection at least – are a close-knit group, for all their variety of
tone, town, period, and language (language which runs from the
impressive Sybilline oracles of *The Streets of Pompeii* itself to the
fluently naturalistic chats and scats of *Return to Naples*). Of course
Italy helps to unify the plays: Reed describes them in his Foreword as 'memorials, however ephemeral, to the love I have
always felt for her'. Twenty-five years before, he had declared
that 'it is a tempting preciosity to say that the Englishman's
education and sensibility are incomplete without Mediterranean
experience. It is also a palpable falsity; they are equally incomplete without experience of the South Seas, China, Russia and
India. But to the English artist (to say nothing of anyone else) Italy
has a strange power of benediction.'[26] The degree of benediction
communicated to the listener varies from one play to another, but
then they have more than simple geography to link them. For
instance, Reed fashions climaxes for all of them which, however

different in mood, raise a similar lump in the throat. Shake-speare's elation at a future of fulfilment across a knife-edge of risk; the pathos of Margherita Farnese as Vincenzo Gonzaga's death condemns her a second time to the arms of the Church; the brave compassion of Monaldo Leopardi's decision that his son shall go to Rome and the mingled triumph and defeat of Giacomo Leopardi's death; the solace for 'H' in the awareness of his adopted family's perennial welcome; the sense of a transcendent love when a young Italian couple and an elderly English one speak to each other in the dusk at Pompeii: these things are presented with a common warmth and humanity which come within an ace of sentimentality without actually succumbing. Again, the ordering of the plays in the *Pompeii* collection chains them firmly together. First comes the Leopardi diptych which bites its own tail, so to speak, in that it ends with a powerful scene of the poet at the moment of his death carried back to his happy childhood. The death-scene is set near Mount Vesuvius, where the historical Leopardi wrote one of his last poems, an elegy for the citizens of the buried Pompeii, so it is apt that the Leopardi plays should be followed by *The Streets of Pompeii*, especially since in it the Sibyl comes from the shades at Cumae to speak choruses which translate lines from Leopardi's poem ('La Ginestra') and also from his 'Chorus of the Dead'.[27] Reed's dead city is visited by English tourists and Italian lovers (contrasted rather as in Fors-ter's *A Room with a View*); and *Return to Naples*, the play which follows *Pompeii* in the collection, is concerned (rather as is Fors-ter's *Where Angels Fear To Tread*) with a young Englishman's visits to an Italian family. At the very end of the *Return* Virgil and Leopardi are both evoked, which glances back to the Cumaean Sibyl at Pompeii; but the fact that the young Englishman has ambitions to be a great writer leads us on to the next play, *The Great Desire I Had*, where William Shakespeare, determined to write an epic on the fall of Troy, comes to the northern Italy of the 1590s for inspiration and a respite from the Globe and his 'dear, brave Anne'. The final scene of *The Great Desire* has Shakespeare waiting in an anteroom at the Gonzaga palace in Mantua, dis-daining to attend a performance by the Gelosi troupe of a magical play which strikingly pre-echoes *The Tempest* ('Did you ever in your life hear of such...*trash?*') and finding himself argued out of the great desire he has to be the English Homer by a total stranger, who is revealed after the event to be Vincenzo Gonzaga himself, just returned unexpectedly from Vienna.[28] This scene leads naturally to the final play, *Vincenzo*, though in it the great artists at the Mantuan court are less verbal: Rubens only ventures a deferential monosyllable and Monteverdi does not speak at all.

Equally and more obviously, the Shewin plays of the Winking Reed make a group. Not that he was the first to take as leitmotiv the establishing of the facts of an artist's life. There were *The Aspern Papers*, *The Quest for Corvo*, and *Cakes and Ale*, the last doubtless especially interesting to Reed the intending biographer of Thomas Hardy in that it was generally believed that Hardy's circle provided Maugham with some of his characters. There was also one of Vladimir Nabokov's first English novels, which Reed reviewed just after the war:

In *The Real World of Sebastian Knight*, a novelist who comes to us with the blessing of Mr Edmund Wilson, does what Mr Maugham has done in one way or another several times already. He attempts to reconstruct the life of an imaginary famous artist, who has been misrepresented by another biographer. He collects material here and there, and unfolds his version with a cunning casualness. Unfortunately, neither Sebastian nor the other characters comes to life, and the amount of incident in the book is extraordinarily small. And though the outlines of Sebastian's books are engaging, the specimens of his prose which Mr Nabokov is daring enough to show us do not suggest a great writer. Nevertheless...one feels curiosity about Mr Nabokov's other novels, several of which apparently exist in Russian.[29]

Whether or not Reed remembered Sebastian when he started *A Very Great Man Indeed*, he certainly gave any demonstration of Richard Shewin's 'greatness' a wide berth by making all the specimens of his prose parodic of different twentieth-century authors. (Joyce is a significant exception, but then instead – as far as one can work out – Shewin more or less shares Joyce's dates of birth and death.) The greatness of Shewin is as much an unknown quantity as his true character in these plays. Their focus, at least until Hilda Tablet intervenes, is what we can learn from a naive scholar's investigations about the genteel-bohemian intellectual world Shewin left behind; and Miss Tablet's intervention serves to open the world out by enabling her unwilling Boswell to meet that many more artists, critics, gentry, and professionals. Although the amount of incident in the plays is as small as in Nabokov's novel, the characters certainly do come vividly alive, helped by obsessions which spring in part from Freud and in part from traditional farce, and by catch-phrases which recall Tommy Handley's *ITMA* of the 1940s: General Gland's 'Say?', Stephen Shewin's 'A hedge, a dartboard', the 'I shall go back to Vienna' of Hilda Tablet's resident soprano, Elsa Strauss.[30] Of course, someone writing such a cycle now would doubtless not make so much play with the *roman à clef*, psychoanalysis, Schönbergian serialism, *musique concrète* (*renforcée* in Hilda Tablet's case), girls' public schools and the little idiosyncrasies of BBC Radio. Genteel intellectual bohemia is not what it was, and listeners in the 1980s may well find something quaint about a world where Karl Marx is never mentioned, where American culture, the cinema, and television hardly impinge, and where the pop music (though 'faintly terrifying' according to one stage direction) now seems very thin gruel. But that world is recorded with real wit in these plays, as when the Duchess of Mulset quizzes Mr Reeve about Miss Tablet's latest opera –

DUCHESS. You know the score of *Emily Butter* backwards, I'm sure, Sir Herbert.
REEVE. Well, only the parts of it that are played backwards, of course.

– and monomania, lack of self-knowledge, hypocrisy, the crossed purpose, and the tensions between public and private morality are comic springs which do not date.

How far the considerable bawdiness of the cycle dates is hard to say. Reed's Freudian-farcical view of a society which affected pretty strict notions of propriety (particularly on Reithian radio) leads to much outrageous fun being had with cracking of taboos and hintings at the unmentionable. So it is with Stephen Shewin's castration-complex, for example ('he knew as well as I did that I *had* a you-know-what'), and with Miss Tablet's lesbianism ('for ee mus' unnerstand, sir, as *Miss Ilda were hall-ways a bit of a tom-boy*'). On a larger scale, the whole intrigue of one of the pieces (*A Hedge, Backwards*) is built round the première of Shewin's Rattiganesque play about A Certain Subject, the climactic line of which – 'The law may be against us, but ordinary people aren't' – becomes splendidly bizarre when most of the play has been rewritten to conform with heterosexual norms. *The Primal Scene, As It Were...* even has a double entendre for a title (as do at least three of Reed's five 'Lessons of the War'). To Herbert Reeve and most of the passengers on Aeschylus Aphanisis' yacht the *Jokasta*, the 'primal scene' is the Mediterranean cradle of their civilisation; but to the amateur Kleinian psychoanalyst Janet Shewin who eventually marries Herbert, it is Freud's term for an infant's traumatic perception of its parents' sexual intercourse, the parents in Herbert's case being represented by Richard Shewin and Hilda Tablet (though which as father and which as mother Janet is not absolutely sure).

This is the Winking Reed indeed, but the wink throughout the Shewin cycle is quite a genial one. The plays are farcical and satiric, but the satire is not harsh or cynical or dismissive. Take the redoubtable 'composeress' herself. Miss Tablet is certainly something of a monster of egotism and imposition; in Donald Swann's variably successful 'realisations' of it, her music comes over as parodying everything from Tchaikovsky to Webern; and *à clef* she seems to be a blend of Dame Ethel Smyth (the mannish dress, boisterous feminism, gentrified parents, and fondness for soldiers), Elizabeth Lutyens (the bohemian life-style and the pioneering of English serialism), and Benjamin Britten (the love-life and fondness for single-sex operas).[31] But she is evidently a genuine creator (and so a *sacred* monster); her parodic music is simply the equivalent of Richard Shewin's novels; Reed's script describes her significantly as having a warm and jolly voice; and we have no reason to assume that Reed disapproved of her 'models', if such they be. Indeed, his admiration for Britten's work is on record, he collaborated with Lutyens over *Canterbury Cathedral*, he must have known his friend Edward Sackville-West's lively and admiring memoir of Smyth, and in an essay on Edith Sitwell's poetic development he writes understandingly about the plight of the woman artist.[32] Again, one does not have to look long at Reed's recorded activities in the 1950s (when the Shewin cycle was being written) to see how close to his own is the world of Herbert Reeve. Reeve is engaged on the biography of a great novelist and so is Reed. Reeve interviews all the contacts he can find and reports on them – a self-centred lot, by and large – over the air; Reed presents an anthology of recorded memories for the BBC called *Thomas Hardy: A Radio Portrait by His Friends*, observing that it is 'characteristic of a great deal of utterance on Hardy' that 'people prefer... to talk at length about themselves'. Reeve tangles with an energetic 'composeress' in search of a libretto and meets her former librettist Harold Reith (note the initials); Reed collaborates with Elizabeth Lutyens on music for radio drama and writes two texts for Arthur Bliss to set, one of them an operatic *scena*. Reeve is involved in the West End rehearsals of a play by a hero of his; Reed has three of his Betti translations staged there in one season. Reeve is in Athens when Evelyn Baxter picks up a Greek boy, as is Reed when Joe Ackerley picks up another.[33] Reeve is attached to a girl who is at first a devotee of *Scrutiny* and then cleaves to Melanie Klein's brand of Freudianism, with its patois of 'splitting off', 'good objects', 'the depressive position'; Reed writes in the *B.B.C. Quarterly* in 1949 that he would like the Third Programme to include at one end of its range 'the standards and tastes of a journal like the admirable *Scrutiny*' and announces in *The Listener* in 1961 that 'I am a Kleinian myself; I have been, for some years'. (He tells us that he has put Mrs Klein's *Narrative of a Child Analysis* 'on the same shelf as *Finnegans Wake* and *War and Peace*, with which it seems to me to have more than mere size and difficulty in common'.)[34]

The blackest view which one can reasonably take of these plays is not that they are malicious caricatures of a world alien to their author, but that they are sharp self-mockery. Reed's own account of Rimbaud's *Saison en Enfer* would be relevant:

It is a painful and complex work... Here are the deep grief and desolation of someone who has come to the simultaneous end of several quests whose quarries have proved to be illusory and despicable. The eye that regards these distresses is capable of the malignest self-satire, is indeed incapable of ignoring the elements of the farcical, the contemptible and the grotesque in them.[35]

But even this is surely too black for the Shewin cycle. A closer analogy to Reed-as-Reeve can be found in the touching passage in *The Great Desire I Had* (full of forward glances to *Othello*) where the comedienne Isabella Andreini describes to Shakespeare her husband's creation of his famous Braggart Captain:

Guglielmo, it is very easy, I know, for English travellers to think that our comedy is artificial and exaggerated, that my husband's Captain Spavento, for example, is only a ridiculous artificiality, because it makes you all laugh so much. But do you think it is founded on nothing?... Everybody laughs when Francesco rants about the base Phrygian Turks and the anthropophagi... But Francesco *knows* about those things. He fought against the Turks as a child, as a soldier in the Tuscan galleys; he was taken into slavery by them and sold to whoever asked for him... He would talk about those things for hours on end, seriously and truthfully, long before the idea of making fun of them on the stage occurred to him. You see only what he has made of them, something to laugh at. I laugh too, but I also see buried beneath it, beneath all the rant and fantasy, the young man who made me fall in love with him as he told me of them.

Captain Spavento is an Othello viewed ironically, Othello a Spavento seen with compassion. In the same way the Thinking Reed at his most intense and the Winking Reed at his most roguish are members one of the other. This is so not just because the straight-faced plays are often funny and the funny ones often concerned with serious issues, but also and more importantly because the two genres have so much common substance, in minute particulars and broad themes. One could instance a tiny turn of phrase: the way both Maddalena Pelzet and Hilda Tablet in *The Monument* and *The Private Life* use 'I like you for saying that' to manipulate their menfolk. Or a name: the apparent descent of the Very Great Man Indeed in the Shewin cycle from the Thomas Shewin of *The Great Desire I Had* ('Thomas Shewin' being a near-anagram of 'what's-his-name').[36] Or a recurring idea: the idea of castration, for example, so dear to the Aristophanic–Freudian mind. Stephen Shewin's fear of stepping off a moving staircase; the dear dotty old Pantalone Pasquati's refusal of the fatal knife which would have preserved his golden voice; the Duchess of Mulset's acknowledgement that although 'we've all *dreamed* of reviving the *castrati* . . . it's needed Hilda to take the first practical steps towards making them a reality': jokey as these are, they connect psychologically with the virtual unmanning of Leopardi by his tyrannical mother and the prospect of life-long thraldom to Hilda Tablet (with attendant dreams of being eaten by her) from which Herbert Reeve narrowly escapes as the lady lights on the *Lysistrata* as the subject of her next operatic triumph. As we have already seen, Hilda Tablet and Adelaide Leopardi are members of a tribe of domineering women who are no respecters of whether a play is a thinking or a winking piece. Equally unconcerned with genre are those other groups of characters which recur from *Pytheas* on: the voyagers to foreign parts, the clans who bring happiness to an outsider by adopting him, the pairs of antithetical men. To these could be added the bevies of spontaneous, lovable children who crop up in various plays: Bruno, Alberto, Leo, and Simone in *Return to Naples*, Nancy's brood in the Shewin cycle, and the precocious young Leopardis who bring such gaiety to the beginning of *The Unblest* (a gaiety which hardly returns in the rest of the diptych until the very end of *The Monument*, when it is the more intense for being regained on the tormented poet's deathbed).

Though Leopardi's torments are presented powerfully enough, the two plays about him were first billed in *Radio Times* as 'Studies of the Italian poet'; and this is a pointer to another characteristic of much of Reed's drama regardless of genre, its unabashed literacy and air of deep learning. Like Reed the critic in *The Novel since 1939*, Reed the dramatist is an intellectual talking to intellectuals. He is also an Eliot afficionado who once wondered 'whether very many people feel that their education began as my own did, with the notes to *The Waste Land*'.[37] So it should be no surprise that most of his plays are either adaptations of great literature or allude extensively to it in various ways or present Portraits of the Artist as a Young Man or mount quests for the truth about the life of the artist in maturity. Further, several plays either show scholars in operation or seem themselves to be highly scholarly; and if the scholars – young Leopardi deforming himself in his father's library, Herbert Reeve, MacFarlane and MacBride in *The Streets of Pompeii* – all tend to be self-punishing or frustrated or pedantic, then equally Reed's own scholarship is not quite as dazzling as it appears. (He makes no bones about this in the Foreword to the *Pompeii* collection, where he records his gratitude for 'the learning of others, which I have stolen, adapted, malformed, sometimes inverted, and almost invariably fantasised over'; and there is certainly not much solid information about, say, the Gelosi troupe in the *The Great Desire* which cannot be found in Kathleen Lea's *Italian Popular Comedy* of 1934, or about Duke Vincenzo which does not appear in 'Il Duca nel Laborinto', the third part of Maria Bellonci's *Segreti dei Gonzaga* of 1947.) With the dramatist's literacy goes his imaginative involvement in the performing arts, and this generates a remarkable number of performances-within-the-performance in Reed's radio work, thinking and winking: the première of Richard Shewin's *opus posthumous* in *A Hedge, Backwards*, Monteverdi's *Arianna* in *Vincenzo*, the hustings in *A By-Election*, Miss Tablet's Shewin Sonata in *A Very Great Man Indeed* and her all-female opera in *Emily Butter*, the sermon in *Moby Dick*, the poetry recital and Act V of *Othello* in *The Monument*, glees and cookery-talks in *Pytheas* (to say nothing of a cantata of Bacchantes), *commedia dell'arte* at Mantua and readings from *The Taming of the Shrew* at Venice in *The Great Desire*, and so on. It is a sign of the high culture of most of Reed's characters that they are never happier than when talking about such things, which as often as not means talking *during* them.

For much of the time, then, the two Reeds take the same material ('love...art...scholarship...the classical heritage', as Herbert Reeve puts its in *The Primal Scene)* and treat it in complementary ways. 'It has been well said', Reed the reviewer once wrote in *The Listener,* 'that it would need a Henry James to do justice to the friends and correspondents of Rilke. There are, however, moments when one thoughtfully puts it to oneself that Mr James Thurber might serve equally well.'[38] Reed the dramatist is both Thurber and James, both Sancho and Quixote, both Ctesiphon and Pytheas. For instance James–Quixote–Pytheas evokes Venice in *The Great Desire I Had:*

The gondolas slide on the fluttering water, a million glances of light sustaining them. A million flames of coolness dance from the sea to her bright palaces. She awaits complacently, the Adriatic whore, her centuries of lovers; they will die in her arms and their flowery hearses will float down the Great Canal.

Thurber–Sancho–Ctesiphon responds in *The Primal Scene*:

Even now as we contemplated the blue waters of the incomparable lagoon flowing from the church of Santa Maria della Salute along the esplan...the front...the...that part of the sea-girt city that...faces the sea – the water of the blue lagoon lapping and...flowing as far as Santa...San...the church at the other end. There was something about her that would have inspired even the most sluggish pen.

The contrasts between the plays, between scenes within single plays and even occasionally between different levels of the same scene (as in the *Othello* episode in *The Monument),* rise from the double vision of Reed the sensitive, observant intellectual, intensity and compassion balancing scepticism and irony. It is not for nothing that his most famous poem, 'Naming of Parts', should be lyrical, satiric, meditative, and risqué all at the same time or that it should involve two voices which contrast with each other yet are very tightly knit together. It may also not be for nothing that, when Reed published a piece on 'The Making of *The Dynasts'* in 1943 (the year after the first appearance of 'Naming of Parts'), it should include a careful account of the Chorus of Hardy's epic-drama: those Phantom Intelligences whose 'comment and debate is itself a drama, with its own climax, which weaves its way about the historical action'.[39] Two of the chief Intelligences are the Spirit of the Pities and the Spirit Ironic, and it is these Spirits who pull Reed the dramatist one way or the other.

The presence of a divided, argumentative chorus in a work he so much admired and eventually adapted for broadcasting may have influenced Reed in developing a personal solution to the problem of preventing the narrative parts of his own radio drama from becoming awkward or obtrusive. His solution is to ensure that the narration 'is itself a drama', or at the least is wholly dramatic. The preacher and the sailor in *Moby Dick*, the brother and sister in *Pytheas*, the formidable Sibyl and more urbane Traveller in *Pompeii*, the two enthusiastic connoisseurs gently arguing their way round Canterbury Cathedral: these duos take away the blandness and buttonholing of conventional narration, as do the grave antics of the BBC personnel in *Emily Butter, Not a Drum Was Heard*, and *Musique Discrète*. Even in those plays with a single narrator, there is a saving dramatic tension. The aureate narrations of *The Great Desire* are counterpointed with the more informal soliloquies of Guglielmo Shakespeare; the Narrator of *Return to Naples* is the older self of 'H', the central figure, and addresses him, not us, throughout; and the pompous inter-locutor of *A By-Election in the Nineties* is clearly a part of the satiric parade, as of course is the Herbert Reeve who introduces four of the Shewin plays.

The most virtuosic choric narration, however, is in *Vincenzo*, where Eleonora, Ippolita, Agnese, and Adriana – a wife and three mistresses of the Duke – take turns in framing those different parts of his history which particularly concern them. The pure technique here, even apart from the insight into aspects of human love, is impressive. As a whole, Reed's radio work is not especially innovative at a technical level. He seems largely con-tent with the classical BBC mode of the 1940s: instrumental mood-music, 'placing' sound effects, the cross-fade, aural pers-pective by way of distance from the microphone, vivid vocal characterisation (most memorably perhaps in the Lizard of *The Streets of Pompeii*), and free exploration of space and time balanced by careful structuring of the total programme. Reed uses the mode with restraint (after a preliminary jamboree in *Noises*) and also with resource; for instance, holding back from his sightless audience until the last and most poignant moment the revelation that young Leopardi has become a hunchback, and holding back indefinitely the crucial details of the screen at Miss Tablet's parish church of Mull Extrinseca:

RECTOR. And that's the new altar screen she gave us; the subject's a bit unusual for a church, as you can see, rather unusual. Artistic, of course, but rather unusual.

REEVE. My word, yes, it is, rather.

RECTOR. Rather unusual for a *church*. And if you step outside again for a minute you can see the two new finials she gave us for the porch...

But there is little in Reed's work to extend the medium (with a few fine local exceptions like the reprising multivoice montage at the end of *The Monument* and the deliciously silly solo montage in *Vincenzo*: Adriana the Neapolitan *diva* in the foreground streaming her consciousness of simultaneous affairs with the Duke and his son while in the background she sings an *exalté* duet with herself). Little, that is to say, apart from the use of choric narration. This must be Reed's most individual contribution to the technique of radio; and the fact that it is at its most complex in the later scenes of *Vincenzo* where the Joycean–radiophonic Adriana also has her moments of glory makes these scenes in some ways the richest of his oeuvre.

If one asks finally what is the most individual contribution of the oeuvre to the *mythology* of radio, a simple answer is less easy to find. The creation of a twentieth-century *grande dame* in the Wishfort–Malaprop–Bracknell line? The contriving in *Pompeii* of a dramatic poem of Hardy-like substance and strength ('The Convergence of the Twain' and 'In Time of "The Breaking of Nations"' married, so to speak, and honeymooning in the Bay of Naples)? Perhaps. But perhaps also the memorable celebration of Giving Up the Quest. The quest-motif itself is hardly unique to Reed, but his specialisation in Quests Thwarted, Quests Diverted, and Quests Abandoned is individual. His first large-scale pieces, *Moby Dick* and *Pytheas*, rehearse the theme. Pytheas is sent by the Massilians on a quest for trade, but it is really the song of the wind which draws him, and when he gets to Britain he realises that his is a different quest: 'All my life I have wanted a ship. All my life I have wanted to explore deep into an unknown world: that which now opens, perhaps illimitably, before me. It is not trade I am after; it is not gold or slaves. I want to go on to the end.' This good diverting of the quest is something Starbuck in *Moby Dick* dearly wishes for his captain, but Ahab cannot master his obsession with the white whale:

STARBUCK. Oh, my Captain, my Captain! Noble soul and grand old heart!
Why should anyone give chase to that hated fish? Away with me! Let
us fly these deadly waters, this instant let me alter course!...

AHAB. What is it, what nameless inscrutable, unearthly thing is it; what
cozening hidden lord and master, and cruel remorseless emperor
commands me, that against all natural lovings and longings, reck-
lessly makes me ready to do what in my own, proper, natural heart I
durst not so much as dare?

In later plays this idea of doing great things in a dubious quest is
set in the framework of the art world, where it is blended with the
idea of the Writing Block: the not-being-really-able-to-get-
started of the would-be great novelist 'H' in *Return to Naples;* the
'there they all are, gargling away: I can't, as it were, get 'em
down' of a Hilda Tablet deprived for once of inspiration in the
middle of a *Lysistrata* duet at the very end of *Musique Discrète.*
Shakespeare has such a block in *The Great Desire I Had.* He comes
questingly to Italy to escape from theatrical hackwork: 'I hope
that at last I can make some headway with an epic poem on the
Siege of Troy...a poem of dazzling richness with Hector and
Achilles so close to the reader that he could all but smell their
flesh.' But the mastering obsession that says to him 'I am the
Siege of Troy: you have still not written me' only produces
creative impotence; and it takes a chance meeting with the potent
Vincenzo Gonzaga to make him realise that he should Give It Up.

Vincenzo, a less earnest but more successful Starbuck, cures
Shakespeare's self-wounding idealisation of the Great Poem. In
the Richard Shewin sequence, the novelist's psychoanalytic
niece Janet is Herbert Reeve's good angel in a similar way. Herbert is prepared to spend a rather shrivelled lifetime pursuing
Shewiniana through the jungles of literary bohemia, but the
quest is thwarted by Hilda Tablet's imposition of a biography of
herself, with 'epic scope', in twelve volumes. ('But not *more* than
twelve, Bertie, I beg you. For the love of God, no more than that.
It was good enough for Gibbon, it was enough for Proust. Let it
be enough for you, Bertie.') Soon Herbert is having bad dreams
about Miss Tablet and revenge-fantasies about Richard Shewin
while getting nowhere with writing the life of either. Janet diag-
noses Compulsive Postponement caused by Schizophrenic Idealisation and starts to work on Herbert when farce intervenes and
Miss Tablet takes her *Life* out of his hands, putting it into those of
the scholar–soldier Arthur Gland. But Janet's analysis is, in its

own terms, admirably shrewd, and Reed the Kleinian is certainly not lampooning her. (It is heartening to find that, in *Not A Drum Was Heard*, Herbert can give a firm No to General Gland when he asks for help with ghosting his splendidly fatuous war memoirs.)

That Janet is talking Reed's own language comes over in his critical work: most interestingly perhaps in a review of Jean-François Revel's *As for Italy* in 1960, since there Reed's view of that country is as antithetic to his other accounts of its lovability as the tone of his second Veronese poem, 'The Town Itself', is to that of 'A Map of Verona':

The germs of a capacity for schizophrenic idealisation are probably to be found in all but the very sanest people. Nothing illustrates this tendency better than the attitude that many English, French and German tourists preserve towards the pleasant land of Italy...M. Revel tells us that he too has had his narcissistic feelings for Italy. But, my word, he does not have them now! The idealised object has become an internal perse-cutor...I have known and loved Italy – whatever one means by that name – for many years. I think I do still. But to anyone who actually contemplates going there for the first time, all I can say, and that with caution, is that the place may well prove worth a visit; though after reading M. Revel's book, and agreeing with a good deal of it, I must be pardoned if I am momentarily at a loss to suggest quite why.[40]

Giving Up the Quest if it is a misguided one is not an idea restricted to the plays. It is to be found in Reed's work outside them; perhaps in his life too. His earliest important critical essay appeared in 1943 with the significant title, 'The End of an Impulse'. Its burden is that Thirties Poetry as a genre is writing itself out and would be well advised to shut up shop altogether. Is it not better to choose silence than go on writing for writing's sake? Reed quotes Rilke's *Letters to a Young Poet*, pointing out that the young poet in question

is now hardly known save as the recipient of these replies. It is small wonder indeed that Herr Kappus is almost unknown as a poet, for he appears to have taken Rilke's advice almost literally, advice which includes this: 'Withdraw into yourself; seek out the necessity that makes you write, and see if its roots push down into the furthest reaches of your heart; and say honestly if you would die if you were forbidden to write. This above all: ask yourself in the deadest hour of your night: *must* I write?' This is a question so exacting that few poets will ever have the courage to ask it of themselves, and fewer still to answer it.[41]

There are signs that Reed himself *has* asked it more than once, as poet, dramatist, biographer, and that Give It Up has been the answer. The fluent and quite prolific lyric and dramatic poet of the forties and early fifties largely abdicated from serious verse for fifteen years. The copious and successful radio dramatist of the fifties wrote *Musique Discrète* – its final trill unresolved – in 1959 and has yet to write its successor. The critic and scholar who idealised Hardy (if one may use that verb) is rumoured to have been working on a Hardy *Life* for many years but seems not to have finished it.

Of course, as Herbert Reeve tells us, 'one is always venturing upon dangerous ground in drawing parallels between an author's fiction and what we know of his life'. It may be irrelevant to do so; it is certainly a little impertinent in the case of a living author who has never presumed to parade the actualities of his private life before the public. But there is a sense in which the personal dimension *is* relevant, the sense that most worthwhile drama is likely to spring from the deepest concerns of the dramatist. It was Reed himself who, in 'What the Wireless Can Do for Literature', suggested that

radio-writers would do well to allow themselves a little more subjectivity: the results might be a bit more healthy and a bit more grown-up all round... It is the parts of an artist's self most familiar to himself as puzzles and obsessions and regular preoccupations that really produce anything worth offering to a serious listener or reader. These things are, above all, more likely to give an audience something to bite on. [42]

If we can bite on the myth of Giving Up, this is perhaps because its dramatist could include in his *Personal Anthology* for the BBC in 1970 the poem by W. B. Yeats 'To a Friend Whose Work Has Come to Nothing' –

> Bred to a harder thing
> Than Triumph, turn away...
> Be secret and exult,
> Because of all things known
> That is most difficult

– and could call it his favourite of all Yeats's poems. Reed's radio drama certainly does not come to nothing, and if it is content to leave the medium technically much as it found it and is concerned predominantly with matters of creativity rather than being itself monumentally creative, it is preserved nonetheless by qualities we would be poorer without. Radio has yet to produce its James

Joyce; but when Reed says of E. M. Forster that 'the perfect clarity of his style, his urbanity and passion, his sensitiveness and comic power, have enabled him to survive the presence of Joyce',[43] he cites the qualities which will allow his own work too to survive.

7   Beckett and the radio medium

KATHARINE WORTH

THE PLAYS BECKETT WROTE for radio have had considerably less critical attention than his stage plays. No doubt this is largely, as Martin Esslin suggests, because there have been few opportunities to hear them and they depend for their subtle effects on being heard. There have been few repeat performances by the BBC (*Embers*, for instance, had to wait till 1978), and the recordings are not in any case available for public use. How much we lose thereby may be felt in reading the brilliantly illuminating account of producing Beckett by his first radio producer, Donald McWhinnie, in his invaluable book, *The Art of Radio*. His *All That Fall*, with Mary O'Farrell as a richly robust Mrs Rooney, is one of the unforgettable experiences of radio drama, and there are a host of other haunting sounds from the BBC productions – J. G. Devlin as Mr Rooney, Jack Macgowran as Henry in *Embers*, Patrick Magee as Words to the music of John Beckett in *Words and Music*, and so on.

The BBC superbly fulfilled its role as a national theatre of the air in giving Beckett the opportunity to create these rare master-pieces. I am not attempting an exhaustive account of them, for that has already been done: I would refer readers to the authorita-tive summary of the production history by Martin Esslin and to the full-length, closely documented study by Clas Zilliacus, *Beckett and Broadcasting*;[1] this last has as much detail on casting, repeats, reviews, and so on as anyone could need.

In discussing the plays, along the line indicated by my title, I will of course have the BBC productions in mind, especially Donald McWhinnie's *All That Fall*, but on *Embers, Words and Music*, and *Cascando* I will draw my illustrations chiefly from the new recordings made by the University of London Audio-Visual Centre, since my critical interpretation of these plays is bound up with experience gained in producing them: also, it may be easier for readers to enter the discussion, as these recordings are avail-able for purchase and hire.[2]

'Radio drama' I take to mean plays specifically written for radio. The difficult distinction between radio drama proper and adaptations (such as the BBC dramatisation of *Lessness*) is rather easier to maintain where Beckett's plays are concerned, since he writes so specifically for a particular medium and is usually adamant about refusing to transfer from one to another. An illustration is the stand he eventually took (after some early concessions) against allowing *All That Fall* to be staged, even when pressed by Laurence Olivier for permission to produce it at the National Theatre.

The first of Beckett's radio plays, *All That Fall*, was broadcast by the BBC in 1957. It was also his first published play in English. More plays for the BBC followed: *Embers* in 1959 and *Words and Music* in 1962. The next play, *Cascando*, was written in French and produced by RTF in Paris in 1963: in its English version it was produced by the BBC in 1964 (I shall discuss it in its English version, which is, as usual, by Beckett himself). A curious piece, described by Zilliacus as 'a kind of proto-*Cascando*', *Esquisse radiophonique*, was published in *Minuit* 5 in 1973; the English version, *Radio 1*, was published in *Ends and Odds* in 1977. Its companion piece in the English collection, *Radio 2*, was broadcast by the BBC as *Rough for Radio* in 1976.

This is not a vast corpus, nor were the listening figures vast, even in terms of the Third Programme 'minority' audience. Yet these rare and curious plays with their restricted appeal had an impact out of all proportion to what might have been expected. Donald McWhinnie and Martin Esslin tell how the highly complex and sophisticated sound effects required for *All That Fall* forced radical experiments in the BBC sounds effects department and resulted in the creation of a new Radiophonic Workshop. There were reverberations from these experiments outside England; no doubt Beckett's international prestige contributed to the interest taken in the BBC productions in Europe and America. Donald McWhinnie was invited to Germany to direct a later production of *All That Fall*, and *Embers* was awarded the Italia Prize in 1959. Playwrights such as Pinter and Stoppard have clearly drawn from Beckett inspiration which is reflected in plays like *A Slight Ache* and *If You're Glad I'll Be Frank*. These have had considerable popularity and in their turn have helped to create an atmosphere favourable to experiment.

As he had already done in the theatre, Beckett seized hold of this new medium with extraordinarily sure intuition, making use of its conventions for the most subtle of dramatic effects, turning its supposed limitations to curious advantage. One instance is the use of blindness as a radiogenic device. There was an early prototype here, Richard Hughes's celebrated play *A Comedy of Danger*, set in the dark at the bottom of a coal mine. It was a poignant and adroit use of the 'blind' situation of radio for a fundamentally realistic effect.

Beckett's handling of blindness takes us into a much more dream-like territory. The blind man's stick tapping the way in *All That Fall* contributes to a strange melody in which human voices, animal sounds, and the music of Schubert create the atmosphere of an inner landscape. A cryptic allusion to an old blind man in *Embers* heralds a mediumistic evocation of the invisible. Our attention as listeners is drawn to our own inability to see and to the compensating ability we share with the characters, to 'see' in a different way, with the eye of the mind.

Similarly Beckett exploits the supposed limitations of radio in his original and daring treatment of pauses and silences. In *All That Fall* he humorously draws attention to the characters' dependence on the medium to give them existence, from which it follows that silence may destroy them. Mrs Rooney feels herself very uncertainly there at times – 'Maddy Rooney, née Dunne, the big pale blur' – while in *Embers*, all the pauses are filled with the sound of the sea and we are never quite sure whether the voices which emerge from and fade into that sound are coming out of a memory, dream, or fiction. In *Cascando* Beckett distinguishes between a 'pause' and a 'silence' with an exactness which matches the rhythm of the speaking voice to the rhythm of the music which is its equal partner. It is a rather nerve-racking technique, testing our ability to wait and concentrate, and in this way drawing us closer to the experience of characters who are being similarly racked. It is especially audacious as a radio technique where there is nothing else than sound to hold our attention and silences could well induce thoughts of mechanical failure in the listener. His uneasiness would be part of the scheme, however; he is to be made newly aware of the value of sounds and reminded that, as Donald McWhinnie says, 'silence lies at the heart of the radio experience'.[3]

Beckett has also been seen as a pioneer in using music not just as acoustic wallpaper but as a character in its own right. Martin

Esslin has pointed out that *Words and Music* is 'so totally radiogenic' that 'the printed page cannot represent it . . . the third character, Music, in every way of equal importance with the other two, is of necessity absent on the printed page'.[4] It was consciousness of how much one missed in missing the music that first impelled me to set about trying, with David Clark, for new productions of the radio plays.

Some of the innovations Beckett is noted for, his avoidance of montage, for instance, are part of a larger achievement. He has brought radio drama nearer to modern theatre by introducing elements of self-consciousness and making witty play with the conventions out of which the illusion grows. He has evolved a subtle and often humorous technique for conveying the strange human ability to draw sounds out of thin air and build them up into a world without the aid of sight. He shows how delicate and fragile a process it is, how it all depends on style. One wrong sound and the whole airy structure is liable to collapse, as Maddy Rooney feels herself becoming 'dead' when she overhears her own unconvincing language: 'No, no, I am agog, tell me all, then we shall press on and never pause, never pause, till we come safe to haven' (*All That Fall*, p. 34).[5] When Dan Rooney repeats the last phrase, commenting 'sometimes one would think you were struggling with a dead language', she agrees, adding that the feeling is 'unspeakably excruciating'. The need to get the sound right is closely related to the process of self-expression in which the characters of the radio plays, like those of the stage plays, are endlessly engaged. 'Interiorising', as Irving Wardle has suggested, found a natural home in modern radio drama, having already established itself as the dominant form in modern literature and in the Theatre of the Absurd. It was, incidentally, the experience of seeing a dramatisation of Beckett's *How It Is* partially performed in darkness which brought this idea home to him.[6]

Beckett's radio plays then, are a milestone in the history of radio drama, as *Waiting for Godot* was in stage history. They were also an important landmark in his own career, marking his return to writing in English after years in French: the radio plays were in fact the first plays he published which were written in English and then translated (by himself) into French. Only with *Cascando* was the process reversed. His attitude to the English language is complex; he has spoken at different times of its having too much tone, being too apt to move towards poetry, and of having special value as a theatre language 'because of its concreteness, its close relation between thing and vocable'. To these divisions of feeling, his Anglo-Irishness adds further complexity. A spell of writing in 'no tone' French seemed to have had an invigorating effect on his relationship with English, for when he came back to his first language in the radio plays he was able to make dramatic capital out of the very difficulties he had experienced with too much tone in the past. He took advantage of the 'blind' situation of his audience, which necessarily involves closer listening, to make demands for very close listening indeed, listening such as the artist himself must practise, in order to distinguish the right tones, the natural from the affected, the true from the false, the half realised from the fully realised.

In the first play, *All That Fall,* he adds to the complications and the fun by casting the dialogue in an Irish idiom which allows for easy fluctuations between the natural and the histrionic; stage Irish casts a long shadow, after all. In *Embers, Words and Music,* and *Cascando* there is a rather different wrestling with words, as artist-figures seek to create expressive narratives, often by subduing destructive sounds – the dreaded sea in *Embers,* the pretentious utterances in *Words and Music.* 'In a medium which depends so crucially on the spoken word', says Donald McWhinnie, 'it is difficult, if not impossible, to conceal insincerity or false motivation.'[7] Beckett tests that idea, inviting the reader to recognise the moments when Mrs Rooney's language goes 'dead' ('Just like our own poor dear Gaelic') or when Words and Music begin to abandon their sterile fluency for more broken and genuine expressions of feeling.

It is apparent that in all the plays the soundscape represents an inner landscape. The medium is air and what is communicated is ethereal, though of course that does not mean it lacks the matter of the everyday. A striking feature of this drama indeed is the sense it conveys of minds playing on a range of homely sounds and sayings and converting them into the more subtle patterns required by some inner vision. The balance between the external and the interior worlds shifts somewhat from one play to another, as we shall see, but in all of them the characters are touched by some awareness of their dependence on the medium.

It is in the first place the medium of radio on which they depend, but 'medium' is a key word in all its senses for the reading of these plays. Beckett builds on the simple fact that the radio medium is a means of communicating material sounds and voices from a place which exists but is invisible to the listeners. Other kinds of medium might also be seen in this way. The spiritualist medium commonly relies on voices to communicate, as he claims, a world beyond human vision (visual materialisations seem usually to be a failure, and are more commonly associated with fraudulency). The ability to change voice and mimic can seem a very impressive and mysterious thing, whether in an actor who is deliberately acting or in a spiritualist medium claiming to be 'possessed'. The writer also at times may feel possessed. Beckett continually writes on this theme of the artist as a medium, hearing voices which force him to draw characters out of the world of shadows and embody them if he can. In his television play, . . . *but the clouds* . . . (1976), he depicts such an evocation. A man with great labour calls up the face of a woman and is able just to make her lips move and form the words of the title. He cannot achieve a fuller projection; the lines of verse in which the phrase occurs have to be supplied by himself; appropriately they conclude 'among the deepening shades'.

The quotation is from Yeats's poem *The Tower*, and Yeats's plays are often in Beckett's mind when possession or 'dreaming back' is the theme. One of them, which deals directly with mediumistic evocation, *The Words Upon the Window-Pane* (1934) may well have provided hints for a radio technique; the shades who are evoked – Swift and the two women he loved – establish themselves entirely through the medium's changes of voice. *The Words Upon the Window-Pane* is very much a stage play; its tension derives partly from the contrast between the ordinary appearance of the medium and the tormented alien voices which issue from her lips. But it shows what can be done with the voice to create a type of ambiguity especially interesting to Beckett, the ambiguous processes by which the mind, in a state of possession, projects dramas more real than life itself.

I now want to look at the way Beckett pursues the implications of the word 'medium', beginning with *All That Fall*. This is a play about a journey. Mrs Rooney, elderly and childless, makes a laborious progress to meet her blind husband, Dan, and bring him home. On the outward journey she encounters, in a variety of vehicles, a variety of neighbours who help or harass her; there is talk of the race meeting some are travelling to and of the inexplicable lateness of the expected train. On the journey back she and her husband are alone, except for a brief dialogue at the close with the small boy who sometimes acts as Mr Rooney's guide; he brings Dan a mysterious object he has dropped and tells the reason for the train's delay, a child's death on the line.

This is on the level of daylight reality. But the play came to Beckett as a more Gothic soundscape. As he told Nancy Cunard, it was a new sort of inspiration: 'Never thought about a radio play technique, but in the dead of t'other night got a nicely gruesome idea full of cartwheels and dragging feet and puffing and panting which may or may not lead to something.'[8]

'The dead of t'other night' sets the tone neatly. Though it takes place in daylight, Mrs Rooney's journey has features of those mysterious odysseys into the mental landscape we associate especially with night and dreams. It is an enigmatic region, familiar yet weird, uninhibited to a ludicrous degree and yet pervaded by a sense of awful effort, the need to get to the 'right' place, and the sense, which cannot be explained, that this is not it. The aura of dream is strong in the opening passage: dragging feet, as Beckett first heard them, faint strains of Schubert's 'Death and the Maiden', a woman's voice murmuring 'Poor woman. All alone in that ruinous old house'. Then in comes the noise of Christy with his donkey cart, and a solider, more homely soundscape begins to take shape. It seems we are moving into the real world as the road fills up with local worthies who stop their vehicles – donkey cart, bicycle, car – to chat to Mrs Rooney, offer lifts, indulge in sexual rallying, share lugubrious news of illnesses and operations.

Everyone has been struck by the richer-than-usual realism, the endearing raciness and local colour of *All That Fall*. More of the day-to-day world is allowed into this than into any other of the radio plays. It is the most Irish of all of Beckett's plays: there is a strong sense of real topography (no surprise to learn that it derives from his own childhood home, Foxrock, with its actual racetrack, Leopardstown). The play is full of convincing Irish talk like Mr Barrell's 'That's enough old guff out of you. Nip up to the box now and see has Mr. Case anything for me.'

Yet all this naturalness is there only because it has impinged on the medium, been taken up into the mental landscape and in the process moved quite a distance from everyday reality. For, after all, the characters Mrs Rooney meets on the road are Happy

Family figures: Mr Barrell the station master, Mr Tyler the retired bill-broker, Mr Slocum the Clerk of the Racecourse; and their encounters very soon take off into a dream-like, farcical freedom. Most outrageous is the episode when Mrs Rooney accepts Mr Slocum's lift and is shouldered into his car, protesting all the time that she has done with these physical intimacies but relishing all the same the mild horseplay and sexual double entendres with which he regales her. But farcical exaggeration permeates the whole dialogue. It is farce rather than realism when Mrs Rooney asks Christy why he is walking: 'Why do you not climb up on the crest of your manure and let yourself be carried along? Is it that you have no head for heights?' Or when Mr Tyler is heard cursing God and man and the wet afternoon of his conception because his back tyre has gone down; or when Miss Fitt boasts of being so 'distray' that she has been known to eat her doily instead of the thin bread and butter. There is a manic quality in all this, never more than when the topics are lugubrious: hysterectomies – 'The entire . . . er, bag of tricks'; the loss of Mrs Rooney's little Minnie – 'Forty she'd be now, or fifty . . .' Farce is used to puncture the sentimentality into which Mrs Rooney so readily falls; she lies awake at night brooding on the world's wretchedness, we are told. But when she come up against a disaster on the road, the running over of the hen, her sentimentalism takes an unexpected turn: 'Just one great squawk and then . . . peace. [*Pause*] They would have slit her weasand in any case.'

In other ways too this so real world is tilted away from realism. We are kept aware by the witty handling of the sound effects that all sounds come to us only, as it were, by courtesy of the medium. In the first place, that medium is radio. Beckett allows the characters from time to time to seem on the verge of knowing this. Mrs Rooney disconcertingly forces her way back into the dialogue when she is being ignored, saying 'Do not imagine, because I am silent, that I am not present, and alive, to all that is going on.' Sometimes characters appear to have control over the sound effects, as when Mr Barrell announces the train and we get '*Immediately exaggerated station sounds*'. Or when Mrs Rooney on the homeward journey coos over the rural scene and the noise of sheep, cows, and so forth comes in promptly on cue. However, this is only the most tentative suggestion of full consciousness, far from the perfect knowingness that we get from, say, Pirandello's six characters. One effect Beckett did not care for in the otherwise admired first production by Donald McWhinnie was the device of having the actors themselves mimic the animal sounds. Sounds need to be natural if the strangeness of their timeliness is to register properly, for the stylisation must bring home the uncanny power of the medium to summon up the exact sounds of the natural world and assimilate them into the other world that is being constructed out of air.

Mrs Rooney does not claim to know that she is a character. She does assert, however, her role as medium. It is through her that the scene is transmitted, the invisible made visible for us the listeners as well as for her blind husband. At the halfway point of the play, when she has gone as far as she will go on her road, she realises for us the whole landscape, including the racecourse whose sounds we will never hear:

The entire scene, the hills, the plain, the race-course with its miles and miles of white rails and three red stands, the pretty little wayside station, even you yourselves, yes, I mean it, and over all the clouding blue, I see it all, I stand here and see it all with eyes...[*The voice breaks*]...

(*All That Fall*, p. 23)

It is the function of the medium as artist that she is performing here by filling in the gaps in the soundscape, and this is a function she practises throughout the piece. She often appears to summon up characters for us, for instance when she calls Mr Barrell back into hearing range. She is, as we know, always listening to the way things sound and is sensitive to the wrong tone, especially in her own speech. She is interested in the people she meets, draws out their stories, and is herself an extremely racy and inventive raconteuse, with a fine line in sarcastic jokes, as when she suggests to Miss Fitt, who has been ignoring her again, 'Just prop me up against the wall like a roll of tarpaulin, and that will be all for the moment.'

But if she is the medium by which the drama comes, the drama is also the medium by which she comes over to us. We may recall that her 'voice breaks' as she concludes her survey of the 'entire scene' and personal feeling overwhelms her. It is her mental landscape which is unrolled on that double journey. The external world has vivid place there, as it registers on her acute senses, but it is always subject to fantastic, humorous, and sombre distortions.

Beckett began with the notion of effort, dragging feet and

panting, and this is the impression we continually receive: a mind is struggling over well-worn tracks, never able to get beyond a certain point, conscious of precipices it must confront and of mystifying impasses. 'Why do you halt?' Mrs Rooney says to Christy at the start, and then, 'But why do I halt?' On the homeward journey, when Dan Rooney enters her consciousness and the sense of a composite landscape develops, the compulsion to press on intensifies. 'All this stopping and starting again is devilish, devilish!' Mr Rooney complains. 'I get a little way on me and begin to be carried along when suddenly you stop dead!' And occasionally there seem to be lapses of consciousness, as in the gaps of silence where Mr Rooney's voice should be, when the train has drawn in.

If we are listening well, we recognise the hidden nature of the homeward journey. It is growing late, we are moving towards night and dream; sounds from the daylight context recur in cryptic, fantastic, but revealing forms. 'Do you want some dung?' says Mrs Rooney, out of the blue, and 'That is a true donkey' as a bray is heard, seemingly in a void. Crazy sayings, unless we still have in our mind's ear the morning dialogue, when these thoughts first surfaced, when Mrs Rooney identified Christy's hinny as 'familiar' and refused the offer of dung from his cart with 'Dung? What would we want with dung at our time of life?' The bizarre fragments we hear now suggest an involuntary return to that obsession with procreation and barrenness and the ills the flesh is heir to. It is a ruling theme, though it continually leads into wistful imagining of some experience that might transcend the cruel world of nature – Christ riding into Jerusalem on his donkey (or hinny), the absent Lord.

In this immensely effortful journey, always over the same track, always turned back on itself at the station and haunted by thoughts of 'wretchedness', there are some striking anticipations of a much later play, *Footfalls*. That is Beckett's most ghostly play, and *All That Fall* too, although its life material is so much richer and warmer, has a ghostliness which brings to mind other senses of the word 'medium'. Mrs Rooney is almost, at times, a revenant. Those moments when she draws attention to herself falling silent are funny, but sometimes rather ominous and uncanny too. She has been absent from the scene through illness, we are reminded, when Mr Barrell greets her at the station, and Miss Fitt tells her that she does not look 'normal'. When they are all waiting for the delayed train 'in the shadow of the waiting room', she continues to suffer from the sense of fading from people's view and from other kinds of absence, notably her husband's failure to materialise when the train arrives. 'Was he not on it?' she calls to Mr Barrell, and then after a pause, 'Is anything the matter, you look as if you had seen a ghost.' When Mr Rooney does appear, he greets her strangely: 'Why are you here? You did not notify me.' She has to tell him that it is his birthday, says she wished him his happy returns in the bathroom. But he did not hear her. Strangely, again, he enquires, 'How old am I now?' and later, as they plod home, 'Why are you hanging out of me like that? Have you swooned away?'

Both he and she have some difficulty in hanging on to their material existence. It is a joke about the radio medium, but it extends into their own view of life: the tension between these two ways of taking the idea is brilliantly maintained. The Rooneys are going home, but they do not feel at home. He dreams of 'other roads, in other lands. Of another home, another – [*He hesitates*] – another home'. The word 'home' echoes through the sound-scape, as when Mrs Rooney and Miss Fitt, climbing the formidable station steps, join in the hymn 'Lead, kindly light' and are cut off when they reach the line 'The night is dark and I am far from ho-ome, tum tum . . .' This technique of repetition is one of Beckett's offered aids to help us through the stream of consciousness and draw out its significance. Similarly, the recurrence of the word 'late' suggests a special pressure on the mind, while repeated images of children and childlessness point to one of its deep troubles, its preoccupation with and revulsion from procreation and terrible nature.

In the last phase of the journey the whole soundscape conspires to convey this urge to move away towards another home, into another dimension. It becomes more overtly musical, a melody in which the sounds of wind and rain, dragging feet, and tapping stick are interspersed with pauses, delicately woven with words. Donald McWhinnie was surely right in the first production to make the sound of the blind man's stick a stylised, percussive effect, no longer realistic, but part of a symbolic orchestration. The melody heard at the beginning, 'Death and the Maiden', returns; now at last it is named for us and we are required to listen to it for some time. Of all music Schubert's is, for Beckett, we are told, the most nearly pure spirit. These strains, stronger now than in the opening, tell us how far we have penetrated into the spiritual landscape inhabited by the Rooneys. Even the tough, sardonic blind man yields to the melancholy influence. 'You are crying,' exclaims Mrs Rooney, and after a pause, 'Are you crying?' His 'Yes' is violent and restores robustness; pity for 'Poor Maddy', for the old woman listening to Schubert in the ruinous house, gives way to the outburst of wild laughter, in which his wife joins, at the thought of the text they will be hearing in church next day: 'The Lord upholdeth all that fall and raiseth up all those that be bowed down' (*All That Fall*, p. 39). They seem to be confirmed in their mocking view by what follows. Mr Rooney's young guide pursues them, to give him a mysterious object he has dropped; he will not tell what it is and so we will never know. A way of reminding us, perhaps, that we remain 'blind' interpreters. Then he tells the reason for the train's delay, the death of a young child on the line. We hear Mr Rooney's attempts to silence the messenger, hear Mrs Rooney's unease, remember Dan's black joke about wanting to kill a child, 'Nip some young doom in the bud'. All that divides and torments the Rooneys rises up in this final episode; it seems a crippling blow, yet what are the last sounds we hear? *'Tempest of wind and rain. It abates. They move on. Dragging steps, etc. They halt. Tempest of wind and rain.'* It is the well-established rhythm continuing. They have halted before and moved on and will keep on journeying, so the pattern of the soundscape suggests. She guides him, he leans on her; they uphold each other. We are left to interpret for ourselves that grotesque and touching union; perhaps it is a lesson to the absent Lord – or perhaps a reminder that he works in mysterious ways to uphold those that fall, though they may not recognise it.

All That Fall has been the most popular of Beckett's radio plays, to judge from the number of BBC repeats, the new stereo version made in 1972, and (perverse evidence) all those requests for permission to adapt it for stage performance. The play which followed it, *Embers*, has not attracted so much notice: after its first performances in 1959 it was not broadcast again until 1978. One can only guess at the reasons; perhaps it has been considered a more rarefied piece than its predecessor, less strong in variety of human interest. It *is* rarefied: indeed, this is the play which most strongly suggests that Beckett knew Yeats's play about raising the spirit of Swift.

However, *Embers* is far from lacking human interest and variety. When David Clark and I set about casting the play for the University of London production, we were confronted with a Pirandellian situation, many lively characters, with no more claim to 'real' existence than the celebrated six characters had, clamouring to be given voice; Henry's wife, Ada, their daughter, Addie, her Music Master, her Riding Master; all distinct personalities, though so dubiously there.

We soon realised that it was not possible to cast the play without committing ourselves on the key question, What kind of reality do the characters have; which of them should be allowed the special status represented by having some voice other than Henry's to express them? Should Addie have a voice of her own, for instance? We thought not and gave her voice to Elvi Hale, playing Ada – hard on the actress, who had to maintain a very special tone for Ada – but representing our view of Addie's insubstantial reality. Henry's is the one voice we can depend on, the voice all the other voices depend on. Of all Beckett's radio plays *Embers* is the closest to *The Words Upon the Window-Pane* in making so overwhelming an impression that everything is filtered to us through the powers of an extraordinary medium. Listeners, like producers, are called upon to grapple with the question, who is 'really' there?

In the first place Henry functions as controller of the radio medium. He works through it, as a producer, getting sounds when he calls for them – horses' hooves, a drip, thuds – and seeming to be aware of us as listeners, for he takes pains to establish the soundscape at the start (though it is only a shade he thinks he is addressing).

That sound you hear is the sea.
[*Pause. Louder*] I say that sound you hear is the sea, we are sitting on the strand. [*Pause*] I mention it because the sound is so strange, so unlike the sound of the sea, that if you didn't see what it was you wouldn't know what it was. [*Pause*] (*Embers*, p. 21)

In the original BBC production, this comment was reflected in an overlay of electronic music which totally removed the sea sound from naturalism. We read it differently, as a sardonic reference to the artificiality of all the 'natural' sound effects in the play, and felt free to use a standard vocabulary of sea effects, including the sound of the receding waves taking the shingle with them, this last to suggest the 'sucking' effect which especially troubles Henry.

Because he has so much power over the medium, it is unnerving when he tries to control it and fails; towards the close, for instance, he is no longer able to summon up the sound of horses' hooves. And one sound he cannot suppress, the sound of the sea. It is heard in every pause of a play which has, so Zilhacus tells us, over two hundred pauses. Criticism of the radio plays must pay attention to the impact on the listener of such aggressive sound effects, and that cannot properly be done unless we hear rather than read. It is too easy, in reading, after all, to skip over the pause notation which represents the sea sound. As listeners we are more uncomfortably exposed to its relentless pressure – and so, closer to Henry, better able to appreciate the unnerving reality of his experience.

Why is he so obsessed by the sea's sound? We are given an oblique and riddling explanation in the dialogue and stories he constructs – though an explanation, it seems to me, which he himself never fully grasps. He can lay it out for us but we may well arrive at a different interpretation from his. He loathes and dreads the sea but he cannot stay away from it: it is the 'strange place' where he can be with his dead father, the father who was thought to have drowned, though they never found his body. 'That held up probate an unconscionable time,' says Henry, with the dry, humorous realism which is as much a part of him as his intense fantasies and which makes listening to him a thoroughly lively experience, despite his consuming interest in the dead. The sea is a link between him and the dead; his father is somehow there, though he has no voice and it is a question whether he is listening: 'Can he hear me? [*Pause*] Yes, he must hear me. [*Pause*] To answer me? [*Pause*] No, he doesn't answer me. [*Pause*] Just be with me' (*Embers*, p. 21).

'La parole sort du noir,' Beckett has said. Is Henry 'dark' in the Irish sense of 'blind', as in Synge's play *The Well of the Saints*, where the word is used of the two tramps who construct a world superior to the world of the sighted from their creative dark? This is one of the plays Beckett most admires. There is an ambiguous suggestion at the beginning that it might be so, when Henry senses the presence neither he nor we can see: 'Who is beside me now? [*Pause*] An old man, blind and foolish. [*Pause*] My father, back from the dead, to be with me' (*Embers*, p. 21). The syntax is

inscrutable, but it is possible that we are to think of Henry as a
blind seer; it is perhaps the paradox on which the whole action
depends, for Alec Reid is surely right in saying, 'Ambiguity,
abstraction, these are the possibilities peculiar to sound radio
which Beckett is exploiting here to the full.'[9]

A conversation with the dead must be a monologue, one might
think, but Henry will not allow it to be so. He works with enormous energy and *élan* to construct dialogues which will 'give' him
his father, materialise him. We must suspect the story he is
endlessly telling, the 'great one' about the two old men, Bolton
and Holloway, as an oblique reflection of this preoccupation; also
that some blurring is taking place between his father and himself.
He brings a remarkably vivid scene before us, consciously impro-
vising: 'Before the fire with all the shutters...no, hangings,
hangings, all the hangings drawn and the light, no light, only the
light of the fire, sitting there in the ...no, standing, standing
there on the hearthrug in the dark before the fire...' And in this
scene – seemingly so clearly fictitious – he places an old man 'in
great trouble', heard pleading with another old man, the doctor,
Holloway, for succour: 'Please! PLEASE!' He can visualise their
encounter with remarkable clarity, down to the tiniest detail, 'the
old blue eye, very glassy, lids worn thin, lashes gone, whole
thing swimming, and the candle shaking over his head'. But he
cannot project it as a soundscape: the most striking feature of this
snow-covered 'white world' of the story is its dead silence. 'Not a
sound' is a recurring phrase. There is one exception, a sound of
dying embers, which he tries to makes us hear, though significantly, as I shall hope to show, he cannot project it: '...not a
sound, only the fire, no flames now, embers. [*Pause*] Embers.
[*Pause*] Shifting, lapsing, furtive like, dreadful sound...' (*Embers*,
p. 24). It is associated with the deathliness of the white world, the
agony of the old man, the idea of extinction. In the end, I believe,
we have to set this 'unheard' sound against the sound of the sea
and value the sea accordingly.

Visually alive as the Bolton/Holloway episode is – in that way
more 'there' than anything else in the play – the listener is always
conscious that it is being realised for us by Henry, with virtuoso
ability but also with hesitation and strain. So when a voice which
is not 'done' by him enters the soundscape – the voice of his wife,
Ada – it is almost bound to seem, not just a refreshing change, but
the sign that we have moved into another order of reality. She is

there on the beach, not at a distance in time and space like all the others, warning him against sitting on the cold stones, advising him to put on his jaegers, watching him go down to the edge of the sea. She brings with her too a whole world of mundane and humorous reference to children, music lessons, betting on horses.

Yet though our ears tell us this, they warn us too that this seemingly solid realism is all an illusion: though she sounds so right, she also sounds wrong: there is no noise of shingle when she sits beside him, her voice is low and remote throughout, she goes as abruptly and oddly as she came. She was there, she says, 'Some little time' before she spoke. We, the blind listeners, cannot question this, nor know what form she takes when she does speak. We are aware, however, that he called to her and then we heard her, so there is a strong presumption that he has, through his power as a medium, called her up.

All the same she has achieved a fuller materialisation than any other character in the play. Maddening though Henry finds her, estranged though they seem to be, she stimulates him to recall a rich variety of episodes from a life they have shared. He projects a family drama, in which we come to recognise the dead father who finds his son a 'wash-out' and the child, Addie, who is always kept at a distance, though Henry mimics her to perfection. Those memories of Addie come through in particularly sharp sound insets: here we did need a separate voice for the Riding Master and the Music Master, who are heard giving Addie the comically horrific lessons – 'Now Miss! Elbows in Miss! Hands down Miss!' – which always end in paroxysms of wailing. Henry suffers an especially keen irritation, the sound tells us, from memories of those walks where he tried to make her look at lambs so that he could talk to himself: Patrick Magee renders these passages of recall with great comic exuberance. Sounds from the Addie world keep pushing into the soundscape: hooves trotting and galloping are among the sounds Henry conjures up to combat the dreaded sucking of the sea.

In producing the play, as we did, in stereo, we tried to suggest the different quality of Henry's evocations – the world around Ada, which seems to reflect an actual life, the world of the Bolton and Holloway story – by locating them in different sound zones. The sea, though in the zone of memory, was allowed to sweep right across the soundscape at a high point of evocation, when

Ada recalls the ecstasy she and Henry once enjoyed on the same beach where they now sit, so far from feeling ecstatic. It seemed justifiable to point up the separation of experience in this way, if only to render the full force of the shock we receive when Ada advises him to consult a doctor about his obsession with the sea: 'There's something wrong with your brain, you ought to see Holloway, he's alive still, isn't he?' So we know the distinction between memory and fiction cannot be maintained and must wonder, Does Holloway really belong in the other story which Henry is painfully projecting about his own life? Or is Ada herself a character in a story whose elements of real life and fiction can never be unravelled?

When we reach this stage, the mediumistic dark begins to thicken. Ada becomes a mouthpiece, used by Henry to bring nearer the figure of the dead father. 'I can't remember if he met you', he says, oddly. She puts him right and proceeds to give a curiously precise and yet dreamlike account of his father, which does in a way materialise him, for what she describes is a figure like Henry himself, sitting very still, by the ubiquitous sea: 'He did not see me. He was sitting on a rock looking out to sea. I never forgot his posture. And yet it was a common one. You used to have it sometimes' (*Embers*, p. 36). She gives her Delphic message which she does not understand (for her it is 'rubbish') and then she goes. He returns to his story, the 'great one', but it will not hold up, it is 'no good'. For us, however, it has acquired new meaning; we can understand now why it seems both invented, a fiction, and yet deeply familiar, a thing that has happened. '...that's it, that was always it, night, and the embers cold, and the glim shaking in your old fist, saying, Please! Please!' (*Embers*, p. 39).

There are no other voices now. He calls 'Ada', and there is no reply; 'Father', no reply; 'Christ', no reply. The name 'Christ' occurred earlier as no more than a common expletive (perhaps for this reason it was, rather curiously, cut from the BBC recording along with some other indecorous words). Its recurrence, in this so different context, with such a note of anguish, changes the nature of the darkness around Henry, gives it a spiritual quality and intensifies the sense we received in the opening scene of a mediumistic exploration into the region of the dead.

The play might appear to end in despair, with Henry consulting his 'little book' and finding nothing except, next day, the plumber coming about 'the waste'. He follows that up with a muttered comment 'Words'. So has it all been a waste, all the words he has uttered? There comes a chill echo from the silent story world where the embers are cold (and from Ada's account of the silent depths of the sea) as he concludes: 'Nothing, all day nothing. [*Pause*] All day all night nothing. [*Pause*] Not a sound.'

But then the sound of the sea returns to contradict him and remind us that it stands for life and creativity as well as death. It was the sea that drove him to talk, invent, project voices, and evoke shades. And for the listeners he has succeeded. The spirit of the dead father has been conjured up, as in life, scolding, raging, withdrawing; he could not be contained in the pathetic story about the old man, Bolton. But that world of the old men also became real for us: we saw the snow and the embers, the swimming blue eye. And throughout the play we heard voices so vividly there that we became disorientated about what constituted reality. In the story the fire dwindles to embers and there is the terror of nothing. In the play the sea continues and so, therefore, will the story-telling, we may imagine; 'nothing' is a concept that must be rejected.

The next two plays, *Words and Music* and *Cascando*, share the distinction already mentioned of having music as a character in its own right. In discussing them I shall draw on the experience gained in producing them, with David Clark directing, for the University of London Audio-Visual Centre. In both plays the music is by Humphrey Searle, the composer who was suggested by Beckett when I asked his permission to make these new recordings (John Beckett had withdrawn the music he wrote for the original BBC production). Searle's music seemed to us to match well with the poetic, ebullient theatricality of Words as played by Patrick Magee, who took the same role in the BBC production. We are still engaged in making *Cascando*, so there I can speak of the music but not as yet of the relationship between it and Voice.

Words and Music, like *Embers*, is an evocation, but this time the medium is heard to be dense and recalcitrant. Words and Music are milling around in the dark when we first hear them, playing sterile variations on well-worn themes. 'Sloth' is the current theme, an amusing pointer to what Beckett especially explores in this play, the artist's difficulty in getting started. The directing force, Croak by name, takes a long time to get going. We hear him shuffling slowly nearer in his slippers, an effect we tried to highlight in our stereo recording. He is a comic tyrant, now propitiating his agents, 'Joe. Bob. My balms', and at other times threatening them with his club. He has something he wants to express, but he can only refer incoherently to a face glimpsed on the stairs of his tower. Beckett has fun here with the notion of the ivory tower among other kinds of towers occupied by poets and lovers. He offers his servants the theme 'Love' and gets a facile reproduction of what they have been doing already; Words even begins to say 'Sloth' before hastily correcting himself. It is comic stuff up to here, as perhaps we may appreciate more easily in hearing than in reading: Humphrey Searle's music, for instance, found some droll equivalents for Words' pomposities, including the mocking little catch-phrase which matches Words' 'My Lord'. There are tentative suggestions of an impulse to something more serious, but first Croak has to abandon the idea of slipping easily into a dream of love: the evocation cannot be effected without an immersion in the real world. That comes when, reluctantly, seemingly without conscious intent, he lets slip the word 'Age'. Words picks it up – 'old age I mean ... if that is what my Lord means', and now at last they have something real to express, an unflattering but not unsympathetic view of the self in old age. An image develops – the old man, huddled in the ingle 'Waiting for the hag to put the pan in the bed'. 'And bring the ... arrowroot,' trolls Words. 'And bring the toddy.' The sentimentality which trapped the trio at the start is punctured by this homely bathos; Patrick Magee extracted much comedy from the anticlimaxes by his wholehearted acting out of the direction *'Trying to sing'*. For, as ever, Music is in the lead, offering Words suggestions which he struggles painfully and hesitantly to follow. Finally he stumbles on the lyric moment promised by Music's increasingly melodious strains, and the long-hoped-for face appears 'in the ashes', an image associated with the old man in the ingle, but bringing with it romantic memories of 'that old light ... That old starlight/On the earth again'.

A battle now develops between 'cold' and 'warm' sounds, perhaps set off by Croak's emotional reaction to the evocation they have achieved. Five times he repeats the word 'face', whereupon Music produces a 'warmly sentimental' strain which Words at once combats with a chilly account – tone 'cold', Beckett says – of the face, now seen by moonlight at a moment of ecstasy.

Still, almost despite himself, he conveys tremors of sensuous delight; they are taken up by Music – as ever, closer to what matters – into a great burst of lyricism, spreading and subsiding as if to render more appropriately what is being so clinically described, the rise and fall of the beautiful breasts.

Words has managed to take them a step on the way – Croak is greatly affected and Music has been inspired – but the episode has been only partially realised, is still in danger of seeming no more than what might be described as 'postcoital recuperation', to borrow Zilhacus's dry phrase. The evocation must go beyond that; it is spirit the medium must raise. And Words reaches that goal. The eyes of the moonlit beauty open and everything is transfigured, as we know from his change to low, poetic tones; with the aid of Music he begins to grope towards revelation, down into a dark where there are no words:

> Through the scum
> Down a little way
> To whence one glimpse
> Of that wellhead

> (Words and Music, p. 35)

At last he is singing with increasing confidence, has caught up with Music: they are completely together; the play becomes a little opera. We receive our glimpse of the inexpressible which by coming together Words and Music have at last been able to express. 'Music always wins,' Beckett said to me, apropos of this play. But Words gets there in the end, and so does Croak, although the experience overwhelms him and he leaves them in disorder. Words closes the play with a deep sigh which suggests that the ecstasy is over, cannot be recaptured unless Music will give him a new inspiration.

The emphasis in Words and Music is on the struggle to set in motion the process which leads into a true evocation. There is no such struggle in Cascando: on the contrary, Opener has only to say 'I open' and at once Voice or Music, separately or together, come on stream, always in mid-phrase, telling the tale which is apparently what the Opener wants to hear, for the play ends with his shouts of encouragement. They are entirely dependent on him for being heard, going off immediately, again in mid-phrase, when he says 'I close'. They seem to have no choice but to obey him: when they weaken and he calls 'Full strength' the volume must increase. At least one assumes so, though admittedly there is no direction to confirm this. In planning the music for our production, we did in fact consider the possibility that they might not respond, but decided that the text is against this; the Opener certainly appears satisfied that he has displayed his powers adequately. 'That's not all,' he says: 'I open both.'

The relation of Voice and Music is not tense, personal, and changeable, like that between Words and Music; no doubt that is why the BBC felt it unnecessary to have new music composed for their production of the English version, but simply took over the existing music from the Stuttgart production of the original French version. The character of Music is indeed something of a mystery. There are no clues such as the 'Love and soul music' of *Words and Music;* only a dotted line to stand for the musical entries into the narrative. In our production we have assumed that Music is telling in his own language the same story told by Voice, for they have no difficulty in keeping pace at whatever point they are 'opened', whether separately or together.

This easy harmony between Voice and Music, and indeed the very fact of their existence, is the mystery which perplexes Opener. His problem is the opposite of Croak's; he does not have to exert himself at all – has only to 'open' and there instantly is the tale of Woburn in midstream. Beckett enjoys witty play here with the basic situation of radio drama; someone turns a switch or knob and a flow of sound is heard which has been there all the time, but will come and go as the control is moved. (He uses the same 'on-stream' effect to create a more neurotic situation in *Esquisse radiophonique,* a play not yet broadcast here.) Opener's function at first appears thoroughly mechanical. He opens the play for us in a voice 'dry as dust', giving us necessary data, including the information 'It is the month of May . . .' But there is already a hint here of something more personal, for he hesitates, adds 'for me', and then, as if to assure himself as well as us, confirms, 'Correct.' So at the start we are encouraged to wonder what is the special significance of May for this 'dry as dust' character. Is it only, as some critics have thought, that being no more than a function, he is necessarily stuck forever in this plot, or may we allow him some freedom as a character, including the possibility of change?

The question has to be suspended because at this point he 'opens', and in comes a voice as different as possible from his measured tones; it is breathless, agitated, gabbling, never finishing a sentence nor punctuating, but desperately rushing to catch up with some object that seems always just out of reach. It tells of itself and its need to discover the 'right' story so that it can have done with stories: '– story . . . if you could finish it . . . you could rest . . . sleep . . . not before . . .' (*Cascando*, p. 30).

Yet though they strike the ear so differently the two speakers reveal that they have something in common by being so completely taken up with their function – the same one, to project a story. Voice has no sense of listeners. His business is '. . . to find him . . . in the dark . . . to see him . . . to say him . . . for whom . . . that's it . . . no matter . . .' (*Cascando*, p. 44). Opener says, 'Listen.' But both must, in their different ways, evoke the character of Woburn. Voice even appears to hint at the connection by using the second person – '. . . if you could finish it . . . you could rest . . .' – before shifting to the first person – '. . . but this one . . . is different . . . I'll finish it . . . I've got it . . .'

Then Voice moves into his story and now he too, in his breathless, idiosyncratic way, begins to perform a function required by the medium, that is to narrate and especially to visualise for the listeners. The aim, as he tells us, is 'to see him . . . to say him . . .' The play is about Woburn, a character who never appears, Beckett has said. There is a bit of a joke here, for how does a character in a radio play 'appear'? Well, through his voice, and it is true that Woburn never acquires one. But it is also true that he is more thoroughly visualised than anything in the play and that in that sense he 'appears' as Opener and Voice never will. Voice works hard to bring him into focus: first, an undefined shape, in a shed, waiting for night, we are told, lifting his head, getting up oddly, knees first like a new-born creature (which he is), setting out into a landscape which gradually firms up around him – 'right the sea . . . left the hills . . .' – making his laborious journey down the boreen across the dunes, stumbling, falling, finally lying in a boat and drifting out to sea. He acquires clothes – 'same old broad-brim' – and size – 'huge bulk'. Voice can never manage to see his face; it is always turned away, or he is lying face down in the mud, the sand, the bilge at the bottom of the boat. He will never look up and face the light. Nor can Voice 'change' him enough, nor see what is in his head, though he tries: '. . . his head . . . what's in his head . . .'

Yet so much is brought before the mental eye that we surely keep expecting more to materialise, perhaps even, as Voice hopes, all. There is pressure on us from the rhythm to collaborate in the evocation: '...follow him...don't lose him...Woburn story...' And there is aid from Music, who comes in, supporting, repeating, stressing, helping to make the key motifs familiar. Humphrey Searle's music highlights especially the motifs: Woburn, 'see him...say him', the island. Music also helps to bring out the regular alternations between the story of Woburn (marked in draft by Beckett as 'élément histoire') and the story of the storyteller (marked 'élément soi'). It can emphasise the echoes between the two types of story, plant the suggestion that they are obscurely connected. As Voice is compelled to travel after Woburn, so Woburn is compelled to travel to the sea. Voice reflects on himself – '...all I ever did...in my life...with my life...' – and then reverts to Woburn – '...a long life already...say what you like...a few misfortunes...that's enough...'

And what of connections with Opener? Of course we cannot forget him; he is always there, intervening, opening and closing, separating Voice and Music and bringing them together. But he soon reveals that he is far from being merely a mechanical function. Once he has demonstrated his powers – 'So, at will' – he too, like Voice, reverts to private obsessions, and we hear in them echoes from the stories Voice is spinning. 'It's my life, I live on that,' he says; 'I have lived on it...enough. Till I'm old. Old.' The ear must recall that phrase of Voice, '...a long life already...', which could apply either to himself or to his character. Opener protests that the people who say Voice and Music are in his head are wrong: 'They say, he opens nothing, he has nothing to open, it's in his head... There is nothing in my head.' Again, an echo floats up from the story: '...what's in his head...'

It is *his* life, then, that is being reflected in the tale of Woburn? His vehement denials draw attention to that possibility and he continually reverts to it. Towards the end, when the story is mounting to a crescendo – 'this time I have it...we're there ...Woburn...nearly' – and Music has entered the soundscape in a way which seemingly takes Opener aback, he is galvanised into a statement which seems obliquely to admit that everything proceeds from him, that Voice and Music are there to offer him ways out of himself:

There was a time I asked myself, what is it.
There were times I answered. It's the outing.
Two outings.
Then the return.
Where?
To the village.
To the inn.
Two outings, then at last the return, to the village, to the
    inn, by the only road that leads there.

(Cascando, p. 47)

It is an image, as he says, though not quite as he also claims 'like any other', for in choosing to envisage his creative activity as a journey, he is linking himself with those other travellers, Voice and Woburn.

Beckett brings us to the point where we cannot miss the possibility that Opener, Voice, and Woburn are one. But what of Music? That is a mystery which deeply perplexes Opener. 'Is that mine too?' he says, and later he registers the strangeness of their coming together so easily, 'As though they had linked their arms'. Music gives him his greatest shock, coming in without being specifically invited, after one of those silences which by being carefully distinguished from pauses, seem to have special significance. 'God,' he says, and then, when Music repeats the statement, 'God God.' There is no indication from Beckett as to what Music is conveying here. In producing the play we had to commit ourselves to an interpretation and decided that Music should express something Opener was not prepared to hear: in contrast to the feverish excitement elsewhere, this music should be calm, confident, even majestic, suggesting a certain independence, perhaps even a movement away from the Woburn story to the almost unimaginable next one.

This would fit in, it seems to me, with the Opener's conviction that his function cannot be explained subjectively. 'They' say it is all in his head, but he will not have it so: 'I don't protest any more, I don't say any more, There is nothing in my head' (Cascando, p. 43). He is a medium, he seems to be saying, receiving sounds which, like Voice and Music, come 'from one world to another'. Beckett holds these two warring views in delicate balance, wittily, relying on the medium he is using to embody the ambiguity. The best evidence for the Opener's view is the play itself, as we hear it. For us indeed Voice and Music are always 'out there', coming in at the Opener's call. He realises for us a world beyond our vision, giving it material reality.

Yet he is also – and this is the special tension of the play – a perplexed and uncertain being who is afraid to open, as he says at one point; though 'dry as dust' he wistfully dwells on thoughts of May, season of long days and, as he reminds us towards the end, 'the reawakening'.

And there is a kind of reawakening, as the tide of the story-telling gathers force, reflecting itself in the tide within the story which gathers up Woburn's rudderless boat sand carries him helpless out to sea. Opener too is caught up in the tide. Gone the detachment; he is joining in now with Voice and Music. 'Good,' he says, and 'Come on', as they intensify the effort to realise Woburn and the sense of 'almost there' becomes overpowering. They are cut off, as always, in midstream, but we do not hear Opener say 'I close', and we should not expect to. The three are all one now, the tide is flowing fast, we will never hear the end of the Woburn story, never reach the island, but despite everything against it, we have seen Woburn, seen the island and the lights he did not see, been given an extraordinary glimpse into the complex process by which the medium has been made to communicate.

To turn from *Cascando* to *Rough for Radio*, a play recently given its first broadcast by the BBC, is to move to more grotesque vein: the pains of evocation are represented as a kind of comic Grand Guignol. The arrangement is inquisitorial: Animator and his Stenographer, with the aid of Dick, who is mute but wields an audible pizzle, try to wring out of their victim, Fox, some magic word which must be fresh, never used before by him. We learn from the Animator's opening dialogue with Stenographer that in between sessions Fox is kept tied up, gagged, and hooded so that there is no chance of his letting drop in solitude the precious word which *'may be it'*.

No music enters in here: the activity is clearly literary (we are told that a fresh pad and pencils are laid out ready for the day's writing). The Animator is every inch a bookman: he revels in grotesquely unusual words like 'fodient rodents', cannot resist an allusion – 'Ah these old spectres from the days of book review-ing, they lie in wait for one at every turn' – and is quick to recognise echoes of Dante in Fox's apparently untutored talk.

The examination of Fox proceeds with business-like blandness, punctuated unpleasantly by the sound of Dick functioning, and drolly by the exchange of courtesies and pleasantries between Animator and his recording angel. It seemed uncannily appropriate in the BBC production that Animator should be played by Harold Pinter, for we were well in his line of country in this inquisition scene: one even began uneasily to wonder whether Pinter, having become a Beckett character, was not secretly engaged in rewriting the play.

'Should one note the play of feature?' Stenographer asks, having received from Fox, so she says, a radiant smile: later she observes a tear. The Animator is unsure. There is witty implication here that the listeners would probably like some visualisation but that the business of the medium is, after all, with words, and that this time that is all we will get. When the words do come from the elusive Fox, they are exceedingly odd: he has a style all his own, both countrified and archaic, with a leaning to poetic inversion: 'Ah yes, that for sure, live I did, no denying, all stones all sides...' Animator identifies the echo of Dante, 'There all sigh I was, I was,' hints that this experience too is purgatorial.

We begin to wonder whose purgatory. Fox is suffering, but so is Animator, whose hopes of hearing new words are continually dashed by the all-remembering Stenographer – 'What an idea sir!' It is no easy task for this literary person to tackle the wild quarry. No wonder, perhaps, that what emerges from Fox is so monstrous, a weird distortion of the natural; there is talk of soaping a mole and drying it by the embers, of somehow harbouring a brother, his 'old twin' inside him and of being given advice: 'Have yourself opened, Maud would say... I'll give him suck if he's still alive, ah but no, no no.'

There is something new here at last – the notion of a brother for Fox and the name 'Maud', which seems to be an unconscious contribution from Stenographer – it was her nannie's name, she recalls. She is rapidly becoming less cool as the Fox stories become more bizarre; the Animator has to soothe her: '... such things happen. Nature, you know... [*Faint laugh*] Fortunately. A world without monsters, just imagine!' But he too is becoming excited; creative energy is rising, not unrelated to the sexual warmth which has been creeping into his dialogue with Stenographer. Now he directs that energy on to Fox, by way of Stenographer, slipping her, as he puts it, on to the victim, ordering her to kiss him. We hear a howl, are told that Fox has lost consciousness. And it seems that the work may have been done. Animator and Stenographer are left pondering the achievement of the day, offering each other suggestions for completing the strange story of Maud. Finally Animator corrects the record of Fox's talk, inserting after 'Maud would say', 'between two kisses'.

Not much for a day's writing, but as Animator says to Stenographer at the end, 'Don't cry, miss, dry your pretty eyes and smile at me. Tomorrow, who knows, we may be free.' It is a broad hint, if we need it, that the purgatory of this writing exercise has been the Animator's: a self-imposed torture. As he wrings words out of Fox, so Beckett has wrung a play out of an experience seemingly intractable to dramatic treatment, the artist's silent inner struggle to produce just a few words that are fresh and seem as if they might lead somewhere interesting. We hear for ourselves what a labour it is – though with its amusing side – to prune the luxuriant fancy and decide what words to keep, what to reject or rewrite, what may eventually form the nucleus of a story that will have meaning, though the meaning can scarcely even be glimpsed at the start.

Freshness is the goal in *Rough for Radio*, and a fresh view is what we are given in all the plays I have been discussing: a fresh view of the medium and its possibilities and of our own capacity to follow the artist in his mysterious task of summoning up worlds out of thin air. As listeners we cannot but be involved in the task, for it forms the stuff of the drama; the conventions of the radio play become the element we play with. Beckett pushes to the limit the demand for close listening which is a condition of radio drama. If we listen well enough, we recognise that words are gaining new force from their tense, witty, suggestive relationship with sound effects, music, and – audacious coupling – silences. We are rewarded with a strange paradox; by being without sight, we have been made to see – see, with the mental eye, both the sights of external reality and the meaning they convey about the hidden world of the interior.

DAVID WADE

WORDS ARE BEGUILING. Because I can write down and you can read the three words 'British radio drama', it may persuade us that there is a unity we can discuss, knowing with an agreeable certainty exactly what we are talking about. There is no such unity: radio drama is and, for as long as I have been listening to it, always has been a kind of loose confederation of diverse offerings whose only points in common are that they are usually in the form of dialogue and usually presented by the BBC's Radio Drama Department. But there may be exceptions even to those criteria: a sizeable amount of the Drama Department's work takes the form of story-reading for one voice; Schools Broadcasting and Light Entertainment also put out work in dramatic form, while what to many listeners is the most spellbinding drama of all time, *The Archers,* was for many years the product of Midland Region and had nothing to do with the central department at all. More significantly, during 1978 the term 'radio drama' for the first time ceased to refer exclusively to the activities of the BBC: the contribution to it of Independent Local Radio may as yet be infinitesimally small, but a monopoly of some fifty-six years has been scratched, if not yet dented. Indeed, at the 1978 awards given by the Imperial Tobacco Company and the Society of Authors a production by Manchester's Piccadilly Radio, *The Last Rose of Summer,* reached the last four in the category for single plays and serials. Some of the future of radio drama may be foreshadowed in that event. For the past and present purposes of this essay, however, 'British radio drama' refers almost entirely to the work of the Drama Department of BBC Radio.

What then does this loose confederation consist of? It seems to me I should begin by outlining some sort of answer to that question, not least because in a society which since the mid-fifties has so enthusiastically deserted radio for television I cannot be sure how many readers will be able to provide an answer for

218

themselves. But it is also important to establish the nature of the creature, for on that depends what I can say about it; and besides, some of the history of radio drama in the last twenty years will emerge in the process.

From one point of view, British radio drama is something other than pure British. A phrase 'National Theatre of the Air', coined apparently by J. C. Trewin, has often been used to describe the Drama Department's sweeping range and influence, but it does it less than justice. Radio in fact provides an 'International Theatre of the Air', a part of its output every year being devoted to the classics of world theatre, to productions of plays by living foreign dramatists and even in recent years to the transmissions of productions made in foreign studios: the work of the American sound drama production unit, the hideously named *Earplay*, is a case in point, and British listeners have heard imported productions of work by Arthur Kopit, Edward Albee, and others. In parallel with this radio drama *is* a National Theatre in the sense that a part of its output is the standard theatrical repertoire of British classics, ancient and modern. In both these roles, national and international, it finds itself serving the many people in this country who love the theatre but, for whatever reason – geographical or financial – can never get to it. In doing this, however, in acting, so to speak, as a theatre-substitute, it seems to me that the BBC is engaged not so much in radio drama as in 'drama by means of radio'. This is not a subject with which I particularly want to concern myself, so having drawn attention to its admirable existence, I do not propose to come back to it.

There is another aspect in which Trewin's phrase, by the comparison implicit in it, could be said to understate the role of radio drama. The National Theatre, in its large and costly complex on the South Bank of the Thames, mounted in its first full year of operation ninety-two new productions, of which more than half were of the less ambitious 'Platform' type; just under 700,000 people paid to see them. Radio's tally of new play productions annually is of the order of six hundred, and it is not uncommon of a weekday afternoon – this being radio drama's peak time – for an audience well in excess of 700,000 to hear a single transmission. In both these versions of the National Theatre most productions are of new plays, although in radio an average of one play a week will be by an author receiving his first-ever performance in any medium.

I do not want to stress these differences to what may be taken as the detriment of a live theatre, because it must be obvious that radio is working in quite a different world and faces entirely separate and maybe less acute problems: the comparison is intended purely to illustrate the very large scale of the radio dramatic enterprise. Another way to do this is to draw attention to the fact that those six hundred or so productions are merely the survivors of about ten thousand scripts submitted every year, most of them unsolicited, most of them unusable, but all requiring to be read. The reality of this influx will be plain to anyone who has ever visited the Broadcasting House Play Library in London: there each submission is recorded in an immense card index in which, as the most cursory examination will show, by far the most common entry bears only some perfectly unfamiliar author's name and a couple of rejected titles. Nothing could speak more clearly of BBC Radio's reputation as the one greatest magnet and promoter of hopeful dramatists in the United Kingdom and probably in the world. Other much less common entries present a different aspect of this matter, one nicely summarised in a Schools Broadcasting interview I did with John Scotney, once a Radio 3 Drama Script Editor, who has since gone to be Head of the BBC's Television Script Unit: 'I was talking to one of my ex-bosses and said, "By the way, can you think of the names of important modern playwrights who have started in radio?" He just said, "Yes, all of them." '[1] No doubt there are one or two who could show they did nothing of the kind. Alan Ayckbourn, for example, although a radio drama producer, does not appear to have written original work for radio before entering the theatre. This, however, is not to deny that the existence in radio of an enormous market for plays and its consequent readiness to give new writers, once anyway, the benefit of the doubt has been of incalculable value to many now-famous names (Bill Naughton, Harold Pinter, Tom Stoppard, etc.) who have subsequently gone on to write for the theatre, the cinema, and television. And of course it is not just a matter of size of market: radio can chance its arm for a much smaller financial risk than any of the other media. At the same time it ought to be said that this remarkable situation is in some ways less satisfactory than my description of it might suggest. For example, names like Naughton, Pinter, or Stoppard, whatever they may owe to radio and it to them, do not very truthfully represent it as it is: since they rose to the top of their profession, they contribute to it either very infrequently or not at all. The reasons for this are various and I shall be referring to them as we go along.

The immense amount of material it attracts and consumes is on its own enough to ensure that radio drama is no neat and tidy unity. But sheer quantity does not necessarily give much idea of how diverse it actually is. To grasp that, the simplest method is to look at the several different categories in which it reaches its listeners and which reflect variety not only of material but of audience as well. First there is the very broad division into Radios 3 and 4; after that the allocation of plays to various slots (*Drama Now, The Monday Play, Thirty Minute Theatre,* etc.), each of which will tend to collect work within a certain wide range of sophistication and emotional and intellectual demand. These are what I had in mind when referring to radio drama as a loose confederation, but it is also possible to detect here a kind of hierarchy: Radio 3 is at the apex with its *World Theatre* and *Drama Now* presenting classics and the more testing new work respectively. Then we move down to Radio 4 with its *Monday Play, Thirty Minute Theatre, Afternoon Theatre, Saturday Night Theatre* arranged in what I take to be, very approximately, a descending order of difficulty. At the time of writing (early 1979) there is also a newcomer to the confederation, *Hi-Fi Theatre,* which by its content if not its title appears to be aiming near the top of the pyramid.

However, I am well aware that this idea of hierarchy will not bear much weight. An *Afternoon Theatre* play, for instance, is not a certain kind of beast: a whole menagerie has been shown in that one enclosure, from Pinter to the most conventional domestic drama. Fay Weldon among the better-known (and better) active writers has contributed to it as well as to the *Monday Play* and Radio 3. Indeed, the Monday slot nowadays quite often presents work which once would have been reserved for Radio 3; which – following recent precedent – may even have received its first hearing there. Sometimes the tables have been turned and a play initiated on a Monday night has then, so to speak, graduated to Radio 3. To put it another way, what was once a no-man's land dividing the old Third Programme from the Home Service has now to a very marked extent been occupied, and it is interesting, in the light of what I shall have to say later about Radio 3, that the impetus to do this seems to have come principally from Radio 4. Here then is one rather important development in the recent history of radio drama, for it implies that the level of work to be heard on the more popular of the two channels has gone up. Undoubtedly it has: in theme, writing, production, and acting the general standard of drama on Radio 4 is considerably higher than it was when I first began professional listening in the sixties. John Scotney, at another point in the interview from which I have already quoted, put the matter graphically: 'The afternoon play used to be called "Plays to hoover to", but we've changed the style a lot.'[2] Yes, indeed, and this has been a matter of explicit policy on the part of the Drama Department, partly in acknowledgement of the fact that, in the wake of television, the major audiences for radio plays have migrated to the afternoons and expect a better kind of play, partly as an expression of a sort of latter-day Reithianism, a determination to do to the listener rather better than he would be done by, but with discretion of course, for in these tolerant days to be too explicit about such an intention is to attract charges of being elitist and patronising. None of this should be taken as suggesting that Radio 4 drama in all its manifestations now maintains an unvarying high level, nor that anyone requires it to. The improvement, however, has been great enough to raise doubts about the standards of Radio 3 itself. This has always been seen as a purveyor of innovation, experiment, and general excellence. How far in the period under review has it lived up to its high reputation? This is the particular question about the network to which I want to return.

If Radio 4 has closed the gap between itself and Radio 3, if it has raised its standards generally, what then has actually been the effect of this on its more run-of-the-mill productions? The 'plays to hoover to' may no longer loom large as once they did and as the modest and very conservative expectations of an audience no longer young certainly encouraged, but what are their successors like? I think the upgrading has taken us no higher than what might be christened 'plays for clearing up the lunch to' or 'fixing the supper to' or 'making do and mending to'. There is a distinction here: if you may hoover while your radio is giving you a play, the suggestion is that it really does not matter whether you can hear the thing or not; 'the play for clearing up the lunch to', however, will stand not much more interference than a faint clatter of dishes and the slosh of washing-up. It will be workmanlike, a thriller perhaps or something more socially relevant and it will probably have been written by an experienced writer, but, fatally, it will never quite have received the kiss of life; something 'not quite right' about the dialogue, the story line, or the characterisation, severally or all at once, tells you that this is a photofit play, not a genuine likeness. One can still hear a good many plays like this on radio, and they owe their existence to a number of factors: first, if you have to find up to six hundred broadcastable plays per annum, then by definition about a third of them will be below the going notions of average; secondly, the conservative audience no longer young has not vanished in the last twenty years: it has grown older and even been topped up, and its expectations, if higher than they were, are still comparatively modest; but a third consideration is that the demand for plays for 'clearing up the lunch to' may actually have increased. I have already mentioned the influence of television on radio audiences and intend to do so much more fully later on, but it is this combined with the advent of the now ubiquitous transistor radio which has helped to turn radio from a primary activity (you sit down in front of your large, immovable set and listen) to a secondary one (you take it around with you while doing something else). Broadcasters recognise this: magazine and other programmes are now geared to it, and I am sure its influence has been felt in drama too; a secondary activity calls for secondary plays and will continue to do so. Seen in one light, radio's huge patronage of playwrights is a means of ensuring the supply.

Although there are many instances of 'the play for clearing up the lunch to', I have not named so much as one and do not intend to do so, partly because singling out would be invidious; also, and much more important, because any example I might quote, not only here but at any level of radio drama, would be most unlikely to mean anything to the majority of my readers and indeed in most cases could not do so. Let me illustrate this: if I were conducting a discussion of contemporary drama in the theatre, I should be able to do it by reference to various famous active names. You would expect and I would try to give you an analysis of work most of which you would be familiar with; you would either have seen it or could confidently expect to at some point. Failing that, you could nip along to your public library and find it there in print. In addition you would have read extensive reviews of it in the press and heard or seen discussions on radio or TV. In some cases you could refer to a lengthy critical literature.

Compared with this, what is the situation within radio? In his 'personal recollection', *Prospero and Ariel,* that zestful and very productive man D. G. Bridson wrote of his thirty-five years in broadcasting, 'There had indeed been plenty of empty praise, but no more solid pudding than sitting behind a desk might well have landed on my plate. Few of my scripts had been published and not many of my shows survived, even in recorded form. For the rest they were blowing in the wind indeed.'[3] Bridson's time in radio ended in 1969, so it included the period when the influence and prestige of sound broadcasting were at their peak. If a first-class radio writer's output was so ephemeral then, it is not likely to have become more lasting in the ensuing years, and that is indeed the case. Of most of the authors I might write about, perhaps you would have heard of some of them and might remember the odd play, but your chances of improving that state of affairs would be remote: most radio plays are broadcast once; some twice; a few, a very few, three times or more and after that, if not destroyed, the recordings end up in the limbo of the Tape Library. Few find their way into print. For this last, a recent move by the Drama Department to publish play scripts will, if pursued, provide some remedy; so will the intended annual publication by Eyre Methuen of some half dozen scripts, winners of the new Giles Cooper Award. But these are drops in the ocean; substantially the radio play is and seems likely to remain a literary art without a literature. It is also one that receives scant notice from either press or broadcasting, an anomaly vividly illustrated at the time of writing by Jennifer Phillips's *Daughters of Men*: when this was heard on radio, critical notice was – what shall I say? – restrained. I expect upwards of half a million people heard it. When, however, it appeared at the Hampstead Theatre (one of the smallest in London) notices were lengthy and widespread throughout the press. I can of course safely make reference to this play because of that circumstance and also because it will form a part of the first Eyre Methuen collection. For the great bulk of radio plays, however – and I am now talking of some of the best work – it is as if they had no existence. This is part of the history of radio drama since 1960 and before, and I think it will be evident that it also greatly affects what it is worth the while of anyone to write about the subject: there is surely a certain futility in an examination of the work of authors if one's readers have little or no hope of becoming acquainted with it.

What I have just written is one constraint on how I can proceed; it combines with others I have mentioned (the quantity and bewildering diversity of the output, the commonplace nature of much of it, the tendency of the most successful radio dramatists to move on to higher things) to ensure that various ways forward will be at best unpromising. However, out of it there have emerged somewhat disjointedly several elements in the history of radio drama. I would now like to adopt a rather more orderly approach to that by going back to the beginning of my period and setting out what I believe to have been the state of play, as it were, in and around 1960. I should make it clear at this point that my personal experience of serious radio listening dates only from early 1966 when I became Radio Drama Critic of *The Listener*. For the few years before that I am on shakier ground.

An examination of who was contributing to radio drama in the early sixties suggests that in many respects its condition was exceedingly healthy. There would be no difficulty in compiling a list of writers – Samuel Beckett, Harold Pinter, James Saunders, Giles Cooper, Louis MacNeice, Henry Reed, Barry Bermange, Tom Stoppard, and more besides – and saying without noticeable exaggeration that all were actively involved in writing for radio. Either they had recently done so or would be doing so again or both. The Golden Age of Radio – that term which is rather loosely applied to some of the more brilliant output of the late forties and the fifties – seemed to be continuing with undiminished splendour. Yet memory, reinforced by reference to the weekly reviews I wrote for some eighteen months on end (during which I heard almost every broadcast play and even some that were never broadcast), leaves me with the strong impression that by the mid-1960s radio drama had begun to sound pretty discouraging. How could this have happened?

One possibility which occurs to me is that I discouraged myself. Radio drama was no less plentiful and diverse than now and 'the play to hoover to' was in its heyday. Anyone attempting near-comprehensive listening might well find that he had simultaneously undergone a course of aversion therapy. Perhaps; and I was not the only one in this condition. But there were other less subjective factors, one of which, I would suggest, dominated and even incorporated the rest: I mean the rise to influence and power of the Genghis Khan of Shepherd's Bush – television. With this in mind one can look at the period around 1960 in a rather different light. Even the everlasting *Archers* had already reached the Everest of their listening figures and had begun to descend: Norman Painting's extended diary of the series, *Forever Ambridge*, is filled during the early sixties with, as it were, the nervous glances over the shoulder of a man who hears the thundering hooves of the barbarian hordes. D. G. Bridson, again writing in *Prospero and Ariel*, seems to move through the decade to his retirement in the growing awareness of a once great empire on the wane: he sub-titled his book *The Rise and Fall of Radio*. Many of his colleagues, who in features and drama had helped sound broadcasting to reach a position as influential as that now occupied by television, were themselves entering their last years with the Corporation. And what colleagues they had been: another interesting discovery to be made in the Play Library is by turning up the small wads of cards marked 'Cleverdon' or 'Dillon' or 'Raikes' (to name but three) only to find them crammed with proposals and adaptations and translations and editings and original work. These are the memorials to the vitality of that now almost departed species, the writer–producers; and if other, very much skinnier, wads of cards say anything, the present generation of producers, with all their talent, are unlikely to match them.

By 1960 Henry Reed had completed all his important work: *The Unblessed, The Monument, The Streets of Pompeii, Vincenzo*, and that formidable version of *Moby Dick*, written as if its adapter had conceived it all himself. (These, incidentally, either are or have been in print.) In 1963 Louis MacNeice died. Giles Cooper's allegiance, if never his talent, seemed to be swinging more and more towards the theatre and television, but by late 1966 he too was dead. The other names I grouped with his above were from that time on to contribute less and less to radio. By the 1960s many of the really able and ambitious, the latter-day Cleverdons, Dillons, Bridsons, Raikeses, were going off to television. In early 1964 plans for the dispersal of the Features Department were announced, and this above all sounded a knell, for it was in Features under Laurence Gilliam that much of the best work of the Golden Age had been created. The decade ended with the crisis and near-mutiny that surrounded the publication of *Broadcasting in the Seventies*, that new deal for radio which, as it was read at the time, seemed to recognise and perpetuate its new inferior status by decreeing that it should concentrate its energies (such as they were) on what it could do best, by which was meant 'better than television'. The emphasis was to be on the broadcasting of news, current affairs, and music. There was no actual pronouncement against drama – indeed, I recall protestations to the contrary – but people knew about the high proportion of humdrum work on the Home Service (soon to be Radio 4); they compared the Third with the impending Radio 3 and its eight hours of speech per week; and they saw that many of those who were to lead the New Model Radio had been drafted in from television where their experience had been chiefly in news and current affairs. They were not encouraged. As Bridson put it with characteristic vigour, '*Broadcasting in the Seventies* proved to most thinking people that the seventies were for the Yahoos, so far as responsible broadcasting went.'[4] I do not myself think it has turned out like that, but this undoubtedly expressed a mood of the time: by 1970 radio had lost its way and knew it but did not at all care for the way it had been told to go. That, I believe, was the wretched state of mind I found reflected in the drama of the late sixties and early seventies, preserved in what I wrote first for *The Listener* and later for *The Times*.

I would like to pursue this question of the rise of television and radio's decline because I think it may cast some interesting light on what has happened to the radio play. Why did radio go down so far and fast in the face of television? That is the puzzle, although it may seem that I have already answered it, leaving nothing much to add except a list of consequences which, by a kind of positive feedback, only made the radio position worse: because radio had declined, it drew less attention – and what it did draw in the swinging sixties was often faintly contemptuous; it also drew less talent and less money. All the novelty, the action, the notice, and the riches were with television. How could radio hope to compete? This is all true enough, but I do not think it tells the whole story by any means.

What has to be remembered about radio is that before the growth of television it too had dominated British life, and its audiences were at home with it in a remarkably sophisticated way. They knew how to listen, had grasped by the million the really rather difficult surreal world of *ITMA* and later, if less rapturously, of *The Goon Show* without apparent difficulty. Present-day audiences, and particularly the young – so I am told – have problems with sustained or complex listening: they seem to have lost the knack. When television arrived it sooner or later tried its hand at the things radio had done so well, but it quickly became apparent that in certain areas – and surreal comedy has certainly been one of them – the new medium was undeniably, sometimes embarrassingly, less good at the job than the old. Yet in the event an audience which already had the real McCoy from radio, simply ignored the sensible and true avouch of its own eyes and ears: it came and gawped and was conquered.

What I believe spelled radio's decline was primarily the con-ditioned – or should it be the natural? – preferences of human perception. We are a species in whom, unless we are born blind, the primacy of the visual mode is first established and then reinforced during every day of our lives after birth. Perceiving by hearing is harder, less 'natural', less rewarding, less informative work for the human organism than perceiving by sight. Things heard are commonly signals for sight to be brought into play to interpret them, and rarely do we rely on sound to the exclusion of sight. Our sympathies seem to express this: it is more dreadful, more pitiable, to be blind than deaf, or so we believe. There are exceptions to this primacy of sight, and music – some music – is one of them. Here vision, and especially the restless glass eye of television, may actually be an impediment: how to reconcile the aural sublimities of the obbligato to 'The trumpet shall sound' with the hideous visual reality, probably in full-colour close-up, of the trumpeter's face as he plays it? Even at a distance in the concert hall, it would be wiser not to look. So it may be as a result of this that radio, since the triumph of television, has staked its survival so heavily on the broadcasting of music.

More commonly, however, radio with its reliance on sound alone may seem a medium for the blind to which sighted crea-tures will only adhere as long as there is no visual alternative. It might be said, with an agreeable touch of moralising, that televi-sion drove radio into second place not so much because it was newer and richer and more glamorous and certainly not because it was invariably better at saying all that had to be said – although I do not deny that better it quite often is – but because it always offers the easier option. There are enough examples from other fields to suggest that, given the choice between two activities, it is the easier one that we will go for, even if it is not always strictly appropriate, even if we could actually have some much more interesting experiences by declining it. Radio comedy makes the point: in the unlikely event that the spiritual heirs of Kavanagh or Milligan could be found to work for radio, I am in no doubt that we could have from them many more interesting and indeed hilarious experiences than television comedy has ever given us or ever will. But as long as there existed a *Monty Python*, poor clumping fellow that he is, to be seen, that is where, *en masse*, we would go.

These circumstances have, I believe, had their effect on every branch of radio speech – even news broadcasting where Radio 1's *Newsbeat* has been specially devised to be comprehensible to people unskilled at grasping anything but the simplest messages by word of mouth. In drama it has changed the listening pattern, as we have seen, by monopolising the evening audience, leaving radio with the afternoons. But the effect has been more profound than that. As I mentioned earlier, present afternoon audiences expect a better kind of play, and one reason for this, one reason why 'the play to hoover to' has receded and 'the play to clear lunch to' is not even more plentiful, is that television does not noticeably deal in them: as it was put to me by Ronald Mason, the current Head of Radio Drama, an audience which looks at television wants the same standards of social realism from its radio. No one can possibly object to that, but the coin has another side: I think that, as in comedy so in drama, televison has obscured the fact that there are things, necessary things, which it either does indifferently or not at all, but which radio does both naturally and superbly well.

What kind of things? At this point I really have no option but to come up with an instance, and it is just as well that the one I have chosen comes from the work of Don Haworth, for he is a radio playwright who happens to have had some of his scripts published, and *On a Day in a Garden in Summer* is one of them. Here is its opening sequence:

    [*Birds: a dawn chorus*]
DICK. Nice morning.
JIM. Grand.
    [*Bullocks low and sheep bleat in the distance. Birds near and far dive and tweet. The conversation is leisurely. These country sounds are heard behind it and during the quite long pauses.*]
JIM. Nippy though.
DICK. Morning mist. Morning mist and morning dew. Going to be hot today, young Jack.

JACK. Is it, grandad?

DICK. When the sun strikes through on a hot day, early summer, there's no better thing in creation than to be a dock plant in this garden.

JIM. Because we fear nothing.

DICK. Correct.

JACK. What is there to fear, Uncle Jim?

DICK. Nothing.

JIM. Encroachment.

JACK. What's encroachment, Uncle Jim?

JIM. The other plants encroaching.

DICK. But we don't fear it.

JIM. Attempting to choke us.

DICK. Because we're more than equal.

JIM. Sometimes.

DICK. Always, Jim.

JIM. Not always, Dick. A large number of dock plants have been lost through the years.

DICK. You're here, I'm here, young Jack's here. This is our patch of garden.

JIM. We tried to teach them that.

DICK. Well, then, it's finally sunk in.

JIM [*laughs*]. I don't think those daisies will come again.

JACK. What's daisies?

DICK. Surface leaf, white flower, close up at night. We throttled them.[5]

Unfortunately, I do not have the space to give a synopsis of what turns out to be an enchanting and a forbidding allegory of the perils and uncertainties of existence: there are hints of that, of course, from the sixth speech on. But the point I particularly want to draw attention to will have struck you as early as the speech before that: the very human characters are not two men and a boy, but two dock plants and a young one – characters whom, I think you will agree, television would be quite unable to present but which give radio no trouble at all. It so happens that for the same Schools programmes from which I have already quoted, I also spoke to Don Haworth and was able to discuss with him how radio can do this and why he, as a writer, should want it to. He said:

Obviously if you really thought about talking dock plants, we'd be in a sort of talking horse business, it would be like a comic cartoon. The thing in radio is the value of the ambiguity of existence in this way; one is not always confronted with a picture of a plant, one doesn't think 'Well, where are their eyes, then?' One doesn't examine the naturalistic background, there isn't the embarrassing presence of something that is not a human being taking the human role. But if I think: could I not have done this with human beings? – I don't think I could because I would then be inside a very highly stereotyped situation, we'd be as it were in the cowboy situation: there they are at the Alamo and they've knocked the windows out and they're waiting for the Indians. It's very difficult to resolve this except in some conventional way in which they die heroically or announce war or do something else of this sort; whereas in this play, simply because I had not thought of what the ending might be, it was as it happened to be.[6]

The ending in fact moves perfectly naturally to a crisis involving human beings, weedkiller, and the death of Jim. The play is not reduced by its horticultural setting but gains stature from it. In short, it makes it perfectly plain that if there are things to be said requiring some kind of dramatic form, but which will be most acceptably, most persuasively, most penetratingly conveyed only if there is nothing to see, then among the media you either get them from radio or you do not get them at all. And of course, as Mr Haworth's play shows, there are things like that. His particular theme apart, we are faced with the monumental unlikelihood that the whole of reality – some might say *any* reality – must be visible. Even hard science tells us that this is not so and we know from our own experience that the world of the mind is not visible, no more than almost anything we may imagine or glimpse outside or beyond ourselves. Abstractions are not visible. The world of the future is not visible. Fairy-stories, allegories, legends, myths, space odysseys – all these risk and usually receive reduction by sight.

These then are *par excellence* the worlds of drama in which, if they are to act upon us as they might, radio holds a virtual monopoly, and so you might imagine that the history of radio drama since 1960 would to an appreciable extent be concerned with work of that kind. And yet, within my hearing, it is not so. Don Haworth apart, I would have difficulty listing more than a handful of writers who could be called – if I may be forgiven the expression – radio-active and who seem to me to produce more often than not work that inhabits radio's own worlds. Some names that come to mind here are Rhys Adrian, Stephen Davies, Peter Everett, Gabriel Josipovici, Peter Redgrove; also Jonathan Raban on a good day, and Frederick Bradnum too; and I would add John Antrobus, provided it were made clear that the inclusion related to form, not to content, of which I have never been able to find any to speak of. There is one other name, as well, which I want to add with special emphasis: he may not have contributed extensively in very recent years, but R. C. Scriven has beyond any doubt been one of the most distinguished of that small band of genuine radio writers during the period I am covering, and I would like as it were to halt here for a moment to say something about this exceptional figure in the history of radio drama, particularly as he is now quite an old man who may be nearing the end of his creative life.

The astonishing thing about a writer like Scriven is that he has ever had a creative life at all. From the age of eight, when he contracted an ear infection, he has been almost totally deaf, and the same illness also seems to have laid the foundations for the glaucoma which came to a head thirty years later – in the 1940s – leaving him stone-blind. Yet in 1947 he wrote his first radio play and a year later *A Single Taper* (published in 1953), which was an account in verse of the operations to try to prevent his blindness. Following from this, much of his successful radio writing has been autobiographical and in verse. It has also been set apart by a powerful melodiousness and by the most intense visual quality, which would do credit to a man in full possession of his hearing and his sight. No illustration can really convey the effect his work creates, but what follows will give some idea of it. It is part of a play about his childhood, *All Early in the April*, the first in a collection published under the title of one of them, *The Seasons of the Blind*:

[*Fade up the slow start of a steam train*]
NARRATOR.:   The train departed dead on Bradshaw time.
Late summer and early autumn were so blended,
the swallows seemed reluctant to depart.
The leaves were darker – even the leaves of the lime.
As the smells of all green things blend after rain,
field merged with wood and wood with country lane.
Down the perspective of a half century
I see, I see
that landscape, caught by an artist's brush,
      suspended
for one brief hour – and eternity.
Somewhere between South Milford and Leeds, long
      ago
the train ran out of that landscape and was lost.
Was it at Micklefield? Was it at Barnbow?
No, no. The point's impossible to trace.
The line is marked in time, but not in space,

> an invisible, intangible boundary I crossed
> where the kingdom of boyhood, I shared with
>   Wilfred, ended.
> [*The train stops at the terminus.*]
> Granny met me, stooping to imprint
> kisses of White Heather, and love, and peppermint.
> GRANDMOTHER. My, how you've grown! Let's have a look at you.
> RONALD.   How's Mother, Granny?
> Granny, I've got a friend.
> His name is Wilfred Kemp. I like him no end.
> He can climb the tallest tree you ever knew.
> Wilfred could climb a church tower if he wanted to.
> Wilfred...
> [*Cross fade the terminus with an old cab horse*][7]

And so on: the story moves as the writer wishes, for radio will not hinder him. And notice the setting of that long reflective narrative against the highly evocative steam-train background – stillness and movement combined; the story advances in a kind of glow and everything is tinged, in a manner typical of Scriven's work, with a profound poignancy.

Surely this is an instance where a writer's immense handicaps have in fact been the making of him. Charles Lefeaux, who produced many of Scriven's plays, reported him as saying, 'When a man knows he will soon be blind, what he looks at stays looked at.' This might be taken as implying that by ferocious application (which may be what gives his work a certain grittiness) he has managed principally to recreate what you or I could perceive as well or better merely by going to look. Nothing could be further from the truth: the effect is much more like that of *hearing* an impressionist painting. It conveys what the writer has presumably arrived at through years of concentrating on the remembrance of things seen: the depth of them. Indeed, when I consider Scriven's work, my inclination is to add his name to that earlier catalogue beginning 'Beckett, Pinter, Saunders', for he seems to me to be of that company.

But what of my more recent list? I am aware that, without subtracting any names from it at all, it must already seem parsimonious enough; and then, though I look at it with the maximum benevolence, I do wonder if by any means it matches up to 'Beckett, Pinter, Saunders' and the rest. Am I being impossibly demanding and perverse? Have I not, for example, chosen to mention only a handful of the well established and to ignore the

new generation? Perhaps, but Stephen Davies is of that generation, and as another part of my interview with John Scotney
suggested, it seems that radio writing of the kind I am discussing
is actually not being submitted in any quantity. Here is what Mr
Scotney had to say in relation to his experience selecting scripts
for Radio 3: 'I found that an awful lot of very good plays that came
to me were really stage plays, or if you like visual plays which
worked in terms of words but didn't primarily use the medium of
radio, and this I think is partly because of this concept of gradua-
tion...' – we had been talking about the way in which writers
regard the stage and television as a step up from radio – '... that
people would tend to try things for television or for the stage and
not necessarily get there and then turn to radio. I think the writer
is partly to blame for not recognising the uniqueness of radio.' If
only he recognised its uniqueness, perhaps he would begin to
work more often in the worlds it favours, but how far is he to
blame if he does not? Mr Scotney went on to qualify his statement: 'Radio is a medium of unique opportunities, but I am afraid
writers live by being noticed... radio gets comparatively little
notice.'[8] And as a result radio offers its writers fewer opportunities, smaller reputations, less money. So who can blame the
writer with a living to earn if his priorities are elsewhere? Yet
there remains the unarguable fact that radio offers him the chance
to say what he cannot say by other means; and furthermore it
happens that the worlds in which radio excels are also precisely
those in which the most imaginative writers are traditionally held
to excel. We might think of them as anglers, casting out lines from
the edges of perception and consciousness to see what they can
hook. Is that a proper metaphor? If so, then radio should hook
them, money, prestige, or no – for after all it does not pay them
nothing, nor offer no prestige at all. Far from it.

In fact it does not often seem to work like that. Rather the
reverse, to the extent that one finds writers whose work is radio
to its roots flirting with the stage or television. I have already
mentioned Giles Cooper as an instance; Rhys Adrian might make
another. As I have said, he is one of that select group of indisputable *radio* writers, and, indeed, his *Evelyn* won an Italia Prize in
1970: it was a typical Adrian play – rather small-scale and written
with a slight but very deliberate formality. For this writer the
basic material is everyday speech, not to say cliché, very accurately reproduced, but then its phrases are repeated, varied,

reversed until they gather innumerable and often disquieting implications. The truth of the matter is that people do not actually hold conversations quite like this, but on radio and in the hands of someone like Adrian, that is actually an advantage. *Evelyn*, however, subsequently appeared on television and the mismatch between the all-too-human faces of the actors and the slightly extraordinary dialogue did the play no good at all. A later work, *Buffet* (also intractably 'invisible') suffered a rather similar fate.

As if to counter this drift to television, the Drama Department tries to draw back the writers who have 'stepped up' from radio or to attract the attention of other great names who have never visited it. A joint commissioning scheme has been set up which arranges that several broadcasting organisations will commission the same work simultaneously, thus making it worth the highly successful author's while to write. From the late Sir Terence Rattigan this elicited the original version of *Cause Célèbre* of which, in radio form, one could only say that a funny thing happened to it on the way to the theatre. More successfully, Bill Naughton paid a return visit in 1973 with *The Mystery*, and plainly here was an author who has, and had retained, a real grasp of the medium. Earlier, in 1972, Tom Stoppard contributed *Artist Descending a Staircase*, not a major play – I doubt if Stoppard has written a major play for radio alone – but one which, like his earlier radio work, was well-nigh impossible to realise in any medium but sound. Here, indeed, it was absolutely essential to the action that the audience should not be able to see what was going on, for the central character was a blind girl and much of what happened in the course of the play, as well as what she had experienced before it, hinged on her blind interpretation. This put her and the listeners both in the same boat and both were equally easily misled. Undoubtedly this was a most ingenious use of sound – not trying, as so many authors do, to compensate for the listener's 'blindness', but employing it to serve the ends of the play.

However, whatever its successes, I cannot say that I look back on the results of the joint commissioning scheme so far with undivided satisfaction. Its diagnosis of radio's difficulty in hold-ing or attracting the finest (or at least the most successful) talent is 'Shortage of money'; its prescription, therefore, 'More money than usual'. The treatment has produced some good names and some work highly appropriate to radio, but not, in my view, anything we shall be looking back on twenty years from now as a classic in its field. It contrasts interestingly and vividly – as does much of radio's recent serious work – with some American contributions and in particular two of the *Earplay* presentations: Arthur Kopit's *Wings* and Anne Leaton's *My Name is Bird McKai*. These, together with Martin Esslin's production of John Robinson's *The Hunter Gracchus*, were extraordinarily apt examples of work to be heard and not seen. Perhaps Americans, having just (in the British sense) discovered radio, also grasp its uniqueness in a way which to us who have seen it rise, fall, and now stand up again is no longer quite so real.

But none of what I have just written seems to me to cast much light on why this uniqueness is not more magnetic, more apparent than it is to more writers. Could it be that the models – the performances and printed versions of radio's classics – do not exist? They may be thin on the ground, but enough exists (MacNeice, Reed, Cooper, Beckett, and so on) for any writer to lay hold of it and draw his own conclusions. Very possibly, of course, I am underrating the power of the opposing television magnet and the effect it has, as John Scotney has described, of persuading writers to conform first and foremost to the demands of that overwhelmingly visual medium. Or are there other forces which are at work upon the writer and which militate against the play for hearing only?

In the course of my conversation with Don Haworth, he expressed an interesting opinion which seems to me to bear on this, although before I quote it I should explain that Mr Haworth earns his living not as a radio playwright (few do that) but as a successful writer and director of documentaries for BBC Television. He therefore knows both radio and television intimately from within, and he characterised one element in television drama thus:

There is in television a kind of dominance of a particular kind of play which is that which is felt to be worthy because the agenda to which it addresses itself is socially political. This for the moment is what television tends to do: as a whole it is concerned with politics, it is concerned with news. A great deal of its money is necessarily spent on maintaining the organisation to provide a flow of these things and there is a tendency for drama to be an extension, a next-door department to that. Of course such a thing may happen in radio, but because the spectrum there is so very wide, it is possible to write practically anything...[9]

The spectrum in radio always has been wide and wide it remains, but the thing which Mr Haworth says *may* happen has, in my belief, been happening for some considerable time: plays addressing themselves to the socially political agenda – which I agree prevails in television – have in the last twenty years come to occupy a greater part of that spectrum than they did. If one looks back at many of radio's classics or more recently at the work of Scriven, Adrian, Josipovici, or Haworth himself, it is really very hard to see them as addressed to an agenda of that kind, but this type of work is less common.

It is of course no surprise if the agenda, the ethic which dominates television, should make itself felt in radio: anyone who has ever glanced at BBC Television's list of script requirements for writers will probably agree that the criteria it lays down are more likely to produce social-political themes and treatments than any others, and these have to be added to the influences I have already mentioned which ensure that many writers think of radio, if at all, as a long-stop for their television misses.

Of course radio has not acquired a taste for the social-political theme just because of television. Both of them have acquired it because that particular ethic is dominant in the society of which broadcasting and its listeners form a part. It seems to rest on the belief that if only we apply ourselves hard enough, then all our problems will be, if not solved, then at least substantially alleviated by social and political means: redistribution of goods, reallocation of power, and so forth. A tenet of this doctrine is that man knows what to do about himself and will do it provided he is not frustrated by his less enlightened fellows. At the same time, as the 1978 Reith Lecturer, Dr Edward Norman, has pointed out, the doctrine contains elements which can be equated with Christian teaching, so that, as a kind of bonus, it can also be held to reflect the mind of God. Small wonder then if it recommends itself as the proper concern of dramatists, if respect for it is taken as an unerring criterion of relevance. And yet there is very little in such a doctrine about how anything that is not merely different but qualitatively better can be achieved in the continuing presence of man as he is – perhaps because it holds that 'man as he is' is only the product of the circumstances it wishes to change. Nor does it seem to notice that what may well be other, less subjective, evidence of 'the mind of God' quite frequently bespeaks a very poor divine opinion of the mind of man. For if the mind of man should prove such an unreliable and shifting instrument, where is the doctrine, where is the agenda?

The mind of man, man as he is – these ideas are, I suggest, essentially part of that invisible world which I referred to earlier, and as such they are within the territory which radio with its intimacy and inwardness is particularly suited to explore. But what does such an exploration reveal? The territory was one over which the late Giles Cooper was often delighted to wander, and in an introduction to his *Six Plays for Radio* Donald McWhinnie typifies the Cooper findings as follows:

Cooper deals with inadequate human beings – or at least with people who by trying to resolve their problems create further problems for themselves. Most of his plays are set in an unremarkable domestic interior; his characters are undistinguished and, on the face of it, uninteresting; the individual never wins, however much he asserts himself, and though he may think he is a free agent his chances of fulfilling himself become increasingly remote – even when he asserts his authority, he usually finds a higher authority frustrating his ambition. The Cooper 'hero' may behave extravagantly, but life always cuts him down to size. Unless he happens to be utterly amoral – in which case he might stand a slight chance of survival. It is not a comforting view; in fact it is thoroughly unsatisfactory by text-book or Sunday newspaper rules of thumb, but strangely stimulating, or infuriating beyond belief, depending on the way you look at life.[10]

That frustrating higher authority is not some easily identifiable social or political entity which by appropriate action will be swept away: it is a strand in the fabric of life itself. In *On a Day in a Garden in Summer* (of which Don Haworth characteristically remarked to me, 'It's a deeply pessimistic play and I hope you get a good laugh out of it') one of the dock plants declares, 'Everything's an ever present threat... Life is lived in ever present threats', and the inescapable conclusion is, as it is with Cooper, that this is part of the human condition: it is not going to go away. If this, as I believe, is typical of what may emerge from the kind of writing that radio makes possible, then of course it must appear deeply inimical to a view of society founded on its diametric opposite – that there is no such thing as the inescapable human condition, that sooner or later man will find remedies. Perhaps it is fanciful, but I wonder if that opposition may not suggest a reason why the uniqueness and the peculiar strengths of radio drama are not more thoroughly exploited.

It may appear that I am saying that the social-political trend in radio drama is in some absolute way a 'bad thing'. By no means, if only because, while I do not believe that everything is remediable, neither do I believe its opposite. There can be a balance here, and it is struck in Louis MacNeice's *The Dark Tower*, in which the hero's eventual salvation is brought about both by his own efforts and those of forces outside himself. More immediately, and as I have already mentioned, television's style of drama has unquestionably had a good effect on the radio play, its obvious and often admirable social interest and realism having both acclimatised listeners to the same in radio and led them to expect it. It is true that a great deal of what we hear today is more absorbing, convincing, well-constructed, lively, well-written, and open-ended and displays a much higher standard of dialogue and characterisation than was the case when I began professional listening. If the social-political agenda has done that for radio, then I am for it. My reservation is that at the same time it may be diminishing radio's interest in saying things which are both equally important and, by the means and force with which they can be uttered, unique to the medium.

Earlier I asked the question how far Radio 3 has lived up to what might be expected of one with such a reputation for innovation, experiment, and excellence. First of all, I think it has to be remembered that this channel labours under some difficulties all its own which very much restrict the contribution it is able to make: since *Broadcasting in the Seventies* it has been obliged to concentrate on music and to limit its speech content, a balance which, other considerations apart, the power of the Musicians' Union might now make it difficult to alter radically. In addition to that and until very recently, its hours of mixed programming have been between 7.30 and 11.30 p.m. only. Not surprisingly, it has rarely been able to find room for more than two plays a week, including repeats, and in the period from early June to just before Christmas 1978 it broadcast some fifty actual plays, twenty-seven of them for the second time.

Within these boundaries, what was the repertoire like? Out of that fifty, about one-third were classics or other plays transported from the stage. Overall, the social-political agenda was well represented, while the play that was for radio or nothing did at once both rather poorly and rather better than it should. By that I mean first that there was little here that a Giles Cooper would not have felt he had equalled or surpassed in form and content. The few he might have saluted as of his fellowship were by three writers I have already mentioned: Arthur Kopit, Gabriel Josipovici, and Stephen Davies. This is amongst those I heard, which was 60 per cent of the total.

My second meaning is a good deal less complimentary, and, other reasons apart, I do not want to do any struggling author the disservice of citing his work in illustration of it. Nevertheless, I heard several plays which were for radio only in the sense that it was almost impossible to imagine where other than on Radio 3 they might have found a refuge. They were, you might say, serious drama's equivalent of 'the play to hoover to': they combined in equal measure negligibility and pretentiousness. This, and indeed the general picture I have painted, was no local phenomenon peculiar to 1978: it has been typical of Radio 3 for most of the years I have been hearing it.

How does this come about? It is, of course, inevitable that any network pursuing an experimental, innovative role will come up with some junk. But as I look back over many years of listening, it also seems to me that a faint odour of negligibility emanates from more of the repertoire than it should, that even at the top end of the scale there is an absence of work on which some successor of mine will be able to look back twenty years from now and declare that in the late sixties and the seventies we witnessed a flowering. On the contrary, I consider that what ought to be a beautiful and exciting garden at best maintains a tolerable show, at worst looks faded and run-down.

No survey like this should omit any mention of radio's technology: after all, that sound drama exists at all is by grace of technical invention. I have already referred briefly to the advent of the transistor radio with its effect upon sound broadcasting as a whole and its rather lesser influence on drama; probably the two most important technological events as far as plays have been concerned were the arrival of the tape recorder and the introduction of frequency modulation (FM), or as it is more often called, very high frequency (VHF) transmission.

From the point of view of the listener, the influence of the tape recorder is probably not very noticeable: his radio continues to talk or play to him rather as it has always done, or so it seems. In drama, however, it spelt the end of live transmissions and with that, so many people say, the loss of a certain edge which is given to a performance when actors know the microphone has people at the other end of it. On the other hand, it has given the director a far greater measure of control over the performance he eventually obtains: provided time allows, sequences can be done and done again, mistakes eliminated, balance perfected. The tape recorder has also been the basic instrument of the new art of radiophonics – the processing of natural or artificial sound to create special effects: the signature tune of *Dr Who* and some of the noises are probably the best-known example of the work of what since 1958 has been the Radiophonic Workshop.

Radiophonics is, or ought to be, an immensely powerful aid to certain kinds of imaginative, invisible drama – creating sounds that never were to evoke worlds that might be; yet it has proved extremely difficult to produce convincing results, and this seems to be chiefly because electronic sound, being itself artificial, tends to dehumanise. This was apparent even in such remarkable features of the early sixties as Barry Bermange's *Inventions for Radio*, where a background of electronic sound set against snatches of recorded interview, though spellbinding to begin with, gradually bled the human voices of all meaning. Radiophonics seems to work best in drama where an original natural sound has been manipulated only rather slightly, but I consider that it has yet to make a really important contribution in the sense of significantly enhancing an author's or director's meaning, let alone creating one of its own.

It may well be that listeners are as unaware of the influence of VHF as of that of the tape recorder, for as recently as 1978, more than twenty years after its introduction, the allocation of Parliamentary broadcasting to the medium wave threw *Afternoon Theatre* listeners up and down the country into a great tizzy. They either did not possess a VHF set or did not know how to use it. In their defence it should be said that radio manufacturers have been astonishingly slow in promoting their beautiful invention and that it is marginally more difficult to use than medium wave, but the compensations are impressive: reception virtually free from all kinds of interference, unaffected by night-time deterioration and delivering words and music with an almost uncanny clarity. When I first heard a telephone on VHF, I ran to answer it.

A play received on VHF can then be heard as its performers and director intended – every nuance of speech, every sound effect, even uneasy silences. These weapons are now at the writer's disposal as never before, and I would take some persuading that the current very high standard of radio acting does not owe quite a lot to the actor's knowledge that even if they cannot hear him out there as he speaks, when at last they do, they will hear in merciless detail.

Yet VHF never really rose in the world purely on its own abundant merits: it did, however, do so more indirectly. One other effect of the transistor radio has been to ensure that almost every set now on the market has a VHF facility. Many of the more ambitious models also offer stereophony, and this, through the influence of the gramophone as well as for reasons of gimmickry and commercial promotion, has caught the public fancy where VHF did not. The minor irony is that stereo and its derivatives, binaural stereo and quadraphony, need VHF in order to exist.

Of these three related developments I think it is really only necessary in this context to say anything about stereo itself. Quad (all-round sound) and binaural stereo (stereo for one in headphones) are available only to a tiny minority; in any case, what I have to say of stereo in drama would also apply to them.

Stereophonic broadcasting of plays and music does one marvellous and beneficial thing: it spreads the sound so that it appears to emanate from an area rather than a point. In play-production this gives far greater clarity and definition to 'large' scenes involving many voices and dense sound effect. The technique is valuable for that alone. But it also does something else. Sound has always had a certain depth on radio which was achieved by distance from the mike. Stereo 'places' voices and sounds in general in the two other dimensions: a voice will be stage-left or -right and there will also be a quite marked sense of vertical placing; moreover, as speakers or objects move, they will appear to transverse the 'sound screen' between the two loudspeakers – assuming in all this that the listener is sitting at more or less the correct point of intersection relative to the speakers. Note that in describing stereo I have to adopt the terms not of sound but of vision.

As the technique became more widely used during the later sixties, it was for this placing, this effect of visual compensation, that it was above all recommended to listeners. I recall a play, a two-hander for a masseuse and her female patient to which we were invited to listen first because, for the sake of verisimilitude, the actress playing the patient had done so more or less naked, second because it would be possible for us to tell with some exactitude on what part of the body the masseuse was operating. It was not a very remarkable play, and stereo did nothing to improve its quality: indeed, it introduced a rather unfortunate element of farce. The length of the patient's body being the same as the distance between the twin loudspeakers, the masseuse appeared to be working on a giantess. This is admittedly a slightly grotesque example; but more commonly what stereo productions did and still do is to invite the listener first to place and then to follow the movements of actors on a stage he cannot and never will see. For this reason it has been described as 'Theatre for the Blind', and its effect, in my experience, is not to enlarge the listener's view but to induce a kind of frustration. My powers of visualisation are well equipped to do all the placing necessary; they do not want to be fed with information which they have to decode and which in any case quite often contradicts and baffles them.

To do radio drama directors justice, I do not think they any longer use stereo quite as literally as they did. But why was it ever felt necessary to do so? The placing effect attempts to compensate for the blindness of radio as a medium, yet – as I hope I have shown – that blindness was and still is one of radio drama's greatest assets. I wonder if this, like the prevalence of the visual play, was not also brought about by the influence of television. That was the rich and dominant broadcasting medium and it was sighted. Perhaps it seemed that radio, in order to compete, must sell its birthright and get as near to sight as possible. If this is so, then, in parallel with its benefits, the effect of stereo has been to reinforce those (in radio terms) negative factors which I have been discussing, those which work against the medium's unique inwardness in favour of the outward and the visible.

This then is one listener's account of the changing shape – or should it be sound? – of radio drama during the last twenty years, years in which it felt the full impact of television's dominance, reeled under it, steadied, learned some lessons, and began the slow climb back. The recovery has been heartening and I hope in all the criticisms I have made that I have not left any reader with an impression to the contrary. But in case I have, let me end by correcting it and hope that last impressions will abide.

When I first became seriously acquainted with it, radio was downhearted, and that went for drama too. Today in no respect does it give off the gloomy emanations that it did, and that also goes for drama: the department is active and successful. This of course is not to say that it does not transmit some very ordinary things indeed – it always has and doubtless always will. It is unfortunately true that some of the most successful recipients of its patronage cease to give it much of their attention, but between such high-fliers and the purveyors of bread and butter there exists, as I have already mentioned, a small body of writers who can generally be counted on to express themselves in the language of radio, and this shades off into a somewhat larger group whose work, if not so reliably attuned to sound, is generally accomplished and often very good. Names that come to mind here might be Rachel Billington, Shirley Gee, John Kirkmorris, Philip Martin, Jennifer Phillips, William Trevor, Elizabeth Troop, Fay Weldon, and so on. Were he still alive, Tom Mallin's name would certainly have to be included. At the same time as all this – and here is the nub of what I have been saying – radio drama, which was once by virtue of quite a small group of remarkable writers not merely very good but highly distinguished and an art in its own right, has not regained that peak. The reasons for this are various and have to do with money and television and reputation as well as with the values of the society in which we live. I would dearly like to see radio ascend as high again – in a manner appropriate to changed times: my doubt is whether that kind of distinction, with all the often disquieting qualities of inwardness that go with it, is these days what we want to hear.

AUTHOR'S NOTE: Since this chapter was completed, the Radio 3 categorisations *World Theatre* and *Drama Now* referred to on page 221 have been discontinued.

Appendix 1
List of plays with broadcast dates

The following list covers only those authors whose work is discussed in
this volume

Chapter 2. Louis MacNeice

Alexander Nevsky	9.12.41
Christopher Columbus	12.10.42
The Death of Marlow	21.6.43
The Nosebag	13.3.44
He Had a Date	28.6.44
Sunbeams in His Hat	16.7.44
The Golden Ass	3.11.44
Cupid and Psyche	7.11.44
The March Hare Resigns	29.3.45
The Dark Tower	21.1.46
Salute to All Fools	1.4.46
Enter Caesar	20.9.46
The Careerist	22.10.46
The Agamemnon of Aeschylus	29.10.46
The Heartless Giant	3.12.46
The Death of Gunnar	11.3.47
The Burning of Njal	12.3.47
Grettir the Strong	27.7.47
Trimalchio's Feast	22.12.48
The Queen of Air and Darkness	28.3.49
Goethe's Faust 1–4	30.10–17.11.49
One Eye Wild	9.11.52
Prisoner's Progress	27.4.54
All Fools at Home	1.4.55
Nuts in May	27.5.57
East of the Sun and West of the Moon	25.7.59
They Met on Good Friday	8.12.59
The Administrator	10.3.61
Let's Go Yellow	9.12.61
The Mad Islands	4.4.62
Persons from Porlock	30.8.63

Chapter 3. Dylan Thomas

Under Milk Wood   25.1.54

Chapter 4. Susan Hill

Miss Lavender Is Dead (adapted by Guy Vaesen)   31.8.70
A Change for the Better (adapted by Guy Vaesen)   7.8.71
The End of the Summer   25.8.71
The Visitor Taking Leave   28.8.71
Lizard in the Grass   7.11.71
The Cold Country   3.10.72
Winter Elegy   31.3.73
Consider the Lilies   18.9.73
Strange Meeting (adapted by Guy Vaesen)   22.4.74
Window on the World   9.6.74
Strip Jack Naked   1.12.74
Mr. Proudham and Mr. Sleight   5.12.74
The Summer of the Giant Flowers   1.10.75

Dorothy L. Sayers

He That Should Come   25.12.38
The Man Born To Be King
Kings in Judaea   21.12.41
The King's Herald   25.1.42
A Certain Nobleman   8.2.42
The Heirs to the Kingdom   8.3.42
The Bread of Heaven   12.4.42
The Feast of Tabernacles   3.5.42
The Light and the Life   31.5.42
Royal Progress   28.6.42
The King's Supper   26.7.42
The Princes of this World   23.8.42
King of Sorrows   20.9.42
The King Comes to His Own   18.10.42

Chapter 5. Giles Cooper

Thieves Rush In   29.3.50
The Forgotten Rotten Borough   19.6.50
Never Get Out   3.7.50
The Timbimbo Craze   18.11.50

Small Fortune	14.4.51
The Private Line	6.8.51
The Owl and the Pussy Cat	15.2.53
The Sound of Cymbals	16.1.55
The Volunteer	21.4.56
Mathry Beacon	21.6.56
The Disagreeable Oyster	15.8.57
Without the Grail	13.1.58
Dangerous Word	12.5.58
Under the Loofah Tree	3.8.58
All for Three Days	26.10.58
Unman, Wittering and Zigo	23.11.58
Part of the View	12.2.59
Caretaker	20.4.59
Before the Monday	4.6.59
Crown of Gold	7.7.59
Pig in the Middle	4.10.60
The Return of General Forefinger	25.7.61
A Perfectly Ghastly Joke	27.4.62
I Gotta Universe	15.8.63
All the Way Home	13.9.63
The Object	17.4.64
The Lonesome Road	22.5.64
The Freewheelers	6.1.65
Where the Party Ended	24.3.65
Something from the Sea	18.3.66
Carried by Storm	19.12.66

Chapter 6. Henry Reed

Noises On	4.3.46
Herman Melville, *Moby Dick* (adaptation)	26.1.47
Pytheas: A Dramatic Speculation	25.5.47
The Unblest: A Study of the Italian Poet Giacomo Leopardi as a Child and in Early Manhood	9.5.49
The Monument: A Study of the Last Years of the Italian Poet Giacomo Leopardi	7.3.50
Return to Naples	17.8.50
Canterbury Cathedral: An Exploration in Sound	7.11.50
A By-Election in the Nineties	12.3.51
Thomas Hardy, *The Dynasts* (adapted in six parts)	3–9.6.51
Henry de Montherlant, *Malatesta* (translated and adapted)	26.2.52
The Streets of Pompeii	16.3.52
The Great Desire I Had: Shakespeare and Italy	26.10.52
A Very Great Man Indeed	7.9.53
Luigi Pirandello, *All for the Best* (translated and adapted)	22.11.53
The Private Life of Hilda Tablet: A Parenthesis for Radio	24.5.54

Jules Laforgue, *Hamlet, or The Consequences of Filial Piety*
(translated and adapted)   20.6.54
Virginio Puecher, *The Battle of the Masks* (translated
and adapted)   6.9.54
Ugo Betti, *The Queen and the Rebels* (translated and adapted)   17.10.54
Emily Butter: An Occasion Recalled   14.11.54
Ugo Betti, *The Burnt Flower-Bed* (translated and adapted)   23.1.55
Vincenzo: A Tragicomedy   29.3.55
Ugo Betti, *Holiday Land* (translated and adapted)   5.6.55
A Hedge, Backwards: A Discovery for Radio   29.2.56
Ugo Betti, *Crime on Goat Island* (translated and adapted)   7.10.56
Samy Fayad, *Don Juan in Love* (translated and adapted)   5.11.56
Jaques Audiberti, *Alarica* (translated and adapted)   22.9.57
Ugo Betti, *Irene* (translated and adapted)   20.10.57
Ugo Betti, *Corruption in the Palace of Justice* (translated
and adapted)   19.1.58
The Primal Scene, As It Were: Nine Studies in Disloyalty   11.3.58
Not a Drum Was Heard: The War Memoirs of General Gland   6.5.59
Silvio Giovaninetti, *One Flesh* (translated and adapted)   12.6.59
Henry de Montherlant, *The Land Where the King Is a Child*
(translated and adapted)   3.10.59
*Musique Discrète: A Request Programme of Music by Dame Hilda
Tablet*   27.10.59
Ugo Betti, *The House on the Water* (translated and adapted)   3.2.61
Dino Buzzati, *A Hospital Case*   22.11.61
Dino Buzzati, *The American Prize* (translated and adapted)   18.6.64
Dino Buzzati, *Larger Than Life* (translated and adapted as
Zone 36)   22.3.65
Natalia Ginzburg, *The Advertisement* (translated and adapted)   24.9.68
Romain Weingarten, *Summer* (translated and adapted)   3.10.69
Luigi Pirandello, *The Two Mrs Morlis* (translated and adapted) 8.11.71
Natalia Ginzburg, *The Strawberry Ice* (translated and adapted) 24.1.73
Luigi Pirandello, *Room for Argument* (translated and adapted)   7.1.74
Natalia Ginzburg, *The Wig* (translated and adapted)   23.3.76
Guiseppe Giacosa, *Like the Leaves* (translated and adapted)   24.5.76
Natalia Ginzburg, *Duologue* (translated and adapted)   3.1.77
Giuseppe Giacosa, *The Soul Has Its Rights* (translated and
adapted)   22.6.77
Giuseppe Giacosa, *Sorrows of Love* (translated and adapted)   23.10.78

Chapter 7. Samuel Beckett

All That Fall   31.1.57
Embers   24.6.59
Words and Music   13.11.62
Cascando   6.10.64

Texts for Nothing	12.6.75
Rough for Radio	13.4.76
For to End Yet Again	4.10.76

Chapter 8. British radio drama since 1960

Rhys Adrian

The Man on the Gate	19.11.56
The Passionate Thinker	27.9.57
The Prizewinner	14.7.60
Betsie	3.8.60
The Bridge	19.7.61
Too Old for Donkeys	29.1.63
Room To Let	19.5.63
A Nice Clean Sheet of Paper	24.10.63
Helen and Edward and Henry	28.8.66
Between the Two of Us	15.6.67
Ella	26.9.68
Echoes	24.10.69
Evelyn	24.10.69
The Gardeners of My Youth	17.7.70
I'll Love You Always	30.10.70
A Chance Encounter	5.7.72
Memoirs of a Sly Pornographer	19.12.72
Angle	1.7.75
Buffet	29.9.76
The Night Nurse Slept in the Day Room	5.10.76
The Clerks	28.11.78
No Charge for the Extra Service	10.7.79

John Antrobus

Captain Oates Left Stock	7.11.70
The Dinosaurs	12.12.74
LMF	10.7.76
Haute Cuisine	6.1.77
The Lie	16.2.78

Barry Bermange

The Voice of the Peanut	14.12.60
Never Forget a Face	4.3.61

A Glass of Lemonade	28.2.62
Nathan and Tabileth	10.6.62
No Quarter	1.12.62
The Dreams	5.1.64
The Mortification	3.4.64
Amor Dei	16.11.64
The After-Life	1.4.65
The Evenings of Certain Lives	5.10.65
Scenes from Family Life	27.9.71
Oldenberg	16.11.77
SOS	13.6.78
Social Welfare	6.5.79

Rachel Billington

Mrs. Bleasdale's Lodger	4.11.76
Mary Mary	12.10.77
Sister Sister	19.6.78

Frederick Bradnum

Private Dreams and Public Nightmares	6.10.57
No Going Home	12.11.57
Chloroform for Mr Bartlett	21.11.57
Mr Goodjohn and Mr Badjack	11.6.58
The Cave and the Grail	7.7.59
The Fist	26.1.63
The Crack of Doom	10.1.64
Appearances Deceive	13.4.64
Pennicotte's Truth	13.8.66
A Lonely Place in a Dark Wood	10.7.67
The Pallingham Depression	13.12.69
Goose with Pepper	7.9.70
A Terribly Strange Man	28.1.71
Alive and Well and Living in London	12.3.71
The Recruiter	7.6.71
A Putney Christmas	24.12.71
You Are Not Alone in the House	16.1.72
The Final Solution	12.8.73
A Dead Man on Leave	2.9.74
The Death of a Revolutionary	2.9.74
The Young Lady from Midhurst	15.10.74
Degas, Cellini, Ming	19.5.75
Springer's England	5.7.76

Craven's Stone	25.2.77
The Girl Who Didn't Want To Be	16.9.78
Reception	15.12.78

Stephen Davies

The Dissolution of Marcus Fleischmann	29.8.76
Events in Heroes Square	16.12.76
Man in Space	9.4.78

Peter Everett

Night of the March Hare	7.4.59
Day at Izzard's Wharf	31.7.59
Private View	3.5.66
The Cookham Resurrection	11.5.75
Me and Mr. Blake	12.8.76
Buffo	5.9.76
Harmonium	10.12.78

Don Haworth

There's No Point in Arguing the Toss	6.4.67
We All Come to It in the End	5.6.68
A Time in Cloud Cuckoo Land	12.7.69
The Prisoner	5.9.69
Where Is This Here Building – By What Route Do I Get There?	5.9.70
The Illumination of Mr Shannon	27.4.71
Simcocks Abound Across the Earth	8.10.71
The Eventful Deaths of Mr. Pruin	11.10.72
The Enlightenment of the Strawberry Gardener	13.10.72
A Damsel and Also a Rough Bird	20.5.74
Fun Balloons	3.5.75
Events at the Salamander Hotel	28.7.75
On a Day in a Garden in Summer	19.8.75
Episode on a Thursday Evening	21.9.78

Gabriel Josipovici

Playback	30.1.73
Words	22.5.73
A Life	26.3.74

Death of the Word	29.10.76
Ag	14.11.76
The Present	10.4.77
Virgil Dying	29.3.79

Anne Leaton

The Heathcliffe Data	6.8.75
My Name Is Bird McKai	21.3.76
Monsters and Other Events	26.12.77

Tom Mallin

Curtains	8.11.71
Rooms	19.11.73
Vicar Martin	27.7.75
Two Gentlemen of Hadleigh Heath	30.12.75
The Lodger	11.5.76
Spanish Fly	18.9.77
Halt! Who Goes There?	26.3.78
Rowland	21.8.78

Bill Naughton

Timothy	28.10.56
My Flesh My Blood	17.8.57
June Evening	29.7.58
She'll Make Trouble	13.12.58
The Long Carry	23.4.59
Late Night on Watling Street	3.10.59
On the Run	13.2.60
Wigan to Rome	29.9.60
Seeing a Beauty Queen Home	8.11.60
Alfie Elkins and His Little Wife	7.1.62
Somewhere for the Night	8.9.62
Jacky Crowe	9.10.62
Looking for Frankie	9.2.63
November Day	19.7.63
The Mystery	9.10.73
All in Good Time	8.6.74

Harold Pinter

A Slight Ache	29.7.59
A Night Out	1.3.60
The Dwarfs	20.12.60
The Caretaker	20.3.62
The Collection	12.6.62
The Examination	7.9.62
Sketches	28.4.64
Tea Party	28.8.64
Landscape	25.4.68
Mac	25.6.68
Monologue	3.12.75

Jennifer Phillips

The Fixed Smile	21.1.75
Birdman	20.8.75
The Antique Baby	20.10.75
Your Tiny Hand Is Frozen	13.3.76
Blow Your House In	7.3.77
Venus at the Seaside	6.8.77
Daughters of Men	1.5.78
The Camera Often Lies	6.2.79
Past Appearances	13.2.79

Jonathan Raban

A Game of Tombola	30.6.72
At the Gate	29.8.73
The Daytrip	20.4.76
Will You Accept the Call?	24.3.77
The English Department	22.5.77
Falling	8.4.79

Peter Redgrove

The Sermon and *The Anniversary*	24.8.64
The God Trap	4.9.66
In the Country of the Skin	19.6.73
Dance the Putrefact	20.11.75
The God of Glass	21.7.77

James Saunders

Women Are So Unreasonable	7.12.57
Dog Accident	26.8.58
Barnstable	20.11.59
Alas Poor Fred	7.9.60
Gimlet	1.1.63
It's Not the Game It Was	1.4.64
The Pedagogue	19.5.64
Pay As You Go	26.1.65
After Liverpool	2.7.71
Random Moments in a May Garden	20.1.74
Bye Bye Blues	1.10.74
Poor Old Simon	13.1.79

R. C. Scriven

The Seasons of the Blind	22.10.68
All Early in the April	18.3.70
The Peacock Screamed One Morning	25.3.70
Dandelion and Parsnip, Vintage 1920	2.8.71
The Peacock City of P'Tzan	7.7.72
Claudia Procula	6.8.72
Give Me London Weather	10.4.74
A Measure of Sliding Sand	30.11.74
Nocturne of Provincial Spring	12.11.75
A Blind Understanding	4.10.77

Tom Stoppard

The Dissolution of Dominic Boot	20.2.64
M. Is for Moon Among Other Things	6.4.64
Walk on the Water	8.11.65
If You're Glad I'll Be Frank	8.2.66
Albert's Bridge	13.7.67
Where Are They Now?	18.12.70
Artist Descending a Staircase	14.11.72
Rosencrantz and Guildenstern Are Dead	24.12.78
Professional Foul	11.6.79

William Trevor

The Original Sins of Edward Tripp	16.3.67
The Old Boys	25.4.67
The Penthouse Apartment	16.8.68
Going Home	29.5.70
The Boarding House	14.6.71
A Perfect Relationship	5.6.73
Scenes from an Album	29.9.75
Attracta	25.9.77

Elizabeth Troop

A Little like Orson Who?	13.11.74
P.S. Wish You Were Here	17.12.74
Send Up	17.8.76
A Fine Country	11.10.76
The Year of the Great Betrayal	21.11.77
Not Waving	10.9.78

Fay Weldon

The Spider	13.8.72
Housebreaker	7.4.74
Mr. Fox and Mr. First	13.8.74
The Doctor's Wife	2.6.75
Polaris	16.6.78

Appendix 2

Plays published

The volume of plays first broadcast and then subsequently published during the period 1924–79 is such that despite every attempt to provide a comprehensive list of published playscripts, what follows cannot claim to be complete.

Adrian, Rhys, *A Nice Clean Sheet of Paper*, in *BBC New Radio Drama* (London, 1966)

Adrian, Rhys, *The Clerks*, in *BBC Radio Playscripts* (London, 1979)

Agar, Anthony, *Break: A Radio Play* (Ilfracombe, 1942)

Arden, John, *The Bagman, or The Impromptu of Muswell Hill*, in *Two Autobiographical Plays* (London, 1971)

Arden, John, *Pearl* (London, 1979)

Baker, D. V., *Cornwall for the Cornish* (Falmouth, 1964)

Barker, George, *Two Plays* (London, 1958)

Barstow, Stan, *We Could Always Fit a Sidecar*, in A. Bradley (ed.), *Out of the Air* (London, 1978)

Bax, C. and L. M. Lion, *Hemlock for Eight: A Radio Play* (London, 1946)

Bax, Clifford, *The Buddha: A Radio Version of His Life and His Ideas* (London, 1947)

Beckett, Samuel, *All That Fall* (London, 1957)

Beckett, Samuel, *Krapp's Last Tape and Embers* (London, 1959)

Beckett, Samuel, *Play and Two Short Pieces for Radio* (London, 1964)

Beckett, Samuel, *Radio II, Ends and Odds* (London, 1977)

Behan, Brendan, *The Complete Plays* (London, 1978)

Bermange, Barry, *Nathan and Tabileth* (London, 1967)

Bermange, Barry, *No Quarter*, in *New English Dramatists 12* (Harmondsworth, 1968)

Betti, Ugo, *Three Plays*, trans. Henry Reed (London, 1956)

Betti, Ugo, *The Queen and the Rebels*, trans. Henry Reed, in *Three European Plays* (Harmondsworth, 1958)

Betti, Ugo, *Crime on Goat Island*, trans. Henry Reed (London, 1960)

Bloom, U., *Displaced Persons*, in V. Gielgud (ed.), *Radio Theatre: Plays Specially Written for Radio Broadcasting* (London, 1946)

Bonett, E., *One Fine Day*, in V. Gielgud (ed.), *Radio Theatre: Plays Specially Written for Radio Broadcasting* (London, 1946)

Bonett, E., *The Puppet Master*, in Henryk Mund (ed.), *Five Radio Plays* (London, 1948)

Borchert, W., *The Man Outside:* in *The Man Outside: The Prose Works of W. Borchert*, trans. D. Porter (London, 1952)

Bowen, E., *Anthony Trollope: A New Judgement* (London, 1946)

Bradley, A. (ed.), *Worth a Hearing: A Collection of Radio Plays* (London, 1967)

Bradley, A. (ed.), *Out of the Air* (London, 1978)

Bridson, D. G., *Aaron's Field* (London, 1943)

Bridson, D. G., *The Christmas Child: A Collection of Broadcast Plays and Poems* (London, 1950)

Bronowski, J., *The Face of Violence* (London, 1954)

Brook, J. C. W., *Giving Up*, in *BBC Radio Playscripts* (London, 1979)

Brophy, Brigid, *The Waste Disposal Unit, London Magazine*, April, 1964

Bryan, Con, *Radio Plays* (London, 1950)

Buzzati, Dino, *Larger Than Life*, trans. Henry Reed (London, 1962)

Cameron, James, *The Pump* (published as a short story) in *Winter's Tales*, ed. A. D. MacLean (London, 1973)

Campton, David, *Don't Wait for Me*, in A. Bradley (ed.), *Worth a Hearing* (London, 1967)

Cavender, Kenneth, *The Iliad and the Odyssey of Homer* (London, 1969)

Churchill, Caryl, *The Ants*, in *New English Dramatists 12* (Harmondsworth, 1968)

Clarke, A., *As the Crow Flies: A Lyric Play for the Air* (London, 1943)

Compton, David, *Relics*, in A. Bradley (ed.), *Out of the Air* (London, 1978)

Constanduros, Mabel, *On the Run* (published as a novel) (London, 1943)

Constanduros, M. and H. Agg, *The Tunnel*, in V. Gielgud (ed.), *Radio Theatre: Plays Specially Written for Radio Broadcasting* (London, 1946)

Cooper, Giles, *Six Plays for Radio*, ed. Bennett Maxwell (London, 1966)

Cooper, Giles, *The Object*, in *New English Dramatisists 12* (Harmondsworth, 1968)

Cooper, Giles, *Unman, Wittering and Zigo* (London, 1971)

Dane, Clemence, *The Saviours: Seven Plays on a Theme* (London, 1942)

Davey, C. J., *Thomas Coke: A Radio Play* (London, n.d.)

Dickinson, P., *Stone in the Midst and Poems* (London, 1948)

Drinkwater, J., *Midsummer Eve: A Play Primarily Intended for Wireless* (London, 1932)

Durban, Alan (ed.), *Playbill Three* (London, 1969)

Edwards, M., *Smash and Grab*, in V. Gielgud (ed.), *Radio Theatre: Plays Specially Written for Radio Broadcasting* (London, 1946)

Fane, Guy, *Over the Garden Wall: A Series of Comedy Episodes* (London, 1939)

Farrington, C., *The Death of Don Juan, Icarus* (University College, Dublin), 1952

Finbow, C., *Tonight Is Friday*, in *BBC New Radio Drama* (London, 1966)

Flatteau, R. (ed.), *Three Plays Broadcast in Saturday Night Theatre* (London, 1947)

Gamlin, L., *You're on the Air* (London, 1947)

Gielgud, V., *How To Write Broadcast Plays* (London, 1932)

Gielgud, V., *The Right Way to Radio Playwriting* (Kingswood, 1948)

Gielgud, V. (ed.), *Radio Theatre: Plays Specially Written for Radio Broadcasting* (London, 1946)

Goodrich, L., *Anne and Harold: One Act Radio Scenes* (London, 1933)

Gore-Brown, M., *Music for Miss Rogers*, in V. Gielgud (ed.), *Radio Theatre: Plays Specially Written for Radio Broadcasting* (London, 1946)

Grenfell, S., *16 Lives of a Drunken Dreamer*, in *BBC New Radio Drama* (London, 1966)

Griffiths, Ll. Wyn, *The Barren Tree* (Cardiff, 1947)

Griffiths, Trevor, *Occupations and The Big House* (London, 1972)

Guthrie, Tyrone, *Squirrel's Cage and Two Other Microphone Plays* (London, 1931)

Guthrie, Tyrone, *Squirrel's Cage*, in P. R. Smith (ed.), *On the Air: Five Radio and T.V. Plays* (London, 1959)

Hackforth-Jones, G. and M. Hackforth-Jones, *Sweethearts and Wives* (London, 1952)

Hadlington, R., *Plays for Performance* (London, 1959)

Hadlington, R., *More Plays for Performance* (London, 1961)

Hamilton, G. R., *Crazy Gaunt and Other Dramatic Sketches* (London, 1946)

Hamilton, P., *Money with Menaces and To the Public Danger: Two Radio Plays* (London, 1939)

Hardill, M. and R. C. Walton, *Christianity in a Great City: Five Plays on the Epistles to the Corinthians* (London, 1959)

Harris, Richard, *Is It Something I Said?* in *Best Radio Plays of 1978* (London, 1979)

Hastings, Charlotte, *The Soft September Air* (London, 1979)

Hatton, C., *Radio Plays and How To Write Them* (St Ives, 1949)

Haworth, Don, *We All Come to It in the End and Other Plays for Radio* (London, 1972)

Haworth, Don, *On a Day in a Garden in Summer*, in *Contemporary One-Act Plays* (London, 1976)

Haworth, Don, *There's No Point in Arguing the Toss* in A. Bradley (ed.), *Out of the Air* (London, 1978)

Haworth, Don, *Episode on a Thursday Evening*, in *Best Radio Plays of 1978* (London, 1979)

Heath, T., *Spinney Under the Rain*, in Henryk Mund (ed.), *Five Radio Plays* (London, 1948)

Henderson, D. L., *The Trial of Lizzie Borden and Other Radio Plays* (London, 1946)

Heppenstall, Rayner, *Imaginary Conversations: Eight Radio Scripts* (London, 1948)

Heppenstall, R. and M. Innes, *Three Tales of Hamlet* (London, 1950)

Hill, Susan, *The Cold Country and Other Plays for Radio* (London, 1975)

Hoddinott, Derek, *Hello Goodbye* (London, 1979)

Hoffe, M., *Permanent Way*, in R. Flatteau (ed.), *Three Plays Broadcast in Saturday Night Theatre* (London, 1947)

Hughes, Richard, *A Comedy of Danger* (London, 1924)

Hughes, Richard, *Plays* (London, 1966)

Hughes, Ted, *Wodwo* (London, 1967)

Hughes, Ted, *The Coming of the Kings and Other Plays* (London, 1970)

Hulme-Beaman, S. G., *The Cruise of the Toytown Belle* (London, 1953)

Hyem, Jill, *Remember Me*, in *Best Radio Plays of 1978* (London, 1979)

Jenkins, R., *Boy Dudgeon*, in Alan Durban (ed.), *Playbill 3* (London, 1969)

Jones, Glyn, *The Dream of Jake Hopkins* (London, 1955)

Kesser, H., *Nurse Henrietta*, in Henryk Mund (ed.), *Five Radio Plays* (London, 1948)

Kevin, D., *Radio Playwriting* (London, 1947)

Kirkmorris, John, *Dancing Dolly*, in *BBC Radio Playscripts* (London, 1979)

Kissen, F., *Plays for the Loudspeaker* (London, 1952)

Kitchin, L., *Three on Trial: An Experiment in Biography* (London, 1959)

Lang, H. and K. Tynan, *The Quest for Corbett* (London, 1960)

Laski, M., *The Off-Shore Island* (London, 1959)

Lee, Laurie, *The Voyage of Magellan: A Dramatic Chronicle for Radio* (London, 1948)

Linklater, E., *The Cornerstones: A Conversation in Elysium* (London, 1941)

Linklater, E., *The Raft and Socrates Asks Why: Two Conversations* (London, 1942)

Linklater, E., *The Great Ship and Rabelais Replies: Two Conversations* (London, 1944)

Livings, Henry, *The Day Dumbfounded Got His Pylon*, in A. Bradley (ed.), *Worth a Hearing* (London, 1967)

Lloyd, A. L. and I. Vinogradoff, *The Shadow of the Swastika: A Radio Drama in Six Parts* (London, 1940)

McGivern, Cecil, *The Harbour Called Mulberry* (London, 1945)

MacLeish, A., *Air Raid* (London, 1939)

MacLeish, A., *The Great American Fourth of July Parade* (London, 1975)

MacNeice, L., *Christopher Columbus: A Radio Play* (London, 1944)

MacNeice, L., *The Dark Tower and Other Radio Scripts* (London, 1947)

MacNeice, L., *India at First Sight*, in L. Gilliam (ed.), *BBC Features* (London, 1950)

MacNeice, L., *Goethe's Faust, Parts I and II: An Abridged Version* (London, 1951)

MacNeice, L., *The March Hare Resigns*, in P. R. Smith (ed.), *On the Air: Five Radio and T.V. Plays* (London, 1959)

MacNeice, L., *The Mad Islands and The Administrator: Two Plays for Radio* (London, 1964)

MacNeice, L., *One for the Grave: A Modern Morality Play* (London, 1968)

MacNeice, L., *Persons from Porlock and Other Plays for Radio* (London, 1969)

Mallin, Tom, *Halt! Who Goes There?* in *Best Radio Plays of 1978* (London, 1979)

Mathias, Roland, *Snipe's Castle* (Llandysul, 1979)

Mella, Agathe, *Grand Slam*, in Henryk Mund (ed.), *Five Radio Plays* (London, 1948)

Mercer, David, *Folie à Deux* (published as a short story), *Stand*, 4, 4 (n.d.)

Milligan, Spike, *The Book of the Goons* (London, 1975)

Morris, Colin, *Quiet Revolution*, in P. R. Smith (ed.), *On the Air: Five Radio and T.V. Plays* (London, 1959)

Mortimer, John, *Three Plays* (London, 1958)

Mortimer, John, *Lunch Hour and Other Plays* (London, 1960)

Mortimer, John, *The Dock Brief*, in A. Bradley (ed.), *Worth a Hearing* (London, 1967)

Mortimer, John, *A Voyage Round My Father* (London, 1971)

Mund, Henryk (ed.), *Five Radio Plays* (London, 1948)

Naughton, Bill, *Alfie Elkins and His Little Wife* (London, 1963)

Naughton, Bill, *Spring and Port Wine* (originally *My Flesh My Blood*) (London, 1967)

Naughton, Bill, *She'll Make Trouble*, in A. Bradley (ed.), *Worth a Hearing* (London, 1967)

Naughton, Bill, *June Evening* (London, 1973)

Nye, Robert, *Penthesilea, Fugue, and Sisters* (London, 1971)

Obey, N., *The Silent City*, in Henryk Mund (ed.), *Five Radio Plays* (London, 1948)

Orton, Joe, *The Ruffian on the Stair*, in *BBC New Radio Drama* (London, 1966)

Peach, L. du Garde, *Ever Ready Plays: Short Sketches* (London, n.d.)

Peach, L. du Garde, *More Ever Ready Plays: Short Sketches* (London, 1926)

Peach, L. du Garde, *Broadcast Sketches* (London, 1927)

Peach, L. du Garde, *Crook's Christmas* (London, 1931)

Peach, L. du Garde, *Radio Plays: Broadcast Sketches* (London, 1931)

Peach, L. du Garde, *Plays for Young Players Broadcast in Children's Hour* (London, 1937)

Peach, L. du Garde, *A Dramatic History of England* (London, 1939)

Peach, L. du Garde, *Storytellers of Britain*, 3 vols. (London, 1941)

Pearn, V. A., *The Devil in the Cathedral* (London, 1942)

Phillips, J. B., *A Man Called Jesus* (London, 1959)

Phillips, Jennifer, *Daughters of Men*, in *Best Radio Plays of 1978* (London, 1979)

Pinter, Harold, *A Slight Ache and Other Plays* (London, 1961); reissued 1966, 1968

Pinter, Harold, *Landscape*, in *Landscape and Silence* (London, 1968)

Pinter, Harold, *Tea Party and Other Plays* (London, 1969)

Pirandello, Luigi, *All for the Best*, trans. Henry Reed, in *Right you Are! (If You Think So) and Other Plays* (Harmondsworth, 1962)

Plater, Alan, *The Mating Season*, in A. Bradley (ed.), *Worth a Hearing* (London, 1967)

Plater, Alan, *Excursion*, in Alan Durban (ed.), *Playbill 3* (London, 1969)

Pollock, S. and W. Grantham, *Men of God* (London, 1947)

Ratcliffe, D. U., *The Spanish Lady: A Comedy in One Act* (Leeds, 1929)

Raven, S., *Royal Foundation and Other Plays* (London, 1966)

Raven, S., *The Sconcing Stoup*, in *BBC New Radio Drama* (London, 1966)

Read, Herbert, *Lord Byron at the Opera: A Play for Broadcasting* (North Harrow, 1963)

Read, Herbert, *Moon's Farm*, in *Selected Writings* (London, 1963)

Ready, S., *I Want To Be an Actor* (London, 1940)

Redgrove, Peter, *In the Country of the Skin: A Radio Script* (privately published in Northants., 1973)

Redgrove, Peter, *The God of Glass* (published as a novel) (London, 1978)

Reed, Henry, *Moby Dick: A Play for Radio* (London, 1947)

Reed, Henry, *Hilda Tablet and Others: Four Pieces for Radio* (London, 1971)

Reed, Henry, *The Streets of Pompeii and Other Plays for Radio* (London, 1971)

Richardson, A. L., *Casson's Boy: A Play for Women* (London, 1956)

Robertson, A. S., *The Luck of the Draw*, in *BBC Radio Playscripts* (London, 1979)

Rodger, I., *A. Voice like Thunder*, in *BBC New Radio Drama* (London, 1966)

Rubinstein, H. F., *Shylock's End and Other Plays* (London, 1971)

Rudkin, David, *Cries from Casement As His Bones Are Brought To Dublin* (London, 1974)

Sackville-West, E., *The Rescue* (London, 1945)

Sandford, Jeremy, *The Whelks and the Chromium*, in *New English Dramatists 12* (Harmondsworth, 1968)

Sandford, Jeremy, *Smiling David: The Story of David Oluwale* (London, 1964)

Saunders, James, *Dog Accident*, in *Ten of the Best British Short Plays* (London, 1979)

Sayers, Dorothy L., *The Man Born To Be King* (London, 1943)

Sayers, Dorothy L., *Four Sacred Plays* (London, 1948)

Scriven, R. C., *The Single Taper and The Inward Eye* (London, 1953)

Scriven, R. C., *The Seasons of the Blind and Other Radio Plays* (London, 1974)

Sharp, Alan, *The Long-Distance Piano-Player*, in *New English Dramatists 12* (Harmondsworth, 1968)

Sherriff, R. C., *The Telescope*, in J. C. Trewin (ed.), *Plays of the Year*, vol. 15 (1956) (London, 1957)

Sieveking, Lance, *The Stuff of Radio* (London, 1934)

Sieveking, Lance, *The Strange Case of Dr. Jekyll and Mr. Hyde*, in J. C. Trewin (ed.), *Plays of the Year*, vol. 15 (1956) (London, 1957)

Simpson, C., *Six from Borneo* (London, n.d.)

Smith, P. R. (ed.), *On the Air: Five Radio and T.V. Plays* (London, 1959)

Smith, S. G., *The Wallace* (London, 1960)

Spain, George, *Bridge of Tyne: A Fantasy in Five Acts* (Newcastle, 1929)

Spark, Muriel, *Voices at Play* (Harmondsworth, 1961)

Stoppard, Tom, *Albert's Bridge and If You're Glad I'll Be Frank: Two Plays For Radio* (London, 1969) (*If You're Glad* also published separately, London, 1976)

Stoppard, Tom, *Artist Descending a Staircase and Where Are They Now? Two Plays for Radio* (London, 1973)

Taylor, Cecil P., *Happy Days Are Here Again*, in *New English Dramatists 12* (Harmondsworth, 1968)

Thiele, Colin, *Burke and Wills*, in P. R. Smith (ed.), *On the Air: Five Radio and T.V. Plays* (London, 1959)

Thomas, Dylan, *Under Milk Wood* (London, 1954; 3rd edn, 1976)

Thomas, H., *The Brighter Blackout Book* (London, 1939)

Traill, G. M. (pseudonym of G. M. Morton), *Madeline* (published as the novel *Mutation Mink*) (London, 1950)

Tremain, R., *Don't Be Cruel*, in *BBC Radio Playscripts* (London, 1979)

Turner, Alexander, *Hester Siding*, in W. Moore, and T. Inglis (eds.), *Best Australian One-Act Plays* (Sydney, n.d.)

Turner, Alexander, *Royal Mail and Other Plays* (London, 1944)

Tuson, N., *The Doubtful Misfortunes of Li Sing: A Spot of Chinese Bother in One Act* (London, 1938)

Wade, P., *Mild and Bitter*, in R. Flatteau (ed.), *Three Plays Broadcast in Saturday Night Theatre* (London, 1947)

Wade, P., *Wedding Group and Other Plays* (London, 1936)

Walke, B., *Bethlehem: A Christmas Play* (London, 1936)

Walke, B., *Plays from St. Hilary* (London, 1939)

Walton, Robert, *Into the Dark: The End and the Beginning* (London, 1967)

Walton, Robert, *Twelve Hours of Daylight: Six Plays About Jesus* (London, 1967)

Watkyn, A., *Portsmouth Road*, in R. Flatteau (ed.), *Three Plays Broadcast in Saturday Night Theatre* (London, 1947)

Weldon, Fay, *Polaris*, in *Best Plays of 1978* (London, 1979)

Whitmore, Ken, *Jump!* in A. Bradley (ed.), *Out of the Air* (London, 1978)

Williams, Herbert, *A Lethal Kind of Love: A Play for Voices* (Ruthin, 1968)

Williamson, H. R., *Stories from History: Ten Plays for Schools* (London, 1938)

Williamson, H. R., *Paul, a Bondslave: A Radio Play* (London, 1945)

Wilson, Ivor, *Take Any Day*, in A. Bradley (ed.), *Out of the Air* (London, 1978)

Wright, D., *A Cradle of Willow: A Nativity Play* (London, 1952)

Wymarck, Oliver, *The Child*, in *BBC Radio Playscripts* (London, 1979)

Notes

Chapter 1. Introduction

1 *The Elements of Drama* (Cambridge, 1960), p. 287.
2 Terence Hawkes, 'Postscript: Theatre Against Shakespeare?', in *The Elizabethan Theatre*, ed. David Galloway (Toronto, 1969), pp. 117–26. See also Ian Trethowan, 'The Development of Radio', *BBC Lunchtime Lectures*, no. 4 (January 1975), 11, where this distinction seems to be implied.
3 Styan, *The Shakespeare Revolution* (Cambridge, 1977) pp. 47 ff.
4 Tyrone Guthrie went on to write plays for radio in 1929, and John Gielgud was regularly involved in Shakespeare productions at the BBC.
5 Styan, *Shakespeare Revolution*, pp. 62–3.
6 Cited by Asa Briggs, *The History of Broadcasting in the United Kingdom* (Oxford, 1961–79), vol. 1, *The Birth of Broadcasting*, p. 282.
7 Bertold Brecht, 'The Radio As an Apparatus of Communication', *Brecht on Theatre*, trans. John Willett (London, 1964), pp. 51–3.
8 BBC Written Archives, Drama Broadcasts File, Acc. 44986.
9 Val Gielgud, *British Radio Drama 1922–1956* (London, 1957), p. 21.
10 Anthony Smith, *The Shadow in the Cave* (repr. London, 1976), p. 66.
11 Peter Black, *The Biggest Aspidistra in the World* (London, 1972).
12 BBC Written Archives, Drama Broadcasts File, Acc. 44986.
13 Gielgud, *British Radio Drama*, p. 20.
14 Black, *Biggest Aspidistra*, p. 37.
15 Tyrone Guthrie, *Squirrel's Cage and Two Other Microphone Plays* (London, 1931), p. 11.
16 Rudolph Arnheim, *Radio*, trans. M. Ludwig and H. Read (London, 1936), p. 102.
17 Briggs, *History of Broadcasting*, vol. 2, *The Golden Age of Wireless* (Oxford, 1965), p. 166.
18 M. McLuhan, *Understanding Media* (repr. London, 1967), p. 31.
19 Lance Sieveking, *The Stuff of Radio* (London, 1934), p. 21. See also his Appendix B, pp. 397–404, for a full explanation of how the dramatic control panel worked.
20 Raymond Williams, *Television Technology and Cultural Form* (London, 1974), p. 26.
21 *Ibid.* p. 27.

22 Tyrone Guthrie, 'The Future of Broadcast Drama', *BBC Yearbook*, 1931, p. 189.
23 Guthrie, *Squirrel's Cage*, p. 11.
24 *Ibid*. See also V. Gielgud, 'The Play from the Armchair', *The Listener*, January, 1931, p. 62.
25 Gielgud, *British Radio Drama*, p. 36.
26 Gielgud, 'Drama', *BBC Handbook*, 1929, p. 75; see also *British Radio Drama*, p. 87.
27 Gielgud, *British Radio Drama*, p. 42.
28 *Ibid*. p. 73.
29 For example, the work of the Italian dramatist Ugo Betti was first introduced to British audiences through the broadcast translations of Henry Reed in the 1950s, while more recently Martin Esslin has introduced the work of Czech dramatists in the same way.
30 Martin Esslin, 'The National Theatre of the Air', *BBC Lunchtime Lectures*, 2nd ser., 4 (8 January 1964).
31 D. G. Bridson, *Prospero and Ariel, The Rise and Fall of Radio: A Personal Recollection* (London, 1971), p. 62.
32 Briggs, *History of Broadcasting*, vol. 1, p. 282.
33 Bridson, *Prospero and Ariel*, pp. 57 ff for a fuller account; see also Louis MacNeice, *Christopher Columbus. A Radio Play* (London, 1944), p. 15: 'This programme followed Prince Charles Edward from his landing in the Hebrides to his final defeat at Culloden, peaking the action with bagpipes and Jacobite songs and covering the transitions with a quick-fire verse commentary skilfully varied in form to match the changes of mood. This achieved a total effect unattainable on the stage and less simply attainable on the screen.'
34 *British Radio Drama*, p. 48.
35 *Ibid*.
36 J. Burroughs, 'The People Versus Johnny Jones', BBC Written Archives, Entertainment Features, Acc. 37645, memo (13 October 1947).
37 *The Growth of Milk Wood* (London, 1969), p. 17.
38 MacNeice, *Christopher Columbus*, p. 12.
39 Bridson, *Prospero and Ariel*, pp. 52–4.
40 See Douglas Cleverdon, 'Radio', *Cassell's Encyclopaedia of World Literature*, vol. 2 (rev. edn, London, 1973), p. 475. In this revised definition of a feature Cleverdon excluded 'dramatic plot' as an option, since its presence would, in fact, transform the feature into a 'radio play'. But his own earlier association of the radio play with 'the tradition of the theatre' allows by implication the claim of the feature to be 'pure radio'.
41 Gielgud, *British Radio Drama*, pp. 66–7.
42 *Ibid*. p. 116. There was no question but that Gielgud thought of radio drama exclusively in terms of live broadcasting. He demurred at the prospect of actors being dominated in the future 'by the mechanism of the scissors and the recording tape'.
43 See BBC Written Archives, Drama Policy File 1937–9, Acc. 44987/3

(October–December 1937). In an internal memo Gielgud referred back to an earlier experiment undertaken in 1928 which failed because it omitted what he called 'entertainment value'.

44 Gielgud, 'Considerations Relevant to Broadcasting Drama Based upon Experience in the Years 1929 to 1948', BBC Written Archives, Acc. 44986 (28 June 1948).

45 Black, *Biggest Aspidistra*, pp. 174–5.

46 Cited by Briggs, *History of Broadcasting*, vol. 2, p. 273.

47 BBC Written Archives, Acc. 44986 (28 June 1948).

48 Bridson, *Prospero and Ariel*, p. 70.

49 D. Stephenson, 'Undesirable Aspects of Drama Output', BBC Written Archives, Drama Policy File 1947–8, Acc. 37311 (17 March 1948).

50 Sir William Haley in *The Responsibilities of Broadcasting*, cited by Harman Grisewood, *Broadcasting and Society* (London, 1949), p. 66.

51 'Profanity in Plays', BBC Written Archives, Drama Policy File 1947–8, Acc. 37311 (6 December 1948).

52 See Rudiger Imhof, 'Radioactive Pinter' in Peter Lewis (ed.), *Papers of the Radio Literature Conference 1977*, vol. 2 (Durham, 1978), pp. 199–217.

53 'The Third Programme in 1950', BBC Written Archives, Acc. 38010 (28 June 1949), para. 7 'Drama'.

54 'Castle on the Air', *Time Was Away: The World of Louis MacNeice*, ed. Terence Brown and Alec Reid (Dublin, 1974), pp. 88–9.

55 Freddy Grisewood, *My Story of the BBC* (London, 1959), pp. 55 ff.

56 'Drama in Sound and Vision', BBC Written Archives, Drama Policy File 1949–54, Acc. 37312 (20 March 1952).

57 Gielgud, *British Radio Drama*, p. 30.

58 See Martin Esslin, *The Theatre of the Absurd* (Harmondsworth, 1968), p. 41.

59 Black, *Biggest Aspidistra*, pp. 182–3.

60 See Leslie Stokes's letter of 28 February 1956 to the Controller of the Third Programme concerning a series of ribald references in Reed's play *A Hedge, Backwards*; BBC Written Archives, file WAC Reed, Henry S/W 1C.

61 Bridson, *Prospero and Ariel*, p. 227.

62 *Ibid*. p. 331.

63 Harold Pinter was given his first part in a broadcast of Shakespeare's *Henry VIII* which was commissioned in honour of Sybil Thorndike's Jubilee year in the theatre. He read the part of Lord Abergavenny.

64 See p. 219 above.

65 Annan Report: *Report of the Committee on the Future of Broadcasting* (London (HMSO), 1977), p. 326.

66 *Drama in a Dramatised Society* (Cambridge, 1974), p. 10.

67 Annan Report, p. 325.

68 Jeffrey, 'The Need for a Radio Drama', *Radio Times*, 17 July 1925, p. 151, and also 'Seeing with the Mind's Eye', *Radio Times*, 5 November 1926, p. 325.

69 *Radio Drama and How to Write It* (London, 1926), p. 40.
70 *Squirrel's Cage*, p. 9.
71 'The Future of Broadcast Drama', p. 189.
72 'The Problems of the Producer', *BBC Handbook*, 1929, p. 178.
73 *Ibid*.
74 See G. Wilson Knight, 'On the Principles of Shakespeare Interpretation', *The Wheel of Fire* (London, 1931), pp. 1–17, for a full explanation of this phrase. There are strong similarities between Guthrie's approach to radio drama and Wilson Knight's account of the structure of a Shakespearean play.
75 See also Richard Hughes, 'The Birth of Radio Drama', in Peter Davison, Rolf Meyersohn and Edward Shils (eds.), *Literary Taste, Culture, and Mass Communication*, vol. 9, *Uses of Literacy: Media* (Cambridge, 1978), pp. 257–9. On the question of advice to the listener to simulate the conditions of blindness when listening to a radio play, see R. E. Jeffrey, 'The Need for a Radio Drama', p. 151.
76 P. 55.
77 Cited by Peter Black, *Biggest Aspidistra*, p. 36.
78 Henry Reed, 'Adaptation of Hardy's *The Dynasts*', BBC Written Archives, File 1A, 1944–53 (29 November 1947), p. 2.
79 *Voice and Personality* (London, 1931), p. 90.
80 *Ibid*. p. 93.
81 *Ibid*. p. 99.
82 *Ibid*. p. 100.
83 *Ibid*. p. 120.
84 'Judging Personality from Voice', in J. Laver and S. Hutcheson (eds.), *Communication in Face to Face Interaction* (Harmondsworth, 1972), p. 155.
85 Stoppard, *If You're Glad I'll Be Frank* (London, 1976), pp. 8–10.
86 *Radio*, trans. M. Ludwig and H. Read (London, 1936), pp. 30–1.
87 *Ibid*. p. 35.
88 *Ibid*. p. 15.
89 *Ibid*. p. 38.
90 *Ibid*. p. 25.
91 Bridson, *The Christmas Child* (London, 1950), p. 3.
92 Arnheim, *Radio*, p. 24.
93 P. 3.
94 *Ibid*. p. 8.
95 *Ibid*. p. 202.
96 *Christopher Columbus*, p. 9.
97 *The Art of Radio* (London, 1959), p. 79.
98 *A Slight Ache and Other Plays* (London, 1966), p. 9.
99 See J. Fiske and J. Hartley, *Reading Television* (London, 1978), p. 191.
100 *Art of Radio*, p. 48.
101 *Ibid*. p. 47.
102 Sieveking, *Stuff of Radio*, p. 54.
103 *Art of Radio*, p. 43.

104 *Ibid.* p. 93.
105 Roland Barthes, *Image–Music–Text*, trans. Stephen Heath (London, 1977), pp. 32–51.
106 Fiske and Hartley, *Reading Television*, pp. 38–40. A number of the concepts advanced in this provocative volume can be profitably applied to radio. See esp. ch. 3, 'The Signs of Television'.
107 *Ibid.* pp. 47–50 for definitions of both these terms. They define 'metaphor' as *'constructed equivalence'* (p. 48), and they conflate the two rhetorical terms 'metonymy' and 'synecdoche'. Though their concern is with visual images, their terms can profitably be applied to radio also.
108 *Christopher Columbus*, p. 19.
109 *Ibid.* p. 10.
110 *Ibid.* p. 8.
111 *Ibid.*
112 *Ibid.* p. 9.
113 *Ibid.* p. 11. See also Felix Felton, *The Radio Play: Its Techniques and Possibilities* (London, 1949), p. 94, where this point is made in specific connection with the role of the narrator in Bridson's *March of the '45*.
114 See M. McLuhan, *The Gutenberg Galaxy* (London, 1962), and Walter J. Ong, *Interfaces of the Word* (Ithaca and London, 1977).
115 See David Lodge, *The Language of Fiction* (London, 1966), pp. 6 ff for an analysis of this problem in relation to the novel.
116 MacNeice, *The Dark Tower* (London, 1964), p. 9.
117 *Christopher Columbus*, p. 11.
118 *Ibid.*
119 *Ibid.* p. 12.
120 *Ibid.*
121 *Ibid.* p. 14.
122 *The Dark Tower*, p. 10.
123 *Ibid.*
124 *Ibid.* p. 11.
125 *New English Dramatists 12: Radio Plays*, introduced by Irving Wardle (Harmondsworth, 1968), p. 14.
126 *Christopher Columbus*, p. 8.
127 'Literature on the Air', *BBC Quarterly*, 7, 1 (Spring 1952), 17.

Chapter 2. The radio drama of Louis MacNeice

1 He was born on 12 September 1907 at Belfast of Protestant parents who themselves had been born and bred in Connemara. His mother was a schoolteacher and his father, John Frederick MacNeice, was a clergyman of the Church of Ireland, who in 1906 moved to East Belfast and in 1909 became rector of Carrickfergus. He stayed in Northern Ireland and finally rose to be Bishop of Cashel (cf. *Time Was Away: The*

World of Louis MacNeice, ed. Terence Brown and Alec Reid (Dublin, 1974), pp. 11–34).

2 *Ibid.* p. 9: 'No poet, simply by practising the vocation to which he believes he has been called, can earn his daily bread.'

3 From *The Sunlight on the Garden: The Collected Poems* (London, 1966), p. 84.

4 From *Autumn Sequel* (1954), Canto IV, q.v. in full for an amusing account of MacNeice's war service. Gilliam = 'Herriot', Harding = 'Harrap'.

5 Asa Briggs, *The History of Broadcasting in the United Kingdom*, vol. 3, *The War of Words* (Oxford, 1970) p. 328: 'Recording... was thought of not as a mainstay but as "an invaluable assistant at moments of emergency".'

6 A student at Birmingham when MacNeice was a lecturer, thereafter a life-long friend and later BBC colleague. To the important source book *Time Was Away* he contributed 'Castle on the Air', a short account of the radio plays and features, and the list 'Radio Scripts 1941–1963', which is still the fullest. R. D. Smith is now Visiting Professor of English at the University of Surrey.

7 *Time Was Away*, pp. 98–9.

8 *Ibid.* p. 9.

9 See below.

10 Briggs, *History of Broadcasting*, vol. 3, p. 585.

11 *Time Was Away*, pp. 97–102.

12 *The Strings Are False* (London, 1965).

13 *The Dark Tower and Other Radio Scripts* (London, 1947), p. 17.

14 *The Mad Island and The Administrator: Two Radio Plays* (London, 1964).

15 *The Dark Tower*, p. 69.

16 *Christopher Columbus: A Radio Play* (London, 1944), pp. 89–90

17 MacNeice, *Persons from Porlock and Other Plays for Radio* (London, 1969).

18 *The Dark Tower*, p. 70.

19 *Christopher Columbus*, p. 15.

20 *Time Was Away*, pp. 91–2.

21 *Varieties of Parable* (Cambridge, 1965), p. 24.

22 *The Dark Tower*, p. 21.

23 *Varieties of Parable*, p. 26.

24 *Time Was Away*, p. 12.

25 *The Dark Tower*, p. 22.

26 *Time Was Away*, p. 20.

27 *Ibid.* p. 17.

28 See his Introduction in *Varieties of Parable*.

29 *Ibid.* p. 80.

30 Cf. also Brecht, p. 71 above.

31 *Varieties of Parable*, pp. 81–2.

32 *Time Was Away*, pp. 11–12.

33 *The Strings Are False*, p. 173.

34 *The Dark Tower*, pp. 57–8.
35 *Varieties of Parable*, pp. 110–11.
36 *Ibid.*
37 Improvised in MacNeice's production by Osian Ellis.
38 *Varieties of Parable*, pp. 76ff.
39 *Time Was Away*, pp. 67–71. See also MacNeice, *Goethe's Faust, Parts I and II* (London, 1951).
40 *The Mad Islands and The Administrator*, Introduction.
41 *Persons from Porlock*, p. 7.
42 Bertold Brecht, *Schriften zum Theater I* (Frankfurt, 1963), p. 157.

Chapter 3. The radio road to Llareggub

 1 As I have published two substantial essays on *Under Milk Wood* in recent years, both of which are fairly 'literary' in that they deal with such topics as language, characterisation, comedy, and Welshness and do not concentrate on its more purely radio aspects, I am taking this opportunity to depart from the almost invariably 'literary' approach critics make, by considering it as a work for a specific medium in the light of Thomas's other creative writing for radio. My two previous essays are 'Return Journey to Milk Wood', *Poetry Wales*, 9, 2 (1973), 27–38, and '*Under Milk Wood* as Radio Poem', in P. Lewis (ed.), *Papers of the Radio Literature Conference 1977* (Durham, 1978), vol. 2, pp. 137–56. The latter is also in *Anglo-Welsh Review*, 64 (1979), 74–90.
 2 'Lovely English', *Western Mail*, 17 March 1954, p. 6.
 3 *Dylan Thomas* (Cardiff, 1972), pp. 68–9.
 4 *Ibid.* p. 75.
 5 *Botteghe Oscure*, 9 (1952), 134–55.
 6 *Mandrake*, 2, 10 (1954–5), 354.
 7 *Poetry Review*, 45 (1954), 164–5.
 8 'A Great Humanist', *Poetry Review*, 45 (1954), 166.
 9 Richard L. Faust's informative MA dissertation for Columbia University (1956), 'A Study of Dylan Thomas' *Under Milk Wood*'.
10 'Dylan Thomas's Play for Voices', *Critical Quarterly*, 1 (1959), 18–26.
11 'Polly's Milk Wood and Abraham's Bosom', *Southern Review*, 1, 4 (1965), 33–43.
12 'Sex in Arcadia: *Under Milk Wood*', in W. Davies (ed.), *Dylan Thomas: New Critical Essays* (London, 1972), pp. 262–82.
13 'London Takes Notice of a Welsh Poet' (Melbourne), 20 March 1954, p. 17.
14 *The Growth of Milk Wood* (London, 1969), pp. 17–18.
15 *Dylan Thomas: Poet of His People* (London, 1975), p. 115.
16 *The Growth of Milk Wood*, p. 17.
17 See V. Gielgud, *British Radio Drama 1922–1956* (London, 1957), p. 48.
18 *Letters to Vernon Watkins*, ed. V. Watkins (London, 1957), p. 99.

19 *Selected Letters*, ed. C. Fitzgibbon (London, 1966), p. 250.
20 'Words in Spate', *New Statesman*, 6 November 1954, p. 586.
21 'Welsh Wizardry', *The Observer*, 26 August 1956, p. 10.
22 *Quite Early One Morning* (London, 1954), p. 1.
23 *The Growth of Milk Wood*, pp. 9–10.
24 'The London Model for Dylan Thomas's *Under Milk Wood*', in Thomas, *The Doctor and the Devils and Other Scripts* (New York, 1966), pp. 209–12.
25 See Cleverdon, *The Growth of Milk Wood*, esp. pp. 36–7, and D. Jones, Second Preface, *Under Milk Wood* (3rd edn, London, 1976), pp. 8–9.
26 All quotations from *The Londoner* are taken from *The Doctor and the Devils and Other Scripts*, pp. 213–29.
27 All quotations from *Margate – Past and Present* are taken from the corrected typescript in the BBC Play Library.
28 *Quite Early One Morning*, p. 38.
29 *Ibid.* p. 41.
30 *Ibid.*
31 *Ibid.* p. 42.
32 *Ibid.*
33 *Ibid.* pp. 45–8.
34 *Ibid.* p. 43.
35 *Dylan Thomas* (Edinburgh and London, 1963), p. 86.
36 All quotations from *Return Journey* are taken from *Quite Early One Morning*, pp. 73–90.
37 *The Growth of Milk Wood*, p. 15.
38 'A Wonder of Words', *National and English Review*, 142 (1954), 235–6.
39 P. 196.
40 'Dylan Thomas's Play for Voices', pp. 22–4.
41 'The Orator of Llareggub', *Poetry (Chicago)*, 87 (1955–6), 122.
42 'Sex in Arcadia: *Under Milk Wood*', p. 268.
43 'Prose and the Playwright', *Atlantic Monthly*, 194, 6 (1954), 74.
44 *British Radio Drama 1922–1956*, p. 85.
45 *Botteghe Oscure*, 9, p. 154. The text of this letter in *Botteghe Oscure* is superior to that in *Selected Letters*.
46 'Chalk Sketch for a Genius', *Dock Leaves*, 5, 13 (1954), p. 21.
47 *Selected Letters*, p. 190.
48 'Preface', *Under Milk Wood* (London, 1954), pp. v–viii (3rd edn, 1976), pp. 5–7).
49 *The Growth of Milk Wood*, passim.
50 In E. W. Tedlock (ed.), *Dylan Thomas: The Legend and the Poet* (London, 1960), p. 80.
51 *Botteghe Oscure*, 9, p. 154.
52 'Dylan Thomas's Play for Voices', p. 18.
53 *The Growth of Milk Wood*, p. 19.
54 'The Backward Town of Llareggub', *Saturday Review of Literature*, 6 June 1953, p. 25.
55 *Botteghe Oscure*, 9, p. 154.

56 *Ibid.*
57 *The Art of Radio* (London, 1959), p. 115.
58 'Dylan Thomas's Play for Voices', pp. 19–20.
59 All quotations from *Under Milk Wood* are taken from the third edition (1976).
60 In Tedlock (ed.), *Dylan Thomas: The Legend and the Poet,* p. 80.
61 *Vision and Rhetoric* (London, 1959), p. 216.
62 'Welsh Wizardry'.
63 'Sex in Arcadia: *Under Milk Wood*'.
64 *Collected Poems* (London, 1952), p. vi.
65 *Botteghe Oscure,* 9, p. 154.
66 *Ibid.*
67 *Ibid.* p. 155.
68 *Ibid.*
69 'Welsh Wizardry'.

Chapter 4. Telling the story: Susan Hill and Dorothy L. Sayers

1 BBC Written Archives, Sayers *Children's Hour* file (3) 1942–6, Acc. 48622/3. I wish to thank Jacqueline Kavanagh and her colleagues at the Written Archives Centre, Caversham, for guiding me to BBC files on Dorothy L. Sayers; and the BBC for permission to quote from unpublished papers.
2 *The Cold Country and Other Plays for Radio* (London, 1975), p. 7. I wish to thank Susan Hill and the BBC for permission to quote from this collection of plays.
3 *Radio: A Guide to Broadcasting Techniques* (London, 1977), pp. 123–4.
4 *The Cold Country,* p. 76.
5 *Ibid.* p. 43.
6 *Ibid.* p. 53.
7 *Ibid.* p. 11.
8 *Ibid.* p. 129.
9 *Ibid.* p. 108.
10 *Ibid.* p. 11.
11 'Radio', in *Cassell's Encyclopaedia of World Literature* (rev. edn, 1973), vol. 2, p. 476.
12 Muriel Spark, *Voices at Play* (Harmondsworth, 1961) p. v. I wish to thank Muriel Spark and Penguin Books for permission to quote from this volume.
13 Evans, *Radio,* p. 97.
14 *Voices at Play,* p. 129.
15 *Ibid.* pp. 133–4.
16 Dorothy L. Sayers, *The Man Born To Be King* (London, 1943), p. 41.
17 BBC Written Archives, Sayers Scriptwriter file 1936–62, Acc. 48628, copy of letter of 19 April 1938.
18 *Ibid.* 21 April 1938.

19 *Ibid.*, letter of 3 May 1938.
20 *Ibid.*, letter of 26 October 1938.
21 *Ibid,* Sayers to Gielgud, 22 November 1938.
22 *Ibid.*, Sayers to Gielgud, 2 January 1939; Gielgud to Sayers, 4 January 1939.
23 BBC Written Archives, Dorothy L. Sayers, *Children's Hour* file (1) 1940, Acc. 48622/1.
24 *Ibid.*
25 *Ibid.*
26 *Ibid.*
27 *Ibid.*
28 *Ibid.*
29 *Ibid.*
30 *Ibid.*
31 *Ibid.*
32 *Ibid.*
33 *Ibid.*, file (2) 1941, Acc. 48622/2.
34 *Ibid.*, letter of 22 July 1941.
35 *Ibid.*, Sayers, *Man Born To Be King* file 1941–60, Acc. 48628A.
36 *Ibid.*, Sayers, *Children's Hour* file (2) 1941, Acc. 48622/2.
37 *Ibid.*
38 *Ibid.*, Sayers, *Man Born To Be King* file 1941–60.
39 *Ibid.*, Sayers, *Children's Hour* file (3) 1942–6.
40 *Ibid.*, Sayers, *Man Born To Be King* file 1941–60.
41 *Ibid.*, Sayers, *Children's Hour* file (3) 1942–6. Cf. Nicolls to McCulloch, BBC internal memorandum, February 1941, Acc. 48622/1.
42 *Ibid.*, Sayers, *Man Born To Be King* file 1941–60.

Chapter 5. Giles Cooper: the medium as moralist

1 *Kittens Are Brave*, BBC 2, 26 November 1967; unpublished. Giles Cooper wrote some seventy plays, only a handful of which have received any critical attention since the first review. The one exception to this is, perhaps, *Mathry Beacon*, first broadcast in the Third Programme on 21 June 1956 and generally acknowledged to be Cooper's best play for radio. For a fuller discussion of *Mathry Beacon* see my unpublished MA thesis 'Giles Cooper: An Introduction'. University of Hull, 1975. I wish to thank the staff of the BBC Script Library at Broadcasting House, the staff of the BBC Written Archives at Caversham, and Mrs Gwyneth Cooper who gave me access to a number of Giles Cooper's unperformed manuscripts.
2 See Rollo May, *Existence – A New Dimension in Psychiatry* (New York, 1958), p. 41.
3 *Squirrel's Cage and Two Other Microphone Plays* (London, 1931), p. 14.
4 *Ibid.* p. 87 (*Matrimonial News*).
5 *The Dark Tower and Other Radio Scripts* (London, 1947).

6 *Ibid*. p. 46.
7 BBC Third Programme, 15 August 1957; published in Giles Cooper, *Six Plays for Radio* (hereafter cited as *Six Plays*), ed. Bennett Maxwell (London, 1966).
8 *Ibid*. pp. 123–4.
9 *Ibid*. p. 97.
10 *Ibid*. pp. 103–4.
11 *The Face of the Tiger*; unpublished; unperformed. Consulted in manuscript in possession of Mrs Giles Cooper.
12 *Everything in the Garden*; first performed Arts Theatre, London, 13 March 1962; published in *New English Dramatists 7* (Harmondsworth, 1963).
13 *Pig in the Middle*, BBC Third Programme, 4 October 1960; unpublished.
14 *Ibid*.
15 *Ibid*.
16 *Pig in the Middle*, BBC 1, 18 August 1963; unpublished adaptation.
17 *Before the Monday*, BBC Third Programme, 4 June 1959; published in *Six Plays*.
18 Quoted by C. D. Broad, *The Doors of Perception* (London, 1977), p. 19.
19 *Before the Monday*, pp. 270–1.
20 *Ibid*. p. 265.
21 *Ibid*. p. 289.
22 *The Listener*, 23 August 1962.
23 *To the Frontier*, BBC 2, 4 March 1968; unpublished.
24 *Dangerous Word*, BBC Home Service, 12 May 1958; unpublished.
25 *The Return of General Forefinger*, BBC Third Programme, 25 July 1961; unpublished.
26 *Napoleon's Piano*, *Goon Show Scripts* (London, 1973).
27 *Ibid*.
28 *Without the Grail*, BBC Home Service, 13 January 1958; published in *Six Plays*.
29 *Ibid*. p. 143.
30 *Ibid*. p. 129.
31 *Ibid*. p. 183.
32 BBC 1, 13 September 1960.
33 *Under the Loofah Tree*, BBC Third Programme, 3 August 1958; published in *Six Plays*.

Chapter 6. The radio plays of Henry Reed

1 *Not Without Glory: Poets of the Second World War* (London, 1976), p. 134.
2 *Hilda Tablet and Others: Four Pieces for Radio* (London, 1971), p. 41.
3 As reported by Kenneth Allott in his *Penguin Book of Contemporary Verse* (Harmondsworth, 1950), pp. 236–7.

4 Helen Gardner, *The Composition of 'Four Quartets'* (London, 1978), p. 21.

5 Text as in *A Map of Verona* (London, 1946), p. 28. The original text – *New Statesman* Week-End Competition No. 585, set by G. W. Stonier on 19 April 1941, with results on May 10 – has 'your skins' for 'yourselves'. Of 'Little Gidding' itself, Reed was to write in a later *New Statesman* (15 June 1946, p. 435), 'It is wholly in accordance with what Mr MacNeice has called Eliot's "monumental wit", that a fire-watching episode should have its place in a poem about the fires of Hell, Purgatory and Pentecost.'

6 *The Novel since 1939* (London, 1946), p. 7; *New Statesman*, 2 February 1946, p. 89; 'Imitation' ('Far from the branch it blows...'), *The Listener*, 15 June 1950, p. 1016; *B.B.C. Quarterly*, 3 (1948–9), 218.

7 The Waugh, Bellow, Hartley, and Peake reviews can be found in, respectively, *New Statesman*, 23 June 1945, p. 408; *The Listener*, 16 January 1947, p. 124; *New Statesman*, 13 January 1945, p. 28, and 4 May 1946, p. 323.

8 *The Streets of Pompeii and Other Plays for Radio* (London, 1971), p. 8.

9 *The Listener*, 9 March 1950, pp. 438–9.

10 Martin Armstrong in *The Listener*, 28 November 1946, p. 767.

11 *B.B.C. Quarterly*, 3 (1948–9), 217–19.

12 *Hilda Tablet and Others*, p. 7.

13 *B.B.C. Quarterly*, 3 (1948–9), 219.

14 MacNeice, *Persons from Porlock and Other Plays for Radio* (London, 1969), p. 7.

15 *The Listener*, 28 October 1971, p. 577, illustrating a review of the *Pompeii* and *Tablet* collections by John Carey.

16 The text of these collections is on the whole excellent, though there is an inconsistency on p. 127 of *Pompeii*, where three lines of stage direction *(long decrescendo... at first entrance)* make no sense as things stand, surviving as they do from a version in which there was more spoken material at this point.

17 *As I Remember* (London, 1970), p. 191.

18 Hardiana reviewed in *The Listener*: 9 October 1952, pp. 599–600 *(Our Exploits at West Poley)*; 2 December 1954, p. 975 (R. L. Purdy's *Bibliographical Study*); 1 December 1955, p. 955 (Hardy's *Notebooks*); 26 October 1961, p. 678 (Emma Hardy's *Recollections*).

19 Reed's feature programme *The Making of a Poem: Henry Reed on 'Gerontion' by T. S. Eliot* (broadcast 27 September 1946); see also his 'James Joyce: the Triple Exile', *The Listener*, 9 March 1950, pp. 437–9, and 'Towards *The Cocktail Party*', *The Listener*, 10 May 1951, pp. 763–4, and 17 May 1951, pp. 803–4.

20 *Three Plays by Ugo Betti*, p. 6.

21 14 March 1952, p. 11.

22 *The Listener*, 10 May 1951, p. 763.

23 Second talk, *The Listener*, 17 May 1951, p. 804. In a talk on Eliot's critical prose, Reed makes a similar point by lineating part of Eliot's

essay on Kipling and setting it beside a passage from 'The Dry Salvages' *(The Listener,* 18 June 1953, p. 1017).

24 The source for this and all later quotations from unpublished scripts is the BBC sound and script archive at Broadcasting House, London. Where scripts are published, quotations are always from the published versions.

25 *The Listener,* 27 February 1958, p. 380.

26 *New Statesman,* 31 August 1946, p. 155. C. Day Lewis's sequence of poems *An Italian Visit* (1953) is dedicated to Reed.

27 A complete translation of 'La Ginestra' by Reed was broadcast in a Leopardi anthology, *An Essential Voice,* on 12 January 1975. His translation of the 'Chorus of the Dead' had been published in *The Listener,* 28 April 1949, p. 710. Near the end of *The Monument* Reed's Leopardi invokes the 'hidden ugly Power that orders our common ill': cf. the historical Leopardi's poem 'To Himself', which Reed translated in *The Listener,* 1 June 1950, p. 957.

28 Why is a point made of Duke Vincenzo – 'so mysterious, so unpredictable' – returning unrecognised (by Shakespeare anyway) from *Vienna*? Because it could have led to Shakespeare's calling his own unpredictable incognito Duke *of* Vienna in *Measure for Measure* 'Vincentio'. (The play is full of such curious learning, which makes it the odder – especially in one so knowledgeable about Pirandello – that Reed makes no play of the fact that at least half the Gelosi troupe would have worn masks while performing.)

29 *New Statesman,* 4 May 1946, p. 324.

30 Reed was enough of an admirer of the *ITMA* characters to bestow a Hardy allusion on their creator Ted Kavanagh: 'the president of these immortals' *(New Statesman,* 22 November 1947, p. 409).

31 Why is the villainess of the all-female *Emily Butter* called Clara Taggart? Because (give or take 'a rat') she shares a name with Claggart, the villain of the all-male *Billy Budd*. (Not that Britten's is the only fairly recent opera laid under impress in *Butter*. Tippett's *Midsummer Marriage* probably inspired the modern dress, Stravinsky's *Rake's Progress* the *secco* harpsichord, and Berg's *Lulu* the sequence on film.)

32 Britten: *New Statesman,* 1 November 1947, p. 349, and *The Listener,* 27 January 1977, p. 116; Smyth: *New Statesman,* 20 May 1944, pp. 335–6, repr. in C. St John, *Ethel Smyth: A Biography* (London, 1959), pp. 250–5; Sitwell: *Penguin New Writing,* 21 (Harmondsworth, 1944), pp. 109–22, esp. p. 113.

33 *The Letters of J. R. Ackerley,* ed. N. Braybrooke (London, 1975), p. 165.

34 *B.B.C. Quarterly,* 3 (1948–9), 222; *The Listener,* 9 March 1961, pp. 445–6.

35 *The Listener,* 20 April 1950, p. 703 (reviewing Norman Cameron's translation).

36 Reed in *Radio Times,* 24 October 1952, p. 7.

37 *New Statesman,* 15 June 1946, p. 434.

38 *The Listener,* 8 December 1949, p. 1014.

39 *Penguin New Writing*, 18 (Harmondsworth, 1943), p. 138.
40 *The Listener*, 14 January 1960, p. 93.
41 *New Writing and Daylight*, Summer 1943, p. 122.
42 *B.B.C. Quarterly*, 3 (1948–9), 219–20.
43 *The Novel since 1939*, p. 12.

Chapter 7. Beckett and the radio medium

1 Clas Zilliacus, *Beckett and Broadcasting* (1976).
2 The following recordings have been issued by the University of London Audio-Visual Centre (Director, Michael Clarke):

Words and Music (1973)

Words	Patrick Magee
Music	Composed for this production by Humphrey Searle and played by the Sinfonia of London
Croak	Denys Hawthorne

Embers (1975)

Henry	Patrick Magee
Ada	Elvi Hale
Music Master and Riding Master	Nigel Anthony

Cascando (1980)

Opener	Harold Pinter
Voice	Patrick Magee
Music	Composed for this production by Humphrey Searle and played by the Sinfonia of London

All three plays were directed by David Clark and produced by Katharine Worth. The recordings are available from the University of London Audio-Visual Centre, 11 Bedford Square, London WC1B 3RA. For a brief account of the production history see K. Worth, 'Audio-Visual Beckett', *Journal of Beckett Studies*, Winter 1976.
3 *The Art of Radio* (London, 1959), p. 11.
4 M. Esslin, 'Samuel Beckett and the Art of Broadcasting', *Encounter*, September 1975, p. 43.
5 All quotations from Beckett's radio plays are from the following editions: *All That Fall* (London, 1957), *Krapp's Last Tape and Embers* (London, 1959), and *Play and Two Short Pieces for Radio* (London, 1964).
6 *New English Dramatists 12: Radio Plays* (Harmondsworth, 1968), pp. 12-14.
7 *Art of Radio*, p. 69.

8 Letter of 5 July 1956, quoted in D. Bair, *Samuel Beckett* (London, 1978), p. 474.
9 *All I Can Manage, More Than I Could* (Dublin, 1969), p. 85.

Chapter 8. British radio drama since 1960

1 From *Prospect: The Medium of Radio,* BBC Schools Broadcasting, Autumn 1978, Programme 1.
2 *Ibid.*
3 *Prospero and Ariel: The Rise and Fall of Radio: A Personal Recollection* (London, 1971), p. 333.
4 *Ibid.* p. 331
5 Don Haworth, *On a Day in a Garden in Summer,* in *Contemporary One Act Plays* (London, 1976). First broadcast on Radio 3, 19 August 1975.
6 From an interview recorded for *Prospect.* Part of the quoted extract was included in Programme 3.
7 From *All Early in the April,* in *The Seasons of the Blind and Other Radio Plays* (London, 1974), pp. 41f.
8 From an interview recorded for *Prospect* but not included in the series.
9 *Ibid.*
10 Cooper, *Six Plays for Radio* (London, 1966), Introduction by Donald McWhinnie.

Select bibliography

The following periodicals all contain short articles and reviews which are of specific relevance to the subject of radio drama:

BBC Handbook
BBC Quarterly (1946–54)
BBC Yearbook
The Listener
Plays and Players
Radio Times

In addition the *BBC Lunchtime Lectures Series* contains analyses of particular aspects of broadcasting, while the *Chadwyck-Healey Catalogue* (Cambridge, 1977), vol 1: *Radio Drama* contains details of all scripts submitted to the BBC and of performances of individual plays. Relevant unpublished material up to 1962 is to be found in the BBC Written Archives at Caversham Park, Reading.

Annan Report: *Report of the Committee on the Future of Broadcasting* (London, HMSO, 1977)

Arnheim, Rudolph, *Radio*, trans. Margaret Ludwig and Herbert Read (London, 1936)

Barthes, Roland, *Image–Music–Text*, trans. Stephen Heath (London, 1977)

Berry, Francis, *Poetry and the Physical Voice* (London, 1962)

Bigsby, C. W. E. (ed.), *Approaches to Popular Culture* (London, 1976)

Black, Peter, *The Biggest Aspidistra in the World* (London, 1972)

Brecht, Bertold, *Brecht on Theatre*, trans. John Willett (London, 1964)

Bridson, D. G., *Prospero and Ariel: The Rise and Fall of Radio: A Personal Recollection* (London, 1971)

Briggs, Asa, *The History of Broadcasting in the United Kingdom*, 4 vols. (Oxford, 1961–79)

Brown, John Russell (ed.), *Drama and Theatre with Radio and Television* (London, 1971)

Burns, Tom, *The BBC: Public Institution and Private World* (London, 1977)

Burns, Tom and Elizabeth Burns, *The Sociology of Literature and Drama* (Harmondsworth, 1973)

Carter, M. D., *An Introduction to Mass Communications* (London, 1971)

Chaney, D., *Processes of Mass Communication* (London, 1972)

Curran, J., M. Gurevitch and J. Woollacott, *Mass Communications and Society* (London, 1977)

Davison, P., R. Meyersohn and E. Shils (eds.), *Literary Taste, Culture, and Mass Communication*, 9 vols. (Cambridge, 1978)

Esslin, Martin, 'The Mind as Stage', *Theatre Quarterly*, 1, 3 (July 1971) 5–11

Evans, Elwyn, *Radio: A Guide to Broadcasting Techniques* (London, 1977)

Felton, Felix, *The Radio Play: Its Techniques and Possibilities* (London, 1949)

Fiske, J. and J. Hartley, *Reading Television* (London, 1978)

Gielgud, Val, *How To Write Broadcast Plays* (London, 1932)

Gielgud, Val, *The Right Way to Radio Playwriting* (Kingswood, 1948)

Gielgud, Val, *British Radio Drama 1922–1956* (London, 1957)

Grisewood, Freddy, *My Story of the BBC* (London, 1959)

Grisewood, Harman, *Broadcasting and Society* (London, 1949)

Hawkes, Terence and J. Hartley, 'Popular Culture and High Culture', *The Study of Culture I* (Milton Keynes, 1977)

Heppenstall, R., *A Portrait of the Artist as a Professional Man* (London, 1969)

Hoggart, Richard, *Speaking to Each Other*, 2 vols. (Harmondsworth, 1970)

Hood, Stuart, *The Mass Media* (London, 1972)

Howarth, W. D. (ed.), *Comic Drama: The European Heritage* (London, 1978)

Laver, J. and S. Hutcheson (eds.), *Communication in Face to Face Interaction* (Harmondsworth, 1972)

Lea, Gordon, *Radio Drama and How To Write It* (London, 1926)

Lewis, C. A., *Broadcasting from Within* (London, 1924)

Lewis, Peter (ed.), *Papers of the Radio Literature Conference 1977*, 2 vols. (Durham, 1978)

McLuhan, Marshall, *Understanding Media* (London, 1964; repr. 1967)

McQuail, D. (ed.), *Sociology of Mass Communications* (Harmondsworth, 1972)

McWhinnie, Donald, *The Art of Radio* (London, 1959)

Matheson, Hilda, *Broadcasting* (London, 1933)

Ong, Walter, *Interfaces of the Word* (Ithaca, N.Y. and London, 1977)

Pear, T. H., *Voice and Personality* (London, 1931)

Pilkington Report: *Report of the Committee on Broadcasting* (London, 1962)

Priessnitz, Horst, *Das englische 'radio play': Typen, Themen, und Formen* (Berlin, 1978)

Priessnitz, Horst (ed.), *Das englische Horspiel: Interpretationen* (Düsseldorf, 1977)

Reed, Henry, 'What the Wireless Can Do for Literature', *BBC Quarterly*, 3 (1948–9), pp. 217–22.

Reed, Henry, 'The Making of *The Dynasts*', in *Penguin New Writing* (Harmondsworth, 1943), pp. 136–47

Reith, J. W., *Broadcast Over Britain* (London, 1924)

Sieveking, Lance, *The Stuff of Radio* (London, 1934)

Silvey, R. J., *Who's Listening: The Story of BBC Audience Research* (London, 1974)

Smith, Anthony, *The Shadow in the Cave: The Broadcaster, the Audience, and the State* (repr. London, 1976)

Snagge, J. and M. Barsley, *Those Vintage Years of Radio* (London, 1972)

Thompson, Denys (ed.), *Discrimination and Popular Culture* (Harmondsworth, 1964)

Tunstall, Jeremy, *Media Sociology: A Reader* (London, 1970)

Williams, Raymond, *The Long Revolution* (Harmondsworth, 1965)

Williams, Raymond, *Culture and Society, 1780–1950* (Harmondsworth, 1966)

Williams, Raymond, *Communications* (Harmondsworth, 1968)

Williams, Raymond, *Drama in a Dramatised Society* (Cambridge, 1974)

Index